Laboratory Manual

Computer Service and Repair

A Guide to Troubleshooting, Upgrading, and PC Support

Richard M. Roberts

X

Publisher
The Goodheart-Willcox Company, Inc.
Tinley Park, Illinois

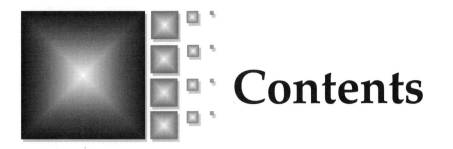

Contents

Introduction

Operating Systems

Motherboards

Power Supplies

Memory

Input Devices

Magnetic Storage

CDs

Printers

Portable PCs

Modems

Troubleshooting

Networking

Windows 2000 and XP

Introduction

This lab manual is designed to give you the basic skills necessary for success in PC repair, upgrade, and support. The order of the labs matches the sequence of the textbook, *Computer Service and Repair*. It is important to complete each lab to the best of your ability. Illustrations and screen captures have been added as necessary to assist you throughout the series of lab activities.

The A+ Certification exam, developed by CompTIA, is designed to test persons with PC support and repair experience. The object of this lab manual is to teach you those skills necessary for the exam and more. The exam is written to test people with approximately six or more months of experience with PCs. Those individuals must also prepare for the examination by classroom instruction in PC theory and operation. These lab activities simulate real-life jobs, and will provide you with the hands-on experience needed to pass the A+ Certification exam.

Let's go over some conventions that will help you understand the information presented in this lab-textbook. There are certain screen images that you will be referred to, such as dialog boxes, menus, radio buttons, check boxes, etc. Look at the illustrations that follow as the information about each type of interface element is covered. This terminology is the same for all of Microsoft's software products, and most of Microsoft's products are similar in design. In other words, many times it will be difficult to distinguish between a Windows 95, 98, 2000, NT, or Millennium edition of the software. Even other operating systems have the look and feel of the classic Windows design.

A menu is a displayed list of commands that you choose from. Look at the following figure. This is the **Shut Down** menu, which is similar in design in all Windows products starting with Windows 95.

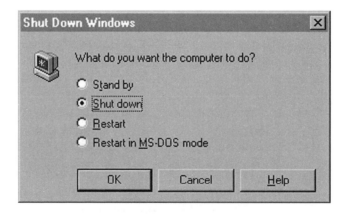

A dialog box requires some type of input. The dialog box on the previous page is used to properly shut down windows. Several options are displayed with radio buttons to the left of the options. Radio buttons are used when only one option is allowed. You cannot pick two items. If two or more items can be chosen, a check box is used. With check boxes, multiple items can be selected. See the following figure.

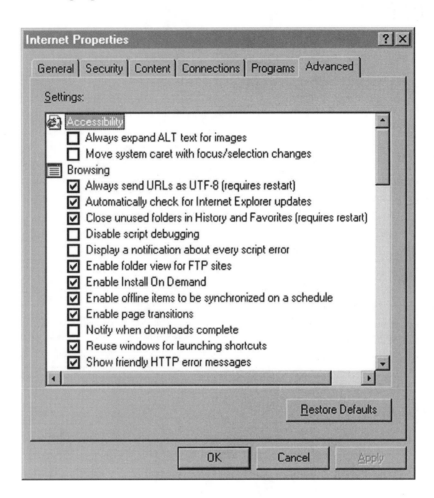

The following figure is an example of a Windows message box. A message box communicates a message to the user, usually when an error occurs. Often a message box will offer the user various options in the form of selectable buttons.

Some dialog boxes contain various types of control buttons and boxes. Look at the Windows **Date/Time Properties** dialog box in the following illustration.

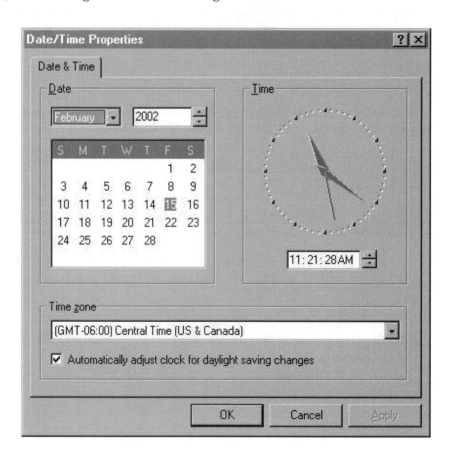

At times you will be instructed to open a certain file or program. Rather than fill the pages with pictures of menus and dialog windows, a simple notation will be given. For example, when you are requested to open the accessories file and activate the Paint program, you will see **Start | Programs | Accessories | Paint**. This serves as an abbreviated set of instructions of how the task can be accomplished. You can use other methods, such as clicking on icons and folders until you reach the program and run it, but previous notation style is used throughout this lab manual and the accompanying textbook. Microsoft and most professional journals also use it.

Windows 98 is the operating system used for most of the lab activities. However, whenever possible, you should repeat the labs on Windows 95, Windows Me, Windows NT, and Win 2000 operating systems. Not all utilities are accessed exactly the same in all these operating systems. While the lab activity textbook centers on Windows 98, most of the activities can be performed, with minor differences, on any of the operating systems noted above. If a lab exercise requires a specific operating system, it will be mentioned in the Equipment and Materials section. For all other labs, Windows 98 is intended.

Again, I must emphasize the importance of completing each of the lab activities.

Using This Manual

Each lab activity begins with a number of learning objectives. These are the goals you should accomplish while working through the activity. In addition to the objectives, each lab activity also contains a brief Introduction section, which presents a brief description of the lab and, in some cases, an overview of the required theory.

Following the Introduction, you will find an Equipment and Materials list. This list provides a general guideline for the material requirements of the activity. A graphic in the upper right-hand corner of each lab activity indicates the operating system requirements for the activity. Most of the activities in this manual can be completed with multiple versions of Microsoft Windows operating systems. The requirement graphic for such activities is simply labeled "Windows." However, if a lab activity requires a particular operating system, the name of that operating system appears in the requirement graphic. Lab activities that are unlabeled can be completed with any available operating system.

The Procedure sections of the lab activities provide step-by-step instructions for completing the labs. You should read through the entire lab activity, including the Procedure section, before beginning a lab. If you have any questions about the requirements or procedures involved with the lab, ask your instructor for help. Some lab activities require you to enter information in the Procedure section. These are not test questions, but simply opportunities to record information about the machine you are using. Often, this information will be required in later steps in the activity.

The final part of each lab activity is the Review Questions. These questions were written to make you think about the material presented in the activity. Not all questions can be answered simply by reading through the lab. Some questions require you to deduce the answer using the knowledge you have gained from working through the exercise. Other questions require you to consult outside sources. Such questions force you to use your new knowledge, reinforcing it.

As you read this text, you will also notice that certain words or phrases stand out. Filenames, such as notepad.exe, student.txt, and io.sys, appear in a roman sans-serif typeface. In this manual, any time you direct the computer to perform a function, whether by entering a line of text at the command prompt or clicking on an element in the GUI, it is considered a command. Commands, such as **dir C:** or **Start | Programs | Accessories | System Tools**, are set in bold sans-serif typeface. Internet addresses appear in the traditional web style, such as www.goodheartwillcox.com.

Be sure to read any Notes or Warnings that you encounter. Such features may alert you to an act that may damage your computer or yourself. Losing all of your data is the most common danger you will encounter with computers. But, you may also encounter some dangerous voltages, especially when dealing with monitors. Those repairs should be left to special technicians.

The lab activities that appeared in the *Computer Service and Repair* textbook are reprinted in this manual in write-in form. These lab activities are nearly identical to their counterparts in the textbook. The following is a list of the end-of-chapter labs in the textbook and the corresponding lab activity in this manual.

Lab Name	Textbook	Lab Manual
Major Part Identification	Chapter 1	Lab Activity 01
Windows XP Upgrade Installation	Chapter 2	Lab Activity 70
Identifying PC BIOS and Operating System	Chapter 3	Lab Activity 26
Replace or Upgrade a ZIF Socket–Type CPU	Chapter 4	Lab Activity 28
Exploring and Replacing the Power Supply	Chapter 5	Lab Activity 30
Determine Amount of RAM	Chapter 6	Lab Activity 31
Keyboard Properties	Chapter 7	Lab Activity 35
Display	Chapter 8	Lab Activity 37
CD Drive Installation (IDE)	Chapter 10	Lab Activity 46
Printer Configuration (Part One)	Chapter 11	Lab Activity 47
Direct Cable Connection	Chapter 12	Lab Activity 49
Modem Installation	Chapter 13	Lab Activity 50
Virus Test Software	Chapter 14	Lab Activity 56
Accessing the Startup Menu	Chapter 15	Lab Activity 51
Network Adapter Card Installation	Chapter 16	Lab Activity 58
Creating a Network Share	Chapter 17	Lab Activity 60
Verify Internet Properties	Chapter 18	Lab Activity 63

General Safety Procedures

1. Before opening a computer's case, turn off all power to the PC and accessories, but leave the power cord plugged into the outlet. This ensures that the chassis is grounded and allows any static charge to drain off.

2. Before working on the computer, discharge static electricity by touching an unpainted, metallic surface. Paint is an insulator, and may prevent a static discharge from the body.

3. Do not touch pin connectors on chips or other components. Pins can be easily bent. Also, when a person touches something, the oils in the person's skin leave a residue, which can hinder a low-voltage electrical connection.

4. Leave parts in their anti-static bags until the parts are needed. When you are done with the parts, return them to the anti-static bags . Do not leave parts on work surfaces or on the PC case.

5. Handle all board-mounted components, such as SIMMs or DIMMs, by the edges. Do not touch bare edge connectors or electrical leads on the board.

6. Never unplug or connect any device while power is applied to the PC. Unplugging a component, such as the hard drive, while power is applied can seriously damage the component.

7. Never open a monitor. A typical monitor can hold an electrical charge in excess of 20,000 volts, even long after the power to the unit has been cut off. In general, a PC technician does not service any parts found inside of a computer monitor.

Name _____ Date_____

Class/Instructor _____

Major Part Identification

After completing this lab activity, you will be able to:

✶   Identify the major components outside of the PC case.

✶   Identify the major parts inside a PC case.

Introduction

One of the first steps to learning PC hardware systems is to be able to identify the major hardware components of a PC. In this lab, you will learn to identify the major components inside a typical PC. You will be asked questions throughout the lab activity that will later be reviewed in your classroom as an instructor-led activity. Answer all questions to the best of your ability. Short answers are acceptable. *Do not* remove any of the major components or disconnect any of the wiring, jumpers, etc., during this activity. This is strictly a visual identification exercise. You may use your textbook to help you identify the components.

Equipment and Materials

✶   Anti-static wrist strap

✶   Pen or pencil and notebook paper

Procedure

1. ___   Report to your assigned PC for this lab activity.

2. ___   Take necessary anti-static precautions. (anti-static wrist strap)

3. ___   Is the assigned PC a desktop model or a tower? _____

4. ___   Put a check mark beside the components listed below if your unit has them.

    ___   Floppy drive

    ___   CD drive

    ___   DVD drive

5. ___ Look at the back of the case and identify the types of port access the unit has. You may use the following illustration to assist you in identification.

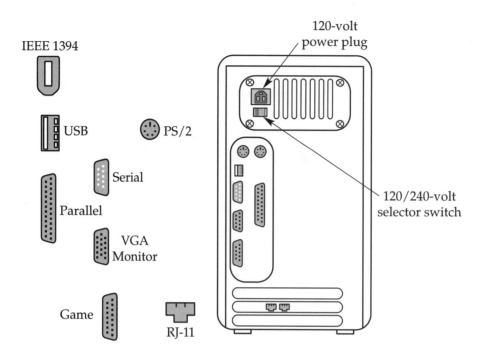

6. ___ Place a check mark beside each port identified on the PC.

   ___ 15-pin D-shell connector used to connect to the monitor

   ___ RJ-11 used to connect to a phone line

   ___ Mouse port (PS/2 or DIN)

   ___ Keyboard port (PS/2 or DIN)

   ___ Parallel port

   ___ USB port

   ___ IEEE 1394 port

7. ___ Watch the instructor as the removal of the case is demonstrated. There are many different case styles used to house the internal components of a PC. The variations can be quite confusing, and damage to the case can result if it is improperly disassembled. Watch closely and do not disassemble the case until given approval by the instructor.

8. ___ After removing the outside case cover, inspect the contents inside. Try to locate and identify the power supply unit. It is usually a large metallic box with many different colored wires running to other devices inside the PC. Another way to identify the power supply is to find where the 120-volt power cord enters the PC. The 120-volt power cord usually connects directly to the power supply.

   Does the power supply have a cooling fan as part of its total assembly? If so, where is the fan located? _____

   Approximately how many sets of power conductors are leaving the power supply unit and going to other components? _____

9. ___ Look on the power supply unit for markings related to the wattage of the power supply. Once you have located the markings, write the wattage rating of the unit here. _____

10. ___ Identify the CPU. It should be mounted on the motherboard and have some sort of heat sink attached to it. It may also have a fan unit. Refer to the following illustration as an aid when attempting to identify the CPU.

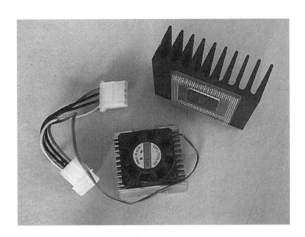

Does the CPU in your unit have a heat sink? _____

Does the CPU in your unit have a fan mounted to it? _____

11. ___ Look for the random access memory modules (RAM). They will be either SIMMs or DIMMs. The following illustration depicts the general appearance of a memory module.

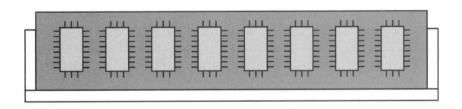

How many memory units are installed? _____

Do the memory modules have chips on both sides or one side? _____

12. ___ Identify the main system board, or motherboard. It is a very large electronic circuit board that covers much of the area inside the case.

How many expansion slots are located on the motherboard? _____

How many of the slots are PCI _____ and how many are ISA _____? PCI slots are usually shorter than ISA slots and white in color. ISA slots are longer than PCI and usually dark brown or black in color.

How many of the expansion slots have adapter cards installed in them? _____

Look closely at how the motherboard is mounted to the case. How much space is between the bottom of the motherboard and the metal case? _____

Why do you think there is a space between the motherboard and the case?

_____

_____

13. ___ Look at the back of the floppy drive.

Does it have any conductors from the power supply connected to it? _____

Does the floppy drive have a flat ribbon cable connected to it? _____

If it does have a flat ribbon cable connected to it, where does the other end of the flat cable connect?

_____

Does the flat ribbon cable have a red or blue stripe on one edge? _____

Does the flat cable going to the floppy drive have any conductors twisted in the cable?

_____

14. ___ Identify the hard drive. It is a box mounted entirely inside the computer case. It will have wires from the power supply plugged into it as well as a wide flat ribbon cable.

Does the hard drive have a flat ribbon cable going to it? _____ If so, where is the other end attached?

_____

Does the flat ribbon cable have a red or blue stripe on one edge? _____

Are there power cables from the power supply going to the hard drive? _____

Does the flat ribbon cable going to the hard drive have a twist in part of the conductors? _____

15. ___ Look at the various chips mounted on the motherboard. Do they appear to be soldered in place or plugged into sockets?

_____

16. ___ Can you locate the CMOS battery? Look for either a circular silver disk approximately 1" in diameter, a blue barrel shaped device approximately 3/4" in diameter, or a rectangular box approximately 2" × 3/4" × 3/4". The battery normally has the voltage printed on it.

17. ___ If you are unable to identify any items, call your instructor for assistance.

18. ___ Lastly, it is often necessary to make a sketch of the PC components' layout. The sketch is used as a guide for reassembly after certain PC components have been disassembled. For example, if you must replace a motherboard, every wire connection point should be identified. Make a sketch of the PC layout. It should look similar to the example that follows. The one shown here is very small and the labeling is limited in order to leave you room to draw. Be sure to identify fan, LED, and switch connections. Draw the sketch with as much detail as possible, as it will help during reassembly. Notice how the red stripe on the flat ribbon data cable going to the hard drive and floppy drive has been identified on each end. Do the best you can, and then turn it in to your instructor for review. Before you begin, see if your instructor wants you to draw it in the workbook or on a separate sheet of paper.

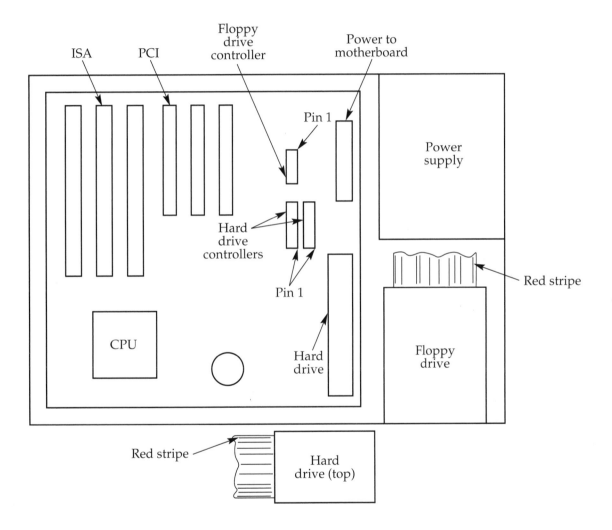

Internet Assignment

1. Find the motherboard layout for the PC you are working on. Go to the manufacturer's web site and see if you can locate the motherboard's schematic diagram. You will need the PC's model number.

Name _____ Date_____

Class/Instructor _____

Lab Activity

02

Finding the DOS Prompt

After completing this lab activity, you will be able to:

✴   Navigate the Windows Start menu selection.

✴   Navigate to and open the DOS prompt.

Introduction

This lab activity will familiarize you with many of the most common functions you will be using throughout the lab activities book. It is imperative that you complete each lab activity. Many of the labs contain information that is not found in the textbook and can only be fully comprehended by completing the lab activity. If you plan to pass the A+ Certification exam at the end of your course of study, you need to complete all labs. Do not skip material, even if you feel you are familiar with the lab activity. Many times you will discover obvious features that you were not aware of before.

This lab activity will introduce the Start menu, located at the lower-left corner of the Windows desktop. You will also learn to access the DOS prompt, which you will need for the next lab activity. Finally, you will be introduced to a quick way to identify the version of Windows that is running.

Throughout this lab activity book, you will be instructed to return the system to the original condition you found it in. Typically, other students may need to use this same PC. Changing system settings, without returning them to there original order when you have finished, may make it very difficult on new users or those studying different features. Please exercise common courtesy.

Equipment and Materials

✴   Typical PC with a Windows 95 or 98 operating system

Procedure

1. ___ Boot the computer. A typical desktop should appear, similar to the one shown.

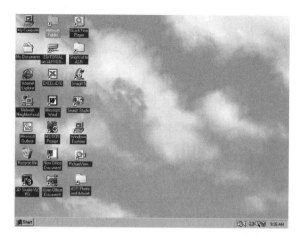

2. ___ The Start menu is located at the bottom left of the screen. Click on the **Start** button only once. The Start menu should appear similar to the one shown.

3. ___ List the options available from the Start menu. The menu options are all listed with a typical icon displayed to the left.

_____

_____

_____

4. ___ Select the **Shut Down** option but do not shut down the computer. List the options associated with the **Shut Down Windows** dialog box.

_____

_____

_____

_____

5. ___ Select each of the options one at a time and try them out to see the effect on the system.

6. ___ The next few lab activities will center on using DOS. The DOS prompt can be accessed by clicking on the **MS-DOS Prompt** option, located at **Start | Programs | MS-DOS prompt** or **Start | Programs | Accessories | MS-DOS prompt**. The route that you use will depend on your operating system.

7. ___ When you successfully access the DOS prompt, you should see a black display or dialog box label "MS-DOS Prompt". In the screen area, you will see messages that are similar to the following.

> Microsoft® Windows 98
> ©Copyright Microsoft Corp 1981-1998
> C:\WINDOWS>

8. ___ Type the **dir** command and press [Enter]. If a list of files scroll from the bottom to the top of the screen, you are at the DOS prompt.

9. ___ To go back to the Windows desktop, type **exit** and press [Enter]. The word "exit" is the DOS command for exiting the DOS program. Since you were in Windows when you started the DOS program, ending the DOS session will return you to Windows.

10. ___ Take special note that when you move the mouse over the Start button and press it, not only are the Start menu items displayed but also the version of Windows that is running. Select the **Start** button now and see the version of Windows you are running on the PC. Write the version below in the space provided.

_____

Review Questions

1. What options are available in the Shut Down Windows dialog box? _____

_____

2. How do you leave DOS and return to the Windows desktop? _____

_____

3. What is a quick method to tell what version of Windows is currently running on the PC?

_____

4. How do you access the DOS prompt? Choose the best answer below.

   (A) **Start | Programs | Options | MS-DOS Prompt**
   (B) **Start | Programs | MS-DOS Prompt**
   (C) **Start | Shutdown | Access Accessories | MS-DOS Prompt**
   (D) **Start | MS-DOS Prompt**

Name _____ Date_____

Class/Instructor _____

DOS Directory Structure

After completing this lab activity, you will be able to:

✱   Navigate a DOS directory structure.

✱   Issue the following commands, **md**, **dir**, **cd**, and **format**.

✱   Format a floppy disk from the DOS prompt.

✱   Explain the 8.3 DOS naming convention.

✱   Determine the active directory.

Introduction

In this lab activity, you will learn to format a floppy disk, and create a directory structure. Also in this lab activity, you will become familiar with several basic DOS commands. DOS can be a very powerful troubleshooting tool when used by a knowledgeable technician.

You will be using the commands **format**, and **dir**. When using the commands **format** and **dir** in conjunction with a drive letter, such as A:, you must leave a space between the command and drive letter.

✱   **format** prepares a disk for storing files.

✱   **dir** displays the directories and files on a disk.

✱   drives are selected by using the appropriate letter followed by a colon.

For example:

dir a:
format a:

When you save a file or create a directory, you must conform to the DOS naming convention. When naming a file, you must use the 8.3 naming convention. In the 8.3 naming convention, all files and directories must have a name that is composed of two parts. The first part can be up to eight characters long and the second part can be up to three characters long. The two portions of the name must be separated by a period. There are certain characters that cannot be used in a DOS file or directory name, such as the back slash (\), which has a special meaning to DOS. For now, use the names as directed in the lab activity. The three-character extension is optional. If you do not add the extension, DOS will automatically add one for you. The extensions usually indicate the type of file. For example, .txt usually indicates a text file.

Equipment and Materials

* A typical PC running DOS 6.0 or higher, or Windows 95, Windows 98, or Windows NT operating systems

* (2) 3 1/2" floppy disks (formatted)

Procedure

1. ___ Boot the system and wait for the desktop to be displayed.

2. ___ Launch the DOS prompt. You may review the last lab activity if you have difficulty remembering how to activate the DOS prompt.

3. ___ Using the Start menu, open the program Notepad located at **Start | Programs | Accessories | Notepad.**

4. ___ Type a short line of text as follows: *This is a test.*

5. ___ Save the file as Test01 on the 3 1/2" floppy in the A: drive.

The following illustration shows Notepad and the **Save As** dialog box, which is used to specify a name and location for the saved file.

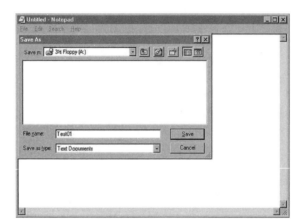

6. ___ Type the name of the file, Test01, into the box below **File name.** The file must be saved to the A: drive. Look at the box below the label **Drives** to see if the drive letter A: is displayed. If not, change the drive letter to A: before saving the file.

7. ___ Close Notepad and launch the DOS prompt as you did in the last lab activity.

8. ___ Type the command **dir a:** followed by [Enter] and observe the screen. The **dir** command will display the directory of files. The **a:** is an option to the **dir** command. It displays all files located in the A: drive.

9. ___ Record the following data, which is displayed on the screen.

Complete file name including the extension _____

The size of the file in bytes _____

Date of the file creation _____

Time of the file creation _____

Amount of free disk space in bytes _____

Do not continue in this lab activity until all information is filled in. Data on the disk will be destroyed in the next sequence of lab steps.

10. ___ At the DOS prompt, type the command **format a:** followed by [Enter]. The **a:** instructs the format command to prepare the disk in the A: drive. Be sure there are no files you need on the floppy disk; all information on the floppy disk will be erased.

The following is a typical sequence of messages that appear when formatting a disk using DOS.

The display first instructs you to place a 3 1/2" disk in the A: drive.

Insert new diskette for drive A:
and press ENTER when ready...

Next, the operating system checks the disk for existing data and then begins to format the disk. A message informs you of the formatting progress.

Checking existing disk format.
Verifying 1.44M
27 percent completed.

Next, you are prompted for a volume label. A volume label is simply a name for the disks. The volume label is optional.

Volume label (11 characters, ENTER for none)?

After the format process is complete, the amount of data available on the disk is displayed. The storage space on a disk is divided into small areas called allocation units. The smallest allocation unit is 512 bytes. When data or files are saved to a floppy disk, they are saved in complete allocation units of 512 bytes. A large file is saved in a cluster of allocation units. For example, three allocation units are required to save a file containing 1,300 bytes of data.

1,457,664 bytes total disk space.
1,457,664 bytes available on disk.
    512 bytes in each allocation unit.
    2,847 allocation units available on disk.

The last screen prompt asks if you wish to format another disk. You must respond with a [Y] for "yes" or [N] for "no," followed by [Enter].

Format another (Y/N)?

11. ___ Use the **dir** command to look at the data on the floppy disk in drive A: once more.

12. ___ Using the **Start** menu, open Notepad, located at **Start | Programs | Accessories | Notepad.**

13. ___ Type four short memos using the following text. Save them as independent files titled memo1, memo2, memo3, and memo4. The content of each memo is displayed below.

> memo1 = This is memo 1.
> memo2 = This is memo 2.
> memo3 = This is memo 3.
> memo4 = This is memo 4.

Save each memo file to the floppy disk in the A: drive.

14. ___ Use the **dir** command to look at the file structure of the disk in drive A: by typing the following command **dir a:**. Remember to leave the space between **dir** and **a:**. The four memos you saved to the disk in the A: drive should be displayed.

15. ___ The contents of text files can be displayed by using the **type** command. The **type** command is followed by the name of the file and the file extension:

type a:memo1.txt

When this command is entered, the contents of the file memo1 should be displayed on the screen.

16. ___ Use the **type** command to display the contents of the other three memos.

17. ___ The **md** command is used to make a directory. It must be followed by the name of the directory that you wish to make. Use the following command to create a directory named level1a.

md level1a

18. ___ Use the **dir** command to display the contents of the disk in the A: drive. A directory structure similar to the one below should appear.

> MEMO1.TXT 16 05-26-00a 10:35a memo1.txt
> MEMO2.TXT 16 05-26-00a 10:36a memo2.txt
> MEMO3.TXT 16 05-26-00a 10:38a memo3.txt
> MEMO4.TXT 16 05-26-00a 10:39a memo4.txt
>
> LEVEL1A <DIR> 05-26-00a 10:45a level1a
>
>   4 file(s) 56 bytes
>
>   1 dir(s) 1,455,104 bytes free

■ **Note:**

The exact file sizes may vary depending on the text-editing program used, and whether returns are included in the message body.

The names, sizes, and creation dates and times, are displayed for the files, including the directory. The amount of free space on the disk is also displayed. You will notice that although the four memo files are only 56 bytes in size, the amount of free space on the hard drive has diminished by 2,560 bytes. Remember that disk space is used in allocation units of 512 bytes even if the file contains only a single byte of data. Also, be aware that the creation of a directory also uses 512 bytes of disk space.

19. ___ Now use the **md** command to create a second directory called level1b.

20. ___ Use the **dir a:** command to verify you have made a second directory called level1b. If it does not exist, call your instructor.

21. ___ Now you will change the directory that you are using as the default directory. The default directory is the directory from which you are issuing commands. The default directory is always displayed on the screen as the DOS prompt. If the DOS prompt is A:\>, then the default directory is the A: drive. If the DOS prompt is C:\>, then the default directory is the C: drive. When only the letter that corresponds with the drive is shown, the root directory is the default directory. If a directory name is displayed as part of the DOS prompt, then you are issuing commands from that directory. To change the default directory to a directory on drive A:, simply type the letter of the desired drive. The DOS prompt should appear similar to the following:

A:\>

22. ___ Type the command **dir** from the new default directory A:. The files named memo1 through memo4, and the two directories level1a and level1b should now appear. Record the screen appearance below.

_____
_____
_____
_____
_____
_____
_____
_____

23. ___ The command for changing directories is **cd** followed by the drive letter with a colon, a back slash (\), and the name of the directory. To change to the level1a directory on the A: drive, type the following command.

cd a:\level1a

The prompt on the screen should now display A:\LEVEL1A>. Take special note of the fact that the root directory name is included in the prompt.

24. ___ From the prompt A:\LEVEL1A type the command to view the directory. Record the appearance of the screen below.

_____
_____
_____
_____

25. ___ Compare the last two screen displays and take note of the differences.

26. ___ Now you will create a subdirectory one level below LEVEL1A. Type the following command at the DOS prompt.

md level2a

Verify the existence of a subdirectory called level2a by using the **dir** command.

27. ___ You can move up and down a directory listing. To move down a directory listing you use the command **cd** followed by the next level directory. To move more than one directory level down, you would have to use a complete path name. Look at the examples that follow.

C:\WINDOWS> **cd:\windows\homework**

This command changes the default directory from windows to homework, which is a sub-directory of windows.

C:\WINDOWS> **cd a:\homework\english\papers**

This command changes the default directory from the C: drive to the A: drive at the level of the directory papers.

C:\WINDOWS> **cd..**

This command (cd followed by two periods) moves the default directory up one directory level.

C:\WINDOWS> **cd**

This command moves you back to the root directory of the drive you are in.

Familiarizing yourself with these commands will assist you in maneuvering around directory structures.

28. ___ Create a third level in the directory structure called level3a and then copy memo1 and memo2 to the level3a directory.

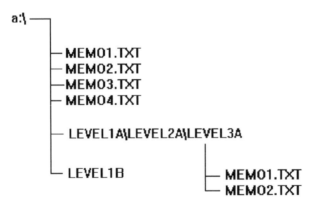

29. ___ Have your instructor check your project.

Review Questions

1. What is the smallest unit allocation size, expressed in bytes, for the floppy disk you created?
   _____

2. A 3000 byte file would require how many allocation units? _____

3. When would the DOS prompt display the word WINDOWS as part of the prompt? _____

4. The DOS prompt displayed on the screen is always the _____ directory. _____

5. What will the DOS command **cd..** (cd followed by two periods) do?_____

_____

6. What does the **format** command do? _____

_____

7. What is the maximum number of characters that can be used for a volume label? _____

8. To change from the C: directory to the A: directory, which of the DOS commands below would you use? _____

    (A) **cd c: to a:**

    (B) **cd a:**

    (C) **cd c:\ cd a:**

    (D) **cd c:/ a:/**

Introduction

Name _____ Date _____

Class/Instructor _____

Help File

After completing this lab activity, you will be able to:

✱ Access the DOS help files.

✱ Use DOS help files to learn more about common DOS commands and switches.

Introduction

The DOS help files are an extremely helpful set of files, especially if you need to know more about DOS commands or DOS command switches. You can access the command by going to the DOS prompt and then enter the name of the command followed by the slash symbol and the question mark. Look at the following examples.

format /?

format /help

Be sure to leave a space between the command and the slash. On some systems you can access DOS help files by simply typing the word **help** at the DOS prompt or by typing the word **help** after the command.

There are two handy commands that will prove valuable to you when using help. The first command is executed by pressing [alt] [Enter] at the DOS prompt. This key combination expands the DOS screen to a larger size. Second, to limit the amount of information displayed on the screen at one time, use the pipe symbol (|) followed by **more** after the help command.

In the following example, the **xcopy** command used with the **/?** switch will provide too much information to display at one time. The addition of the **|more** flag allows the viewer to scroll one screen at a time by pressing [Enter].

xcopy /?|more

Equipment and Materials

✱ Typical PC with Windows 95, Windows 98, or Windows NT 4.0 installed (do not use Windows 2000 or Windows Me)

Procedure

1. ___ Report to your assigned station and boot the PC.

2. ___ Access the DOS prompt. Enter the commands referred to in the questions below. Add the **/?** switch to access information about the commands.

3. ___ After you have answered all the questions, close DOS and shut down the PC.

Review Questions

Answer the following questions after accessing the DOS prompt.

1. What command is equal in function to **del**? _____

   _____

2. What switches may be used with the **attrib** command? _____

   _____

3. What does the **/f:** switch do when used in conjunction with the **format** command? _____

   _____

4. What is the **find** command used for? _____

   _____

5. What other command is equal to **md**? _____

   _____

6. What does the **/s** switch do when used with the **format** command?_____

   _____

7. What does the **sys** command do? _____

   _____

8. What does the **/h** switch mean when using the **xcopy** command? _____

   _____

9. When using the command **prompt**, what does **$q** mean? _____

   _____

10. When using the command **prompt**, what does **$v** mean? _____

    _____

Name _____ Date_____

Class/Instructor _____

Lab Activity

05

DIR Command Options and Switches

After completing this lab activity, you will be able to:

✳ Identify the common switches used with the **dir** command.

✳ Use the **help** command or the **/?** switch to obtain information about a particular command.

Introduction

There are a number of **dir** command options available that can change the way the command displays the data requested. On this worksheet, briefly define what each of the switches used with the **dir** DOS command does. You may use a PC, preferably using Windows 98 or later, to assist you in finding the answers. Remember that the help file can be displayed using the command **dir/?** at the DOS prompt.

Equipment and Materials

✳ Typical PC with Windows 95 (or later) operating system

Procedure

1. ___ Report to your assigned PC station and boot the PC.

2. ___ Access the DOS prompt and then complete the review questions below using the **dir/?** command.

3. ___ When you have completed the questions, exit DOS and shut down the PC.

Review Questions

For Questions 1–10, write a brief description of the switch listed.

1. **dir/?** _____

2. **/p** _____

3. **/w** _____

4. **/a** _____

5. **/s** _____

6. **/b** _____

7. **/l** _____

8. **/v** _____

9. **/4** _____

10. **/o** _____

11. What does each of the attributes below represent?

      h=

      s=

      r=

      a=

12. What are the types of sorting order available and what are their switches? _____

_____

Name _____ Date_____

Class/Instructor _____

Lab Activity

06

File Attributes

After completing this lab activity, you will be able to:

✷   Use DOS to set a hidden file attribute.

✷   Use DOS to remove a hidden file attribute.

✷   Use DOS to set a read-only file attribute.

✷   Use DOS to remove the read-only file attribute.

Introduction

In this lab activity, you will change file attributes to see how a memo file is affected. The two most common file attributes you will be using are hidden and read only. The following is a list of the various switches that can be used with the **attrib** command.

✷   The (**+**) plus sign sets the file attribute that follows it.

✷   The (**-**) minus sign removes the file attribute that follows it.

✷   The **r** switch designates a read-only file attribute.

✷   The **h** switch designates a hidden file attribute.

✷   The **s** switch designates a system file attribute.

✷   The **a** switch designates an archive file attribute.

✷   The **/s** switch follows the pathname, and causes all of the files in all of the directories in the specified path to be assigned the file attribute.

The typical format for using the attribute command is as follows:

attrib +h a:memo1.txt followed by [Enter].

This example sets the file named memo1, on the A: drive, with a hidden file attribute. This means that the file cannot be seen by the command **dir**. It is hidden to the viewer and cannot be accessed. The hidden attribute is commonly used to protect certain files from accidental removal or modification.

Equipment and Materials

✷   A typical PC with MS-DOS 5 or higher, Windows 95 or higher, or Windows NT 4.0 or higher loaded

✷   The floppy disk containing the memo files created in Lab Activity 3

Procedures

1. ___ Boot the PC and wait for the Windows desktop to appear.

2. ___ Access the DOS prompt.

3. ___ Look at the memo1 file on the floppy disk. Change the file attribute to hidden. You may need to access the DOS help file to review the procedures for changing a file attribute.

4. ___ View the directory of the floppy using the **dir** command to see if the memo1 file is still listed.

5. ___ Now, reverse the operation by removing the hidden attribute from the memo1 file. If it was done correctly, the memo1 file should appear again when the **dir** command is issued. Check the floppy by using the **dir** command. The file name memo1 should reappear.

6. ___ Set the file attribute for memo1 to read only.

7. ___ Open the file memo1 in a text editor and try to alter its contents. What happens?

8. __ You can display the attributes of files in the current directory by typing the **attrib** command at the DOS prompt. To see the attributes of files in a different directory, you must first make that directory the default directory using the **cd** command, and then issue the **attrib** command. As an alternative, you may type the entire path following the **attrib** command. You must include the names of files you wish to see the attributes of, or you can use wildcards. The following are examples of the two methods.

   ```
   C:\> a:
   A:\> cd\homework
   A:\HOMEWORK>attrib
   ```

   or

   ```
   C:\> attrib a:\homework\*.*
   ```

9. ___ After answering the questions below, return the PC to its original settings and then shut it down.

Review Questions

1. How can the hidden-file attribute be used for security? _____

_____

2. Why would you give a file a read-only attribute? _____

_____

3. How can the attributes of files in a directory be displayed?_____

_____

Name _____ Date_____

Class/Instructor _____

The DOS File Naming Convention

After completing this lab activity, you will be able to:

★   Identify the special symbols that are valid and invalid for use in a DOS file name.

★   Describe the effects of the invalid symbols when used in a file name.

Introduction

The DOS naming convention is called "8.3" because a file name consists of two parts separated by a period. The first part is a maximum of eight characters in length. The second part, after the period, is called the extension and has a maximum length of three characters. Many special symbols can be used in file names. Many others, such as the colon and back slash, have special meanings to the operating system and therefore cannot be used in file names. The following symbols can be used as part of a DOS file name.

_   (underscore)

^   (caret)

$ (dollar sign)

~   (tilde)

!   (exclamation mark)

(number sign)

%   (percent sign)

&   (ampersand)

-   (hyphen)

{ }   (braces)

@   (at sign)

"   (quotation mark)

'   (apostrophe)

( )   (parentheses)

No other special characters are allowed.

Equipment and Materials

★   Typical PC with MS-DOS operating system

★   3 1/2" floppy disk

■ Note:

A full version of the MS-DOS operating system, not the MS-DOS system that comes with Windows 95 (or later), must be used for this lab activity. The exercise will not work correctly with those versions, and will be misleading.

Procedure

1. ___ Boot the PC and wait for the Windows desktop to be displayed.

2. ___ Access the DOS prompt.

3. ___ Access the DOS Edit program by typing **edit** at the DOS prompt and then pressing [Enter].

4. ___ When the DOS Editor program is on the screen, type "This is a test file." Try saving it a number of different ways using both valid and invalid characters. For example, save the file with the name a:testfile and then try using a:te$tfile. Also, try using a name longer than eight characters. Observe the results.

5. ___ When you are finished with the lab activity, properly shut down the PC.

Review Questions

1. When attempting to save a file, which special characters generate an error when they are part of the file name? _____

_____

Name _____ Date_____

Class/Instructor _____

Lab Activity

08

Copying Files

After completing this lab activity, you will be able to:

✳ Use the DOS **copy** command.

✳ Use the DOS **xcopy** command.

✳ Explain the difference between the **copy** and **xcopy** DOS commands.

✳ Identify the switches used with both the **copy** and the **xcopy** commands.

✳ Identify the use of the wildcard symbol (*) when transferring files.

✳ Identify the use of the question mark symbol when transferring files.

✳ Identify common switches used with the **copy** and **xcopy** commands.

Introduction

In this lab activity, you will use the DOS **copy** and **xcopy** commands to transfer files from one disk to another. You will also learn to use many of the switches associated with these commands. Also you will learn how to use the question mark and the wildcard symbol, the asterisk (*), when transferring or copying files.

Equipment and Materials

✳ Typical PC and two empty 3 1/2" floppy disks

Procedure

1. ___ Boot the PC and wait for the Windows desktop to appear.

2. ___ Mark one floppy disk as disk one and the other as disk two.

3. ___ Open the WordPad program and type the following: "This is a test file for the copy program." Save the file to disk one. Name the file testit.

4. ___ Access the DOS prompt. The **copy** command is used to copy the contents of a file to another disk. The **copy** command can also be used to make a copy of the file with a different name. In the next step, you will copy the file called testit from the floppy drive to the hard drive. It is assumed that the hard drive is the C: drive and that the floppy drive is the A: drive.

5. ___ From the DOS prompt, type **cd** to make the root directory the active directory.

6. ___ Type **dir a:** to verify that the file called testit is on disk one.

7. ___ Type **copy a:testit c:**. Be sure to leave a space between **copy** and **a:testit** and another space between **a:testit** and **c:**. This command will copy the file called testit from floppy disk one to the hard drive. The copy of the file will share the same name as the original. If an error message appears, such as "File cannot be copied onto itself," or "Overwrite file (Y/N)," call your instructor. This means that the file already exists in the directory to which you were attempting to copy it. It was left there by another student who previously completed the same exercise but did not return the PC to its original condition.

8. ___ Type **dir c:/p** to view the contents of the C: drive one page at a time. Verify the file named testit is on the C: drive.

9. ___ Now, we will reverse the operation. Try to copy the file from the C: drive back to the A: drive. This should generate an error. Try it and write the error message below.

_____

10. ___ Respond to the message by pressing [y].

11. ___ This time try the following command **copy c:testit a:testit2**. By adding the number two to the end of the file name, it will appear as a different file. This should allow you to copy the file. Try it now. Use the **dir** command to check the floppy. The files testit and testit2 should both appear.

12. ___ Now try to copy the file using the command **copy c:testit a:testit.bck**.

13. ___ Check the floppy disk in the A: drive to see if testit.bck exists. Take note of the file extension .bck. The file extension .bck is often used for labeling backup copies of files. While the letters .bck do not have to be chosen, they do represent the word *back*. Try copying the testit file from the C: drive again. This time use a different set of three letters for the file extension.

14. ___ Now try to make a copy of the testit file on the same disk. To do this, you must rename the file. Using the exact same name is not permitted. Try the command **copy a:testit a:testb**. This should make a copy of the testit file called testb on the same disk. Verify its creation using the **dir** command.

15. ___ Very carefully delete the file on the C: drive called testit by typing **del c:testit**.

16. ___ Use the **dir** command to verify that you have erased the file called testit on the C: drive.

17. ___ The wildcard symbol is the asterisk (*). When an asterisk is used in a command in the place of a name or extension, it represents all possible names or extension. For example, when you enter the command **copy a:*.* c:**, *all* files on the A: drive will be copied to the C: drive, regardless of their names and extensions. For another example, the command **copy a:*.txt c:** will copy all files with a .txt extension to the C: drive. That is why it's called a wildcard. It is used in place of any name, part of a name, or any file extension. Now try out the wildcard by issuing the command **copy a:test*.* c:**. In this instance, the first asterisk represents any combination of characters after the letters test. This use of the wildcard is helpful when you know how a filename begins, but are unsure of the complete file name, how many characters it has, or what the extension is.

18. ___ Verify that all test files from drive A: have been copied to the C: drive.

19. ___ Another special character is the question mark (?). It can be used to substitute individual symbols in a file name or extension. For example, if you have several files with similar names such as memo1, memo2, and memo3, they could all be copied using the command **copy a:memo?**. This command would copy all files that have the letters memo as the first four symbols and any single symbol in the fifth spot of the filename. Files that have more or fewer symbols in their filenames will not be copied. The question mark can be used to selectively substitute for any symbol. You may also use more than one question mark in a file name.

20. ___ Try copying testit by using question marks to represent some of the letters.

21. ___ The **copy** command is used to copy files from one location to another. The **xcopy** command will copy files and directory structures from one location to another. The **xcopy** command has many more switches than the **copy** command, which makes it much more versatile.

Originally PCs were equipped with two floppy drives. This was standard before hard drives were affordable. It was common practice to copy files from one floppy drive to the other floppy drive. The **copy** command by itself does not verify that both copies are exact duplicates. In the days of standard dual floppy drives, PC technology was still new and at times an error would occur while copying files, causing the copy to be incomplete or corrupt. The **copy** command was designed to copy files but not verify that the file copied was an exact copy. The **xcopy** command was designed not only to copy files and directories but also verify that they were exact copies.

22. ___ Create a small directory structure on the floppy disk and then use the **xcopy** command to copy the structure on to the C: drive. Use the DOS help as needed.

23. ___ Answer the questions in the review. You may use the DOS help to answer the questions.

Review Questions

You may use the DOS help files to answer the questions below. When finished, delete any files you created on or copied to the C: drive, return the PC to its previous condition, and shut down the system.

1. What is the main difference between the **copy** and **xcopy** commands?

   _____

   _____

2. What is the wildcard symbol, and what is it used for? _____

   _____

3. What is the **?** used for? _____

   _____

4. What does the **v** switch mean? _____

   _____

5. What does the **h** switch mean when used with **xcopy**? _____

   _____

6. Is an **h** switch used with the **copy** command? If so, what does it do?

   _____

7. What does the **s** switch mean when used with **xcopy**? _____

   _____

8. Can a file be copied while the **h** attribute is set? _____

9. What does the switch **/d:date** do when used with the **xcopy** command?

   _____

10. What would be the result of issuing the command **copy a:*.txt c:**?

    _____

Name _____ Date_____

Class/Instructor _____

Diskcopy

After completing this lab activity, you will be able to:

✶ Use the **diskcopy** command to make backup copies of a floppy disk.

✶ Explain the switches associated with the **diskcopy** command.

Introduction

This is an easy but useful lab exercise. A single DOS command can be used to make a quick backup copy of a floppy disk. In this exercise, you will copy all the files from one disk to the other using the **diskcopy** command. For example, typing the following at the DOS prompt will copy the entire contents from one floppy disk to the other.

    C:\> **diskcopy a: a:**

The **diskcopy** command automatically formats unformatted disks. While the command transfers data from one disk to the other, there will be a series of prompts on the screen telling you what to do and what is happening at the time. Two terms that will be new to you are source disk and target disk. The disk that contains the data to be backed up is called the source disk, and the blank disk is the target disk. When the **diskcopy** command is issued, duplicates are made of the files on the source disk and are transferred to the target disk. When using this command, you must be very careful not to mix up the two disks. If the source disk is mistaken for the target disk, all data on the source disk will be erased. It is always advisable to label each disk when using this command. Both disks may use the same name for the files, but the target disk should be labeled with the word "backup," so that the target disk and source disk are easily identified.

Equipment and Materials

✶ Typical PC with a 3 1/2" floppy drive

✶ (2) 3 1/2" floppy disks, preferably blank

Procedure

1. ___ Boot the computer and wait for the Windows desktop to appear.

2. ___ Next, access the DOS prompt.

3. ___ At the DOS prompt, type the **edit** command. This runs the MS DOS Editor program. It is a small, handy, text-editing program. Type "this is a test file." Insert a floppy disk into the drive. Save the file as testfile on the floppy disk. Use the **dir** command to verify the file called testfile is saved to the floppy disk. Remember that the file will be saved to the default directory that the command is issued from, unless otherwise specified. It is very easy to accidentally save to the hard drive when you intend to save to the floppy. Unless you change the default directory to the A: drive, you must put the A: in front of the file name when you save the file.

4. ___ Issue the **diskcopy** command at the DOS prompt. Watch the instructions as they appear on the screen. The instructions are easy to follow.

5. ___ Use the **dir** command to confirm that the file exists on both the target and source disks.

6. ___ Now, try this command with the hard drive as the target and then as the source.

7. ___ What were the results when you tried to use the **diskcopy** command with the hard drive? Use the space provided to write your answer.

_____

_____

_____

8. ___ You may experiment with the **diskcopy** command until you are comfortable using it, and then answer the review questions. You may use the DOS help to answer the questions. When finished, return the PC to its original configuration if necessary.

Review Questions

1. Which disk is the target disk, the original or the backup copy? _____

2. What does the **-1** switch do? _____

3. What does the **-v** switch do? _____

4. What does the **-m** switch do? _____

Name _____ Date_____

Class/Instructor _____

Make a DOS Boot Disk

After completing this lab activity, you will be able to:

✶ Start a PC using a DOS boot disk.

✶ Create a system boot disk using the DOS **format** command.

✶ Create a system boot disk using the DOS **sys** command.

✶ Identify the system files associated with a DOS boot disk.

Introduction

In this lab activity, you will make a boot disk. A boot disk consists of all the necessary files needed to boot a computer. It will be one of the first software tools for your PC repair kit. A boot disk can be used to start a computer that has a hard drive failure. It is a standard tool used by all PC technicians.

When you make a boot disk for your personal software tool kit, be sure to label it with the correct version of the operating system it was made from. For example, if you used Windows 98 to make the boot disk, label it "Win98". You will acquire several boot disks, also known as system disks, in your studies. System disks are usually made during an operating system installation. A typical system disk contains many more files than a standard boot disk. Some of the files are specific to the machine. You should only use a system disk that was made using the exact same version of windows you are trying to boot.

Equipment and Materials

✶ PC with Windows 95, Windows 98, or Windows NT 4.0 installed

▇ **Note:**

Do not use Windows 2000 or Windows Me. Windows 2000 and Windows Me do not support making a boot disk from the DOS prompt.

✶ 3 1/2" blank floppy disk

Procedures

1. ___ Insert the 3 1/2″ floppy into the A: drive.

2. ___ Reboot the computer with the 3 1/2″ floppy disk still inserted into the drive. Record the error message displayed on the screen.

_____

_____

3. ___ Launch the DOS prompt.

4. ___ At the DOS prompt type in the following command **format a:/s**. The **/s** switch tells the command.com to not only format the disk in the A: drive, but also transfer all files necessary to create a boot disk. A boot disk is commonly referred to as a system disk. Windows 2000 and Windows Me do not support the DOS **format /s** command. These operating systems require more files on the boot disk than do Windows 95, 98, or NT.

5. ___ After the formatting operation is complete, return to the DOS prompt and use the command **dir** to view the contents of the boot disk you created in the A: drive. List the files that you find.

_____

_____

6. ___ Close the DOS prompt using the **exit** command and return to the desktop screen.

7. ___ Remove the boot disk you just created and shut down the computer.

8. ___ After the computer is totally shut down, place the newly created boot disk into the A: drive.

9. ___ Leave the newly created boot disk in the A: drive while you start the computer. Turn the power switch on to boot the computer system.

10. ___ Did a prompt appear? If yes, proceed to step 11, if not, call your instructor.

11. ___ Next, reveal the hidden files on the boot disk by typing **attrib a:**. List the files hidden on the boot disk and their file attributes.

12. ___ Another way to make a boot disk is by using the DOS **sys** command. Format the floppy disk to delete all programs.

13. ___ After the format is complete, type **sys a:**. The command should transfer the required files for a system boot disk to the 3 1/2" floppy in A: drive. Use the **dir** command and the **attrib** command to verify the files on the disk. List the type of attributes associated with each of the files on the disk.

       _____ IO.SYS

       _____ DRIVSPACE.BIN

       _____ MSDOS.SYS

       _____ COMMAND.COM

14. ___ Type the **exit** command at the DOS prompt to return to Windows desktop.

15. ___ Answer the review questions that follow, and then properly shut down the PC using the Start menu.

Review Questions

1. What does the **/s** mean after the **format** command? _____

  _____

2. How do you reveal hidden files? _____

  _____

3. Which file on the boot disk that you made is not a hidden file? _____

  _____

4. What files on the boot disk have hidden attributes? _____

  _____

5. How does the **/q** switch affect the **format** command? _____

  _____

6. What does the command **format a:/v:testdisk** do? _____

  _____

7. What does the **sys a:** command do? _____

  _____

Name _____ Date_____

Class/Instructor _____

File Management with Windows Explorer

After completing this lab activity, you will be able to:

✻ Open and navigate Windows Explorer file-management program.

✻ Interpret the symbols and structures used in Windows Explorer.

✻ Display hidden and system files.

Introduction

This lab will enhance your skills for using Explorer to navigate directory structures. You will be asked questions about files, such as file locations and types. You will learn how to display files that are hidden from view. You will also learn how to copy, create, and delete files and folders.

The file structure is revealed in two common ways from the desktop. The first method is to simply double click on the **My Computer** icon on the desktop. This action reveals all the storage media devices and the Control Panel icon. The display should be similar to that shown in the following illustration.

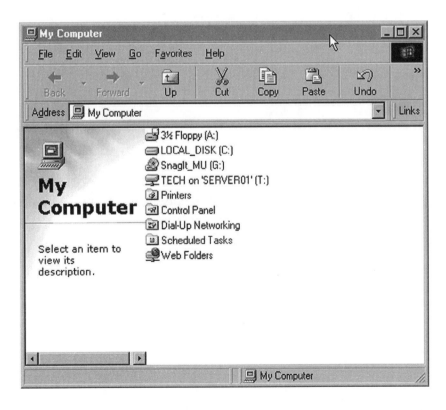

In the first layer of the directory structure, you can see icons for all available storage devices, including the floppy drives, hard drives, and CD drives. An icon also allows access to the Control Panel. Double clicking on a drive or directory's icon reveals the next layer of folders and files for that drive or directory. If the Folder Options settings are set to **Open each folder in its own window**, a new window will appear, listing the contents of the directory. If the **Open each folder in the same window** option is set, then the active window will be updated to display the contents of the directory.

The following illustration shows the layer of files and folders found under the C: drive. This view was created by double clicking the **Local Disk (C:)** icon in the My Computer window. The **Open each folder in the same window** option has been set. This is a typical structure but it may not necessarily match the one on the PC you are using.

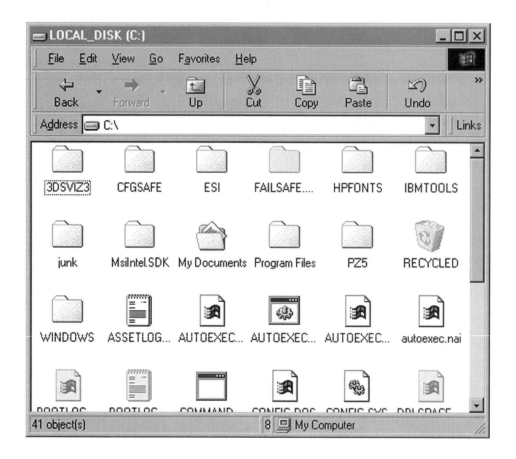

The C: drive is displayed at the left of the window while the folders in the first layer of the directory structure are displayed on the right. All of these folders are in the root directory of the C: drive. The term root directory refers to the first directory on a drive. No directories, or folders, need to be opened to access files saved in the root directory.

The other method of examining the directory structure is by right clicking on the **My Computer** icon located on the desktop, and selecting the **Explore** option from the drop-down menu. This is the preferred method of technicians because it displays the hierarchy of the file-system structure. This means that the Explorer window allows you to see a detailed display of files, directories (folders), and paths all at one time. Look at the following figure.

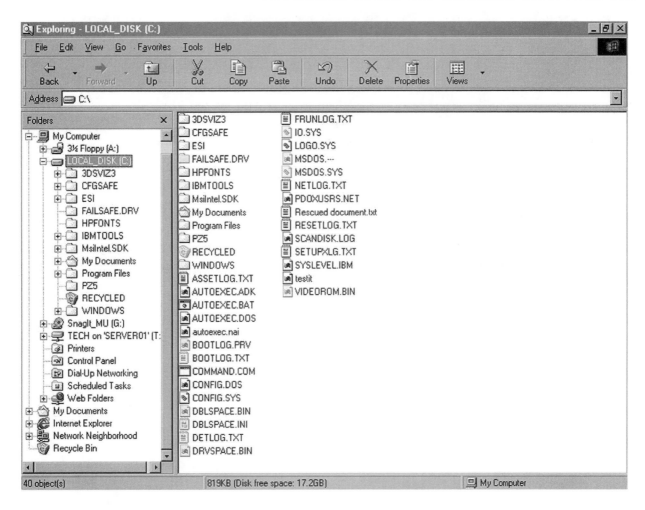

The Explorer window displays information about the files and their structure in two panels. The panel on the left displays the path structure (the available drives, directories, and subdirectories) as an expandable and collapsible tree. The panel on the right displays the contents of the directory or subdirectory selected on the left. To select a new directory, click on the directory's icon. To expand or collapse a branch in the directory tree, double click on the directory's icon or click the box to the left of the folder icon. In the previous screen capture, the C: drive is highlighted on the left. The files and directories contained in the C: drive's root directory are displayed on the right.

Take special notice of the plus (+) and minus (–) signs in the small boxes to the left of the directory structure. A directory that contains unexpanded subdirectories is indicated by a plus sign (+) in front of the directory name. Clicking the box would expand, or reveal, the subdirectories in the directory tree. When the subdirectories have been expanded, a minus sign replaces the plus sign in the box. Directories that contain no subdirectories have no box to the left of their folder icon.

The Folder Options dialog box is used to change the appearance and presentation of files. To open the Folder Options dialog box, double click the **My Computer** icon, select **View** from the menu bar, and then select **Folder Options** from the drop-down menu. Look at the following screen captures to identify the Folder Options locations in the drop-down menus.

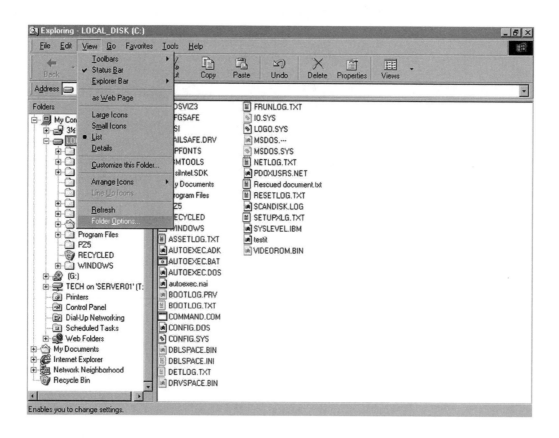

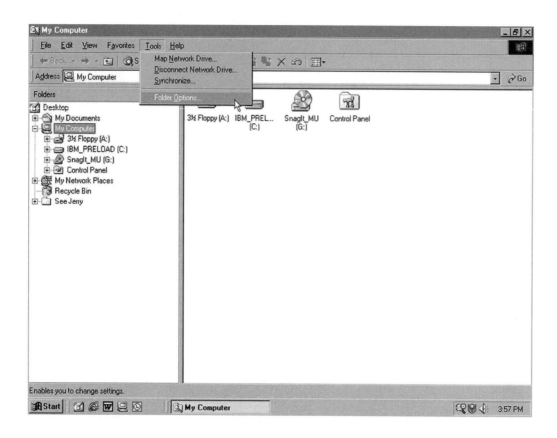

Take special note of where **Folder Options** command is located in each of the two screen captures. In Windows 98, the **Folder Options** command is located in the **View** menu. In Windows Me and Windows 2000, it is located in the **Tools** menu.

Once the **Folder Options** command has been selected from the drop-down menu, a dialog box, similar to the one shown here, appears on the screen. The exact appearance will vary according to the edition of the operating system you are using.

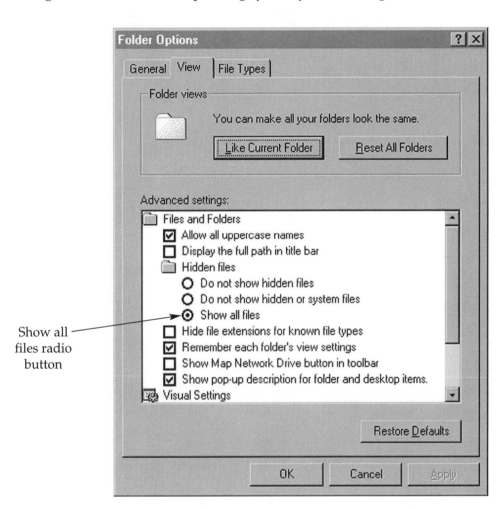

Show all files radio button

To display hidden and system files in Windows Explorer, open the **Folder Options** dialog box and select the **View** tab. Click on the **Show All Files** radio button in the Advanced Settings window. This will be necessary in order to see any hidden or system files in the directory structure. The default setting is **Do not show hidden or system files**. This is done to prevent novice users from deleting system or hidden files, which would have a disastrous effect on the system. Once the option to display all files has been selected and applied, all hidden and system files will be displayed. Compare the following screen captures.

Operating Systems

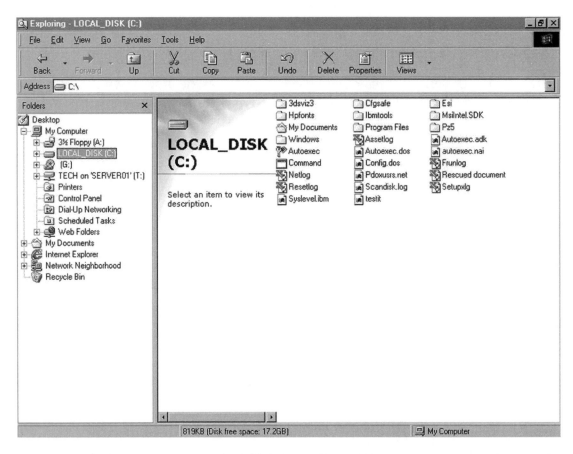

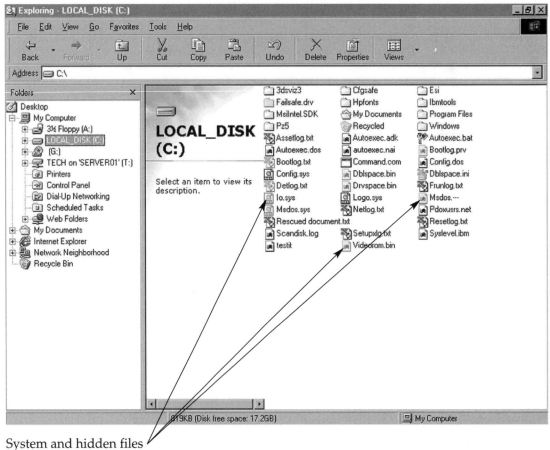

System and hidden files

The hidden and system files are displayed lightly rather than sharp and crisp. This is so they can be easily distinguished from other files.

There are many other folder options that can be selected in the Folder Options dialog box. Files can be displayed or hidden by type. The type of file is identified by its three-letter file extension. For example, a text file extension is .txt and a batch file is .bat.

Equipment and Materials

✳ Typical PC with a Windows 98 operating system

Procedure

1. ___ Boot up the assigned PC and wait for the desktop to be displayed. Follow any logon procedures that might be required to access the desktop.

2. ___ Double click the **My Computer** icon to open the My Computer window.

3. ___ Double click the **Local Disk (C:)** icon and observe the result.

4. ___ Close the My Computer window(s). Right click on the **My Computer** icon, and select **Explore** from the drop-down menu. This opens Windows Explorer.

5. ___ After opening the Explorer window, try clicking on the C: drive to expose the directory structure below it. Click on each of the subdirectories that have plus signs in front of their names. This will show you how the file structure is designed and what files are inside the directories. Each level is connected by a light gray line, which indicates the file or directory path.

6. ___ Right click on the **My Computer** icon and select **Explore** from the drop-down menu. Locate the Folder Options dialog box.

7. ___ Change the **View** tab settings of hidden files to **Show all files**, and **Apply** the setting.

8. ___ Now look at the Explorer directory to see the appearance of hidden files in the viewing window.

    The Folder Option dialog box contains many other features, such as Display the full path in title bar, Hide file extensions for known file types, and a list of registered file types under the File Type tab.

9. ___ Explore the available settings in the Folder Options dialog box. Experiment and note the effects on the files in the Explorer window. Take special note of the location of the control for changing between single click and double click to open an item. While the single and double click option is located in the Folder Options dialog box, it is accessed differently according to the version of Windows being used.

10. ___ When you have finished experimenting, return the folder options to the default settings.

Review Questions

1. What file extension is used to indicate a Help file? _____

2. What file extension is used to indicate a Microsoft program group? _____

3. What file extension is used to indicate an Outlook Express Mail Message? _____

4. What file extension is used for a Dr. Watson log file? _____

5. What file extension is used for a digital ID? _____

6. When Windows is first installed on a computer, what is the default setting for hidden files? _____

7. How can you change the default settings for hidden and system files? _____ _____

8. Why are certain files hidden by default? _____ _____

9. What is displayed in the right side of the Explorer window in relation to the left side of the window? _____

10. What does the plus sign in front of a directory name indicate? _____ _____

Name _____ Date_____

Class/Instructor _____

Using Help

After completing this lab activity, you will be able to:

✱ Access the Windows Help file.

✱ Conduct information searches using Help.

✱ Use the Index feature of Help.

✱ Be familiar with the information available through Help contents.

Introduction

Help for using the Microsoft operating system is available at any time. You can access the Help program using the Start menu. Sometimes the Help file will be accessible with the key combination [Alt][H]. Usually you have to be in a Windows application to access Help using the key combination method. The Help file contains information about many Windows topics. The information can be accessed by one of three easy-to-use methods: search, index, or contents. Look at the following screen capture.

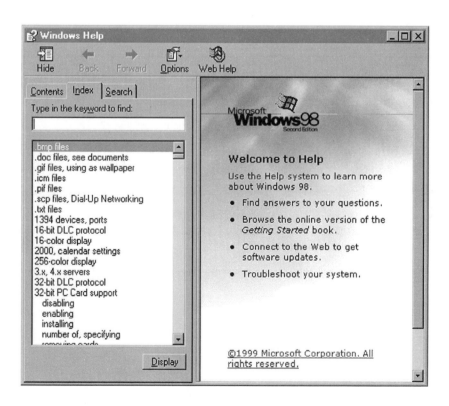

This is a screen capture of a typical Windows 98 Help window. Windows 2000 and Me edition Help screens are quite different in appearance but are used in a similar manner.

Equipment and Materials

✳ Typical PC with Windows 98 operating system (do not use Windows 2000, Windows Me, or Windows XP)

Procedure

1. ___ Boot the system and wait for the desktop to appear.

2. ___ The Help file can be accessed through the Start menu, **Start | Help**. Access the Help file at this time.

3. ___ Now, click on the tab marked **Contents**. A list of subjects should appear on the left side of the window. This may take a few seconds depending on the PC system you are using.

4. ___ In the space provided, list the primary subjects shown in the Contents window. There should be ten listed under Welcome to Help, which is displayed at the top of the list.

_____

_____

_____

_____

_____

_____

_____

_____

_____

_____

5. ___ Click on the **Index** tab and observe the change in the window.

6. ___ What is the name of the first item in the Index list?

7. ___ How do the items appear to be listed in the Index window?

8. ___ Now click on the **Search** tab. You should see a blank text field labeled **Type in the keyword to find:**. Type the word **files** into the blank text field, and then click on **List Topics** button. A list of topics related to "files" should appear in the topic window.

9. ___ Scroll down and select the topic **To change the name of a file or folder**. Click the **Display** button to reveal the contents of the topic. The contents should appear on the right side of the window.

10. ___ Based on the display of the last topic, what characters cannot be used as part of a file name?

11. ___ Do a search for the topic **phone**, and see what appears. List the first five topics in the space provided.

_____

_____

_____

_____

12. ___ Search for and display information about **WebTV for Windows**.

13. ___ The right window should display a small square in front of **New hardware and graphics**. Click on the text to display the information about new hardware. What four types of hardware are listed?

_____

_____

_____

14. ___ Experiment with the Help window for a few minutes, and then go on to your next lab activity if time permits.

Review Questions

1. What key combination can sometimes be used to access Help? _____

2. Describe a situation in which a search by keyword would be the most helpful method of information retrieval._____

_____

3. Describe a situation in which a search through the Help index would be the most useful.

_____

_____

4. If you wanted to quickly browse through information about Windows Accessibility features, which Help window tab would you most likely select? _____

Operating Systems

Name _____ Date_____

Class/Instructor _____

Lab Activity

13

Using Find

After completing this lab activity, you will be able to:

✳   Locate files using the Find feature of the Windows Start menu.

Introduction

In this exercise you will use the Find option, located in the Start menu, to complete the exercise below. In the exercise, you will fill in the blank using the complete path name for each file. The Find option of the Start button can be used to locate various items such as other computers on a network system, locations on the Internet, and people on a computer system. Refer to the following Windows 95 screen capture as some of the options are explained. With the exception of the Containing Text option, which first appeared in Windows 98, the interfaces of file-searching programs are very similar in all advanced operating systems.

The basic Find: All Files dialog box is used to locate files on the computer system. To find a file by its name and location, select the **Name & Location** tab. Type the name of the file you wish to locate in the **Named:** field of the dialog box. The field labeled **Look in:** is the location where the computer will begin searching for the file. If the **Include subfolders** check box is checked, the computer will also search in all of the subfolders of the designated drive or directory. Clicking the **Browse** button opens an Explorer-style window. This window allows you to navigate the directory tree and select a drive or directory in which to begin the file search.

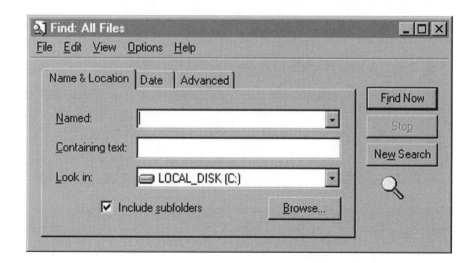

You may use the **Date** tab to search for a file by date. As indicated by the labeled fields in the dialog box, you may search for files that were created, modified, or accessed on a certain day, or between a range of dates.

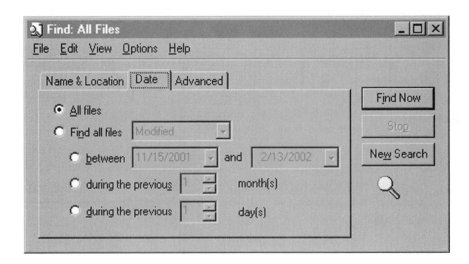

The **Advanced** tab uses advanced criteria, such as file size, to search for desired files.

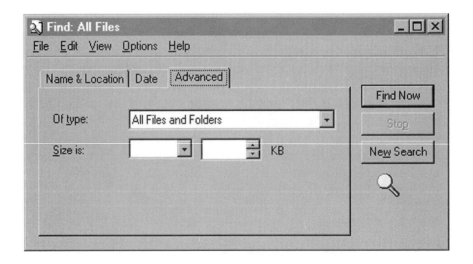

As you can see, this is a very flexible and handy utility.

Equipment and Materials

* Typical PC with Windows 95, 98, or 2000 operating system installed
* 3 1/2" floppy disk

Procedure

1. ___ Boot the computer.

2. ___ Open Notepad on the computer, using **Start | Program | Accessories | Notepad.**

3. ___ Type the following text: "This is a test file."

4. ___ Save the text using the file name NotepadTestFile1. Close Notepad.

5. ___ Launch the Find Files or Folders under the Start menu. **Start | Find | Files or Folders.**

6. ___ Now, you will use the Find: All Files dialog box to locate the file NotepadTestFile1, which you previously created in Notepad. Type the filename into the **Named:** field.

7. ___ Write the complete path of the location for NotpadTestFile1 in the space provided. The results area, at the bottom of the Find: All Files dialog box, will display the name of the located file in the first field, or Name field. The file's location is displayed in the In Folder field, or second field. You must combine the two for a complete file name.

_____

8. ___ Locate the following files and write the complete path name for each. Do not answer with any short cut file names.

himem.sys _____

bootlog.txt _____

config.sys _____

sysedit.exe _____

drvspace.bin _____

pages _____

msinfo32.exe _____

9. ___ Properly shut down the PC.

Review Questions

Indicate in the space provided whether each statement is true or false. Use a "T" for true and an "F" for false.

1. ___ You can limit your search for a file to a specific hard drive.

2. ___ You can limit your search for a file to a specific directory.

3. ___ You can limit your search for a file to a particular creation date.

4. ___ You can search for a particular file by matching part of the file contents such as a string of text characters.

5. ___ Searches are never case sensitive.

Name _____ Date_____

Class/Instructor _____

Taskbar

Operating Systems

After completing this lab activity, you will be able to:

✶ Explain the taskbar properties.
✶ Change the taskbar appearance and position.
✶ Modify the desktop and Start menu.
✶ Create a shortcut using the Task Manager.

Introduction

The taskbar is typically located at the bottom of the screen. The Start button is located at the left end of the taskbar, and the clock is at the right end. Programs that are currently running are also displayed along the taskbar. In the following illustrations, you can see two ways the taskbar can be displayed.

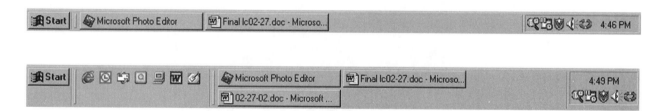

To enlarge the taskbar, position the cursor over the top edge of the taskbar until a double arrow appears. Next, drag the arrow upward to increase the size or downward to decrease the size of the taskbar. You can drag and drop the taskbar to either side or the top of the display as well. There are many service calls that come from people who have lost their taskbar. The taskbar is not really lost; it is simply hidden. Other important features of the taskbar can be accessed by right clicking on the taskbar and selecting **Properties** from the drop-down menu.

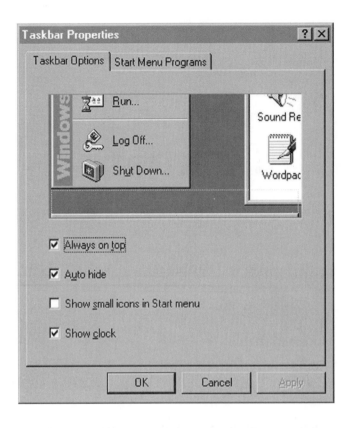

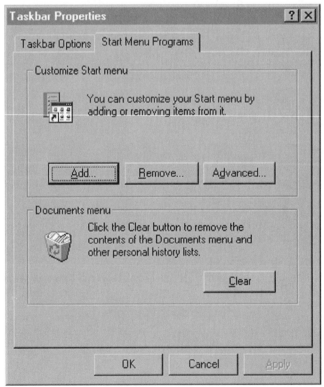

These screen captures are of Windows 98 Taskbar Properties dialog boxes. From these two windows, many features can be changed. Look at the options available under the **Taskbar Options** tab in the dialog box. All of the features found under the Taskbar Options tab of the Taskbar Properties dialog box are explored in this lab activity.

Name_____

Equipment and Materials

✳ Typical PC with Windows 95 (or later) operating system

Procedure

1. ___ Boot the PC and wait for the desktop to be displayed.

2. ___ Locate the taskbar at the bottom of the screen. Move the cursor over any one of the icons in the taskbar, and wait to see if anything happens. Do not click on the icon; simply position the cursor over the icon and wait. Is anything displayed? _____

3. ___ Move the cursor over the clock in the taskbar and double click. The double-click action should open the Date/Time Properties dialog box. If not, call the instructor.

4. ___ In the Date/Time Properties dialog box, click **Cancel**. You may reopen the dialog box and take a few minutes to experiment with the date and time settings. For example, change the time from AM to PM and then click the **Apply** button to see if the change is made immediately. Afterward, return the properties to their original settings.

5. ___ Right click on the taskbar and select **Properties** to open the Taskbar Properties dialog box.

6. ___ There are four check boxes on the left side, under the **Taskbar Options** tab. These check boxes are labeled, **Always on top**, **Auto hide**, **Show small icons in Start menu**, and **Show clock**. Write down the default settings of the check boxes before continuing in this lab activity. Use the space provided.

_____

7. ___ Check the box marked **Auto hide** and then click the **Apply** button. Observe the condition of the taskbar.

8. ___ Move the cursor into the area of the taskbar and see if it reappears; it should. If it doesn't reappear, call the instructor for help.

9. ___ Next, restore the taskbar by clearing the check mark in front of **Auto hide**.

10. ___ Now, remove the check mark in the box labeled **Show clock** and click the **Apply** button. The time should disappear from the taskbar. If the clock does not disappear, call the instructor.

11. ___ Restore the clock to the taskbar once more.

12. ___ Right click on a clear area of the taskbar and a menu should appear. Look for the menu selection labeled Toolbars. Move the cursor over the menu selection **Toolbars** and a submenu should be revealed listing **Address**, **Links**, **Desktop**, **Quick Launch**, and **New toolbar**. The menu selection **Quick Launch** should have a check mark in front of it. The check mark indicates that the Quick Launch toolbar is activated.

13. ___ Remove the check mark in front of **Quick Launch** and observe the change in the taskbar. What program icons disappeared? You can identify the individual icons by using a right click on each of the icons to reveal their properties. List them in the space provided.

_____

14. ___ You can add programs to the Quick Launch portion of the taskbar by right clicking on the taskbar, selecting **Toolbars**, and then selecting the submenu item **New toolbar**. When selected, the New Toolbar dialog box appears. You can navigate the Explorer-style directory tree located inside the New Toolbar dialog box. Select the program you wish to add to the Quick Launch tool bar. If you cannot locate the program you wish to launch, close the dialog box and use the **Find** option from the **Start** menu.

15. ___ Modify the taskbar to enable the Quick Launch of Accessories programs. The accessories are Notepad, WordPad, Paint, etc. Call your instructor when finished so your lab can be verified to this point.

16. ___ Experiment by adding other programs to the Quick Launch area of the taskbar.

17. ___ Windows Explorer can also be used to add programs to Quick Launch. Open Windows Explorer and navigate the path to reveal the contents of Quick Launch. The Quick Launch program is located at C:\Windows | Application Data | Microsoft | Internet Explorer | Quick Launch. The programs located in the Quick Launch area of the toolbar are also revealed in the right side of the Explorer window. You can simply **Copy** the program from the left side and **Paste** it to the right side. If you drag and drop a program to the right side, the program is moved rather than copied.

18. ___ Review the lab activity and then answer all of the review questions.

Review Questions

In the space provided, indicate whether each statement is true or false. Use a "T" for true and an "F" for false.

1. ___ The taskbar can be move to any of the four sides of the display area.

2. ___ The taskbar can be made to hide when not in use.

3. ___ The Quick Launch area of the taskbar can be modified by adding other executable programs.

4. ___ Once programs are added to the Quick Launch area of the taskbar, they cannot be removed.

Answer the questions below with short, precise answers.

5. How can the clock be removed from the taskbar? _____

_____

6. Write the entire path from the C:\ prompt to the Quick Launch directory. _____

_____

_____

Name _____ Date_____

Class/Instructor _____

Lab Activity 15

Create, Copy, Delete, and Undelete Files

After completing this lab activity, you will be able to:

✶ Create a folder.

✶ Copy, delete, and undelete files using Windows Explorer.

✶ Change file locations.

✶ Rename a file.

Introduction

In this lab activity, you will perform common tasks associated with file and directory management, such as deleting, copying, and restoring deleted files. These are simple but vital tasks.

Equipment and Materials

✶ Typical PC with Windows 95 (or later) operating system

✶ (1) blank 3 1/2" floppy disk

Procedure

1. ___ Boot the PC and then open Windows Explorer.

2. ___ Using Windows Explorer, verify that the 3 1/2" floppy disk is blank.

3. ___ Open Windows Notepad. It is located in **Start | Programs | Accessories | Notepad**.

4. ___ Type the following: "this is an original file." Next, save the file as Original File in the My Documents folder. Leave a space between the words "original" and "file" in the filename.

5. ___ Use Windows Explorer to verify that the file has been saved to the My Documents folder.

6. ___ Insert the blank disk into the floppy drive.

7. ___ In the Windows Explorer window, locate and right click on Original File. A drop-down menu should appear with a Send To option. Use the **Send To** option to send a copy of Original File to the 3 1/2" floppy disk.

8. ___ Use Windows Explorer to verify that the file named Original File now exists on the floppy disk.

9. ___ Now, repeat the process again. Open Windows Explorer, locate the file Original File in the My Documents folder. Right click on Original File and try sending it to the floppy disk for a second time. What message appears, and what information does the dialog box contain?

_____

_____

_____

_____

10. ___ You may either copy over the existing file or cancel the copy command by pressing the **No** button.

11. ___ To rename a file, right click on the file in Windows Explorer. A drop-down menu will appear with the **Rename** option in the list. Rename the file to Renamed File.

12. ___ Now, return the file to the name Original File.

13. ___ You can also use Windows Explorer to copy a file. Right click on the folder, and select **Copy** from the drop-down menu.

14. ___ Right click again anywhere in the open white space beside the file named Original File, and select the **Paste** option from the drop-down menu. What is the name of the new file that appeared?

_____

15. ___ Repeat the paste operation again. What is the name of the second pasted file?

_____

16. ___ Double click on the file named Copy of Original File to open it.

17. ___ Does the file named Copy of Original File contain the same information as the file named Original File? _____

18. ___ Type in the line of text, "This is new information," below the existing line of text.

19. ___ Save and close the file named Copy of Original File.

20. ___ Open the file named Original File. Does it match the file called Copy of Original File? _____

21. ___ Delete the file named Copy (2) of Original File. To delete the file, right click on the file and select **Delete File** from the drop-down menu.

22. ___ Resize the Windows Explorer window so that the desktop appears.

23. ___ Open the Recycle Bin by double clicking. Is the file named Copy (2) of Original File listed in the contents? It should be. If it is not there, call the instructor.

24. ___ Right click on the file in the Recycle Bin and select the **Restore** from the menu. This action should restore the file back to its original location in the Windows Explorer window. Restoring reverses the process of deleting the file.

25. ___ Delete the file named Copy (2) of Original File once again.

26. ___ Open the Recycle Bin once more and locate the file named Copy (2) of Original File.

27. ___ Click once on the **File** option in the menu bar at the top of the Recycle Bin window. This opens the File drop-down menu. Select **Empty Recycle Bin**. What happened to the file named Copy (2) of Original File?

28. ___ Creating a folder is easy. First, double click on the **My Computer** icon and select the drive or folder where you wish to create a new folder. To create the actual folder, right click on the white area, select **New** from the shortcut menu, and then click **Folder**. You can also use the menu bar at the top of the window. Simply open the drive where you wish to create the new folder, and then select the **File** option from the menu bar. In the drop-down menu, select **New** and then **Folder**.

29. ___ Open **My Computer** and select the floppy drive. Be sure there is a disk in the drive before selecting it. Create a folder on the floppy disk called This is a New Folder.

30. ___ Create a second new folder called Second New Folder.

31. ___ Now, open the folder called This is a New Folder. The folder should be empty.

32. ___ With the folder called This is a New Folder opened, create another new folder called Second Level. In other words, create a folder that will be a subdirectory of the folder called This is a New Folder. The directory structure should look like the one shown. The following image is a screen capture from Windows Explorer.

33. ___ Open Windows Explorer and verify the directory structure you created looks similar to the one above. If not, call your instructor.

34. ___ Using Windows Explorer, it is possible to change the location of a file. To move the file, simply click on the file and hold the button down while dragging the file to the new location. Move the folder called Second Level from the folder called This is a New Folder to the folder called Second New Folder.

35. ___ Experiment with moving the folders around on the floppy disk. See if you can put one directory under the other.

36. ___ Now, move the files and directories around until they appear similar to the one shown. If you cannot accomplish the task, call the instructor.

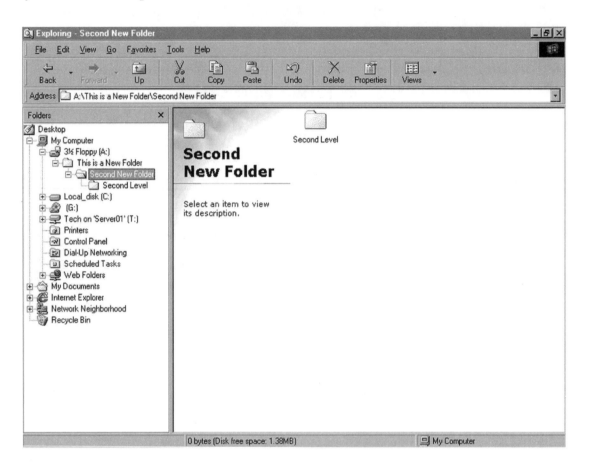

37. ___ Now, you will copy a file in Windows Explorer using the right-click feature. Right click on the file named Second Level and select **Copy** from the drop-down menu.

38. ___ Right click on the folder named This is a New Folder, and use the **Paste** option in the drop-down menu to place a copy of the file named Second Level under the folder named This is a New Folder. You should now have two copies of Second Level, one copy under each of the two original folders. The directory structure should appear similar to the one that follows. If it does not, call your instructor.

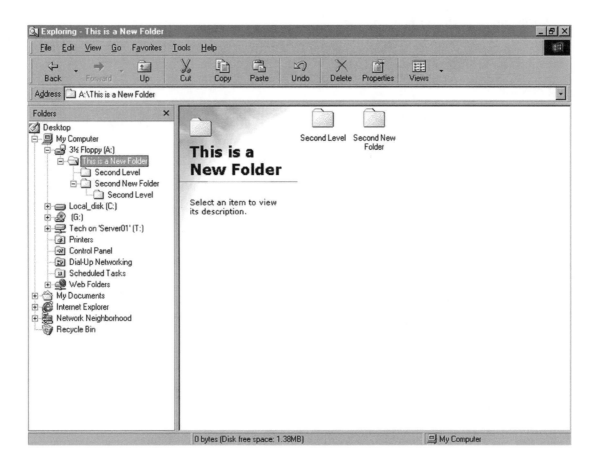

39. ___ Experiment with deleting files on the floppy disk. Does deleting a directory also delete all files in the directory, or must you delete the files one at a time?

_____

40. ___ You may use the PC to assist you in answering the set of questions below. After completing the questions, properly shut down the system and restore everything to its original order.

Review Questions

In the space provided, indicate whether each statement is true or false. Use a "T" for true and an "F" for false.

1. ___ When you rename a file, the content of the file changes.

2. ___ When you copy a file and then make changes in the copy file's contents, the contents of the original file are also changed.

3. ___ When a file is sent to the Recycle Bin, it is permanently deleted.

4. ___ A file can be restored from the Recycle Bin.

5. ___ To permanently delete a file, you must first move the file to the Recycle Bin, and then empty the Recycle Bin.

6. ___ Directories cannot be relocated.

7. ___ You can use the drag-and-drop feature of the mouse to relocate a file.

8. ___ You can copy a file in Windows Explorer by right clicking on the file and selecting **Copy** from the drop-down menu.

9. ___ You can delete folders in Window Explorer by right clicking and selecting **Delete**.

10. ___ When you delete folders from Windows Explorer, they are permanently deleted.

Name _____ Date_____

Class/Instructor _____

Lab Activity

16

Create a File Folder

After completing this lab activity, you will be able to:

✱ Create a new file or folder.

✱ Create a directory structure with Windows Explorer.

Introduction

In this lab activity, you will create a series of new folders and arrange them in a directory structure.

Equipment and Materials

✱ Typical PC with Windows 95 (or later) operating system

✱ 3 1/2″ floppy disk

Procedure

1. ___ Boot the PC and wait for the desktop to appear.

2. ___ Double click on the **My Computer** icon. This action opens the directory structure in the cascading-window style rather than the Windows Explorer style.

3. ___ Place the 3 1/2″ floppy disk into the drive.

4. ___ In the My Computer window, you will see icons of the various drives available. Double click on the 3 1/2″ floppy drive icon to open another window. This window is labeled A:\ (or whatever the drive letter is for the floppy drive), and lists all files contained on the floppy disk. If the disk is new, there will be no files listed.

5. ___ Select the **File** option from the menu bar at the top of the A:\ window. This will activate a drop-down menu with more options. Select the **New** option. This will cause the menu to cascade. Select the **Folder** option from the top of the cascading menu.

6. ___ An icon labeled New Folder should appear inside the window. Rename it Folder1.

7. ___ Double click on the Folder1 icon to open it. It will be empty. Notice that the new window is labeled A:\Folder1.

8. ___ Select **File** from the menu bar across the top of the window. Next, select **New**, and then **Folder** from the cascading menus. Rename this folder to Folder2Level2.

9. ___ Close all windows. Right click on the **My Computer** icon. Select the **Explore** option from the shortcut menu. This opens a Windows Explorer window.

10. ___ While in Windows Explorer, double click on the floppy drive icon to open the floppy disk directory. You should see the folder labeled Folder1. Double click on the **Folder1** icon to expand the directory and reveal the folder labeled Folder2Level2.

11. ___ Now, delete the folders from the floppy disk. To delete the folders, open My Computer and expand the floppy drive directory. Right click on the files you wish to delete and select **Delete** from the drop-down menu.

12. ___ In the next part of the lab activity, you will create a directory structure exactly like the one in the illustrated screen capture. You may use the **Help** feature from the **Start** menu to assist you. When finished, call your instructor to inspect the lab activity.

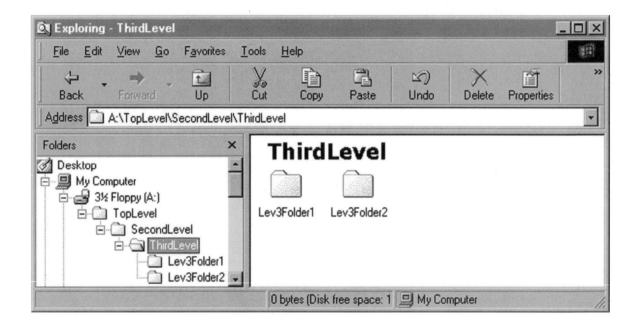

Take note that the directory structure consists of three levels. The top level is a directory called TopLevel. A directory labeled SecondLevel is a subdirectory of the TopLevel directory. A third directory, labeled ThirdLevel, is a subdirectory of the SecondLevel directory. At the bottom of the directory structure are two more folders. One is labeled Lev3Folder1 and one is labeled Lev3Folder2. Both are subdirectories of the ThirdLevel directory.

13. ___ When finished, properly shut down the PC and return all materials to their proper location.

Review Questions

1. What is another name for a directory within a directory? _____

2. What is the significance of the little plus signs to the left of folders in the Windows Explorer directory tree?_____

_____

Name _____ Date_____

Class/Instructor _____

Lab Activity

17

Booting and Shutting down the PC

After completing this lab activity, you will be able to:

✶ Explain the difference between a cold boot and a warm boot.

✶ Closely observe and understand the boot process.

✶ Describe the correct way to shut down a PC.

✶ Activate hibernation and standby modes.

✶ Describe the activities that take place on a system boot after a PC has been shut down incorrectly.

Introduction

There are two main ways to boot a PC, a cold boot or a warm boot. A cold boot is also called a hard boot. A cold boot occurs when power is supplied to a computer that previously had no power. Starting up the computer by activating the power switch is an example of a cold boot. A warm boot is initiated when a PC that is already operating is restarted, usually by pressing [Ctrl] [Alt] [Delete], pressing the reset button, or selecting **Restart** from the **Shut Down** menu. A warm boot may occur when a PC has locked up. Often when installing new software or hardware, the computer will go through a warm boot.

During a cold-boot process, the PC runs a power-on self-test (POST), which checks the system hardware and makes sure everything is working the way it should. It then loads the operating system and drivers, configures the system, and runs the autoexec.bat file if it exists. When the system goes through the warm boot, it skips the POST and the loading of the operating system. Instead, it skips ahead to load drivers, configure the system, and run the autoexec.bat file. As stated earlier, a warm boot is used to restart the PC after it has already gone through a cold boot and there is no need for the complete reboot sequence associated with a cold boot. When a new software or hardware system is installed, drivers may need to be loaded, or the computer reconfigured before the new installation will work. A warm boot would be necessary in such an instance. Also, a warm boot may be required to clear a PC lockup problem caused by software. During the warm reboot, the suspected program is identified by the task manager and blocked out for the reboot.

The PC can be completely shut down, put on standby condition, or put into hibernation. The standby or hibernation features are activated from the **Shut Down Windows** dialog box. In standby condition, the monitor, hard drive, and fan shut down. Before entering hibernation, the computer saves the contents of its RAM (random-access memory) to the hard drive, and then shuts down all of its components. When the computer is brought out of hibernation, the RAM contents are reloaded from the hard drive. This means that the desktop will appear exactly as it did before entering hibernation. Any files that were open when the computer went into hibernation will be open when it emerges from hibernation. A typical PC is set up to go first into standby mode and, after a longer duration of time, to go into hibernation. To bring the PC out of hibernation, you must use the power-on button. To bring the PC out of standby, simply move or click the mouse or press a key on the keyboard. Not all PCs can utilize hibernation mode. If hibernation mode is missing from the **Power Options** dialog box (accessed through the Control Panel), the PC does not support this feature. Note: The system BIOS must support the hibernation feature in order to use it.

Equipment and Materials

✻   A typical PC with Windows 98 operating system

✻   Access to a watch or clock for timing purposes

Procedure

1. ___ Boot the PC and carefully observe the starting sequence. Watch the indicators located at the front of the PC. There are usually light-emitting diodes (LED) located near the floppy drive, and the CD drive. In addition, there are often LED indicators for power and hard drive activity. Observe closely the sequence of activity, which LEDs light up and in what order. Also, write a short description of the messages appearing on the monitor. Repeat the cold boot several times if necessary. Write your findings in the space provided.

_____

_____

_____

_____

2. ___ The proper way to shut down the PC is through the **Shut Down** option on the **Start** menu. Look at the screen capture that follows and study the other options available in the Shut Down Windows dialog box.

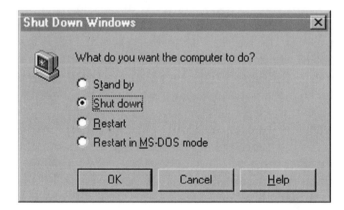

3. ___ Open the Shut Down Windows dialog box and look at the four option buttons listed. Also, take note of the **OK**, **Cancel**, and **Help** buttons. Select the **Help** button, and then do a search for "shutting down". You will notice quite a bit of information pertaining to shutting down the PC system, hibernation, and standby modes. You will use the Windows Help dialog box later in the lab.

4. ___ Close the Windows Help dialog box and return to the Shut-Down Windows dialog box. Select the **Restart** option and then click the **OK** button. Observe the PC's response. The system should have shut down and then restarted similarly to a warm boot.

5. ___ Now, open the Shut Down Windows dialog box once more and select the **Stand by** option. Click the **OK** button and observe the PC's response. Wait approximately 30 seconds after the computer has completely shut down, and then move the mouse or touch any key on the keyboard. The system should respond immediately. There should be no delay as in a system restart.

6. ___ Now, open the Notepad program located at **Start | Programs | Accessories | Notepad** and type a short sentence. Try putting the PC in standby mode without saving the file you just typed in Notepad. Bring the system out of standby mode and observe the desktop display. Was the sentence still in Notepad? _____

7. ___ Repeat the same experiment in step six, but this time shut down the computer rather than putting it in standby mode. Take note of the difference between standby mode and shut down.

8. ___ Open the **Control Panel** and select the **Power Management** icon. A window should appear that closely resembles the following illustration.

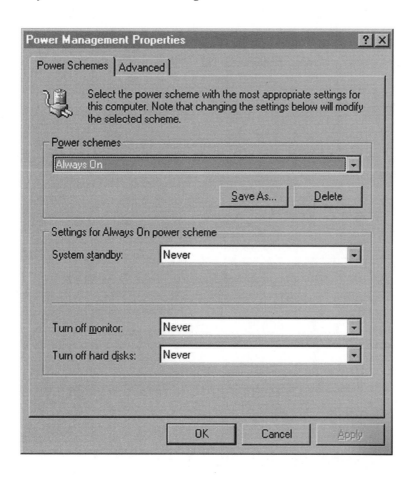

Notice the three main selections listed in the power schemes drop-down list, **Always On, Home/Office Desk,** and **Portable/Laptop.** Select **Always On** for the power scheme and then go on to the **System standby** drop-down list and select **After 1 min.** In the **Turn off monitor** drop-down list, select **After 2 mins**, and in the **Turn off hard disks** drop-down list, select **After 3 mins**. Apply the settings or select the **OK** button.

9. ___ Once again, open the Notepad program and type any short sentence. Wait and observe the actions of the computer. After one minute, it should go into standby mode. After two minutes the monitor should shut down, and after three minutes, the hard drive should shut down.

10. ___ Now, reactivate the desktop by either moving the mouse or touching a key on the keyboard. The desktop should reappear without much delay.

11. ___ This step in the lab activity must be verified by your instructor. In this step, you will shut the PC down by using the power switch. After approximately one minute, reboot the PC by using the power switch and observe the display.

12. ___ What happened when the PC restarted?

13. ___ Leave the PC on while you answer the following review questions. If you did not do so yet, return the power management system to its original settings. Be sure to return the PC to its original setup and shut the system down properly.

Review Questions

You may use the Help program in the Windows Start menu to assist with the review questions.

1. What are the four shut-down options associated with the **Shut Down Windows** dialog box?

2. What is the difference between a cold boot and a warm boot? _____

3. What is the difference between hibernation and standby? _____

4. What warning is stated about a FAT32 file system and using hibernation in Windows 98 operating system? _____

5. How do you set up password protection for standby mode? _____

Again as a reminder, be sure to shut the system down properly and return the PC to its original setup. If you did not do so yet, return the power management system to its original settings.

Name _____ Date_____

Class/Instructor _____

Lab Activity

18

Filenames for Windows 98

After completing this lab activity, you will be able to:

✳ Explain the effects of invalid symbols used in a filename.

Introduction

In this lab activity, you will experiment with various symbols for filenames and observe their effect on the filename. The following symbols are classified as invalid for use as part of a filename when using Windows 98.

$$ \backslash \ / \ : \ * \ ? \ " \ < \ > \ | $$

Equipment and Materials

✳ Typical PC with Windows 98 operating system
✳ (1) blank 3 1/2" floppy disk

Procedure

Open Notepad, type a short message, and attempt to save the file to a floppy disk using each of the filenames listed. This test demonstrates the effect of the invalid symbols. If the name seems to work and the file is saved, check the name in the directory. Record any differences. If an error is generated, write the error next to the filename under the observation column.

Filename   Observation

1. A:Report\June _____

2. A:Report/May _____

3. A:Report:Apr _____

4. A:Report*Dec _____

5. A:Report?Jan _____

6. A:Report"Sep _____

7. A:Report<Feb _____

8. A:Report>July _____

9. A:Report|Aug_____

Note:

In Windows, the maximum number of characters that can be used for a long filename is 255.

Review Questions

1. Make a list of special characters from the keyboard that can be used as part of a filename in the following space.

_____

_____

_____

Name _____ Date_____

Class/Instructor _____

Lab Activity

19

Recycle Bin

After completing this lab activity, you will be able to:

✶ Locate the Recycle Bin Properties dialog box.

✶ Adjust the size of the Recycle Bin.

✶ Recover items from the Recycle Bin.

Introduction

The Recycle Bin icon is located on the Windows desktop. Often the Recycle Bin is referred to as "the trash can," or simply "the trash." The Recycle Bin stores files the user wishes to remove. When the file is sent to the Recycle Bin, it remains there until the Recycle Bin is emptied. This allows a user to see the effect of removing a file, such as a program, before permanently deleting it. System files and other critical files are normally hidden from the typical user. The user may change file attributes to reveal the hidden and system files. After that, they could be accidentally sent to the Recycle Bin. In addition, users sometimes delete files by accident. The Recycle Bin gives them the opportunity to retrieve those files.

Equipment and Materials

✶ Typical PC with Windows 95 (or later) operating system

Procedure

1. ___ Boot the PC and wait for the Windows desktop to appear.

2. ___ Locate and right click on the **Recycle Bin** icon. Select **Properties** from the drop-down list. This should open the Recycle Bin Properties dialog box. It should appear similar to the following illustration.

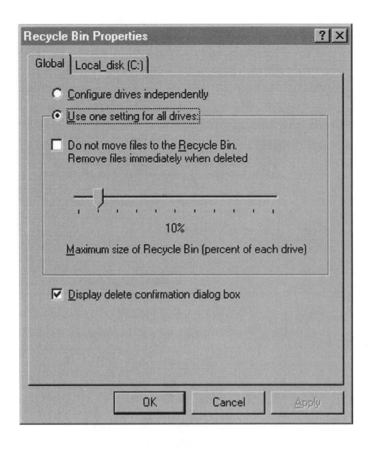

3. ___ Look at the various settings available in the dialog box. There is a slider for adjusting the Recycle Bin's maximum size in relation to the size of the hard drive. The default setting is ten percent. Also, note the radio button labeled **Use one setting for all drives**. Each drive on the PC can have its own individually sized bin, or they can all use the same size, based on percentage.

4. ___ Look at the check box labeled **Do not move files to the Recycle Bin. Remove files immediately when deleted**. When this option is selected, files do not go to the Recycle Bin, but are deleted immediately. Be extremely careful when using this setting. You may want to use it, but should only do so when you are sure of the consequences.

5. ___ Right click on the **Recycle Bin** icon and choose **Open** from the drop-down menu.

6. ___ Are there any files in the Recycle Bin? If there are, check with the instructor. In this exercise, you will be using the Recycle Bin and emptying it.

7. ___ Next, you will create a file, delete it, and then recover the file using the Recycle Bin. Open the WordPad program and type, "This is a test of the Recycle Bin." Save the file under the filename RecycleBinTestFile.

8. ___ Close WordPad and open Windows Explorer. Locate the file.

9. ___ After locating the file, delete it.

10. ___ Open WordPad once more and try to open the file you deleted. The filename should appear in the Recent Documents field, near the bottom of the File menu. When you attempt to open the file, you should receive an error message telling you that the path or filename is invalid.

11. ___ Close WordPad again.

12. ___ Open the Recycle Bin and locate the deleted file called RecycleBinTestFile.

13. ___ After locating the file, right click on the filename and choose **Restore** from the drop-down menu. The file should now be removed from the Recycle Bin and appear back in its original location. Open WordPad to confirm the file does exist.

14. ___ Once again, use Windows Explorer to delete the file.

15. ___ Open the Recycle Bin and confirm that the file is listed.

16. ___ Open the **File** menu on the Recycle Bin's menu bar. Select **Empty Recycle Bin**. This should remove all items from the Recycle Bin. Now the files have been permanently erased.

Note:

To the normal user, the files have been permanently erased. However, there are techniques for recovering the files, which will be covered in later exercises.

17. ___ Create a simple WordPad file once more for experimentation. Make a desktop shortcut for the file, and then drag the shortcut to the Recycle Bin. Did this action delete the shortcut, the file, or both? _____

18. ___ Restore the PC to its original configuration. Do not leave any experimental files on the PC.

19. ___ Properly shut down the PC and then answer the review questions.

Review Questions

1. Place a check mark next to the statement that best describes the function of the Recycle Bin under default conditions.

    ___ The Recycle Bin is used to permanently delete files that are placed in the bin.

    ___ The Recycle Bin is used to temporarily store deleted files until the bin is emptied.

2. How much of the hard drive area is used by the Recycle Bin in its default setting?

    _____

3. How are the contents of a file affected when the shortcut to the file is sent to the Recycle Bin?

    _____

4. This question requires some thinking. Does placing a file in the Recycle Bin affect the amount of free space on a drive? _____

Name _____ Date_____

Class/Instructor _____

Lab Activity

20

[Ctrl] [Alt] [Delete]

Operating Systems

After completing this lab activity, you will be able to:

✱   Access the Close Program dialog box.

✱   Identify and end the program that is causing a system lockup or freeze.

Introduction

When a PC appears to lock up, or freeze, many times the program causing the system lockup can be shut down without interrupting other programs that are running. The standard method to attempt a recovery is to press the [Ctrl], [Alt], and [Delete] keys simultaneously. When the key combination is pressed, a special dialog box is displayed. This dialog box contains such options as End Task, Shut Down, and Cancel. A list of programs currently running is also displayed. This list can help you to identify the program that is causing a system lockup or any such program-generated problem. To demonstrate a system lockup, a program called EndlessLoop.exe will be available from your instructor. Obtain the program from the instructor, and run it from the floppy drive. Do not install the program on the hard drive. To run the program double click on the file in Windows Explorer, or use the **Run** option in the **Start** menu.

■ **Note:**

In Windows NT and Windows 2000, using the key combination [Ctrl], [Alt], [Delete] activates the system logon screen as well.

To become familiar with the way the Close Program dialog box works, press the key combination [Ctrl], [Alt], [Delete] one time only. This should open the Close Program dialog box. Now, open several programs, such as WordPad, Paintbrush, and Notepad. As you start each program, observe the effect on the dialog box. Pay particular attention to the order they appear in the list. Their positions in the list are directly related to the order in which the programs are executed.

Equipment and Materials

✱   Typical PC with a Windows 95 or 98 operating system

✱   Floppy disk with the EndlessLoop.exe program

Procedure

1. ___ Boot the PC and wait for the display to normalize.

2. ___ Press the [Ctrl], [Alt], and [Delete] keys simultaneously one time only. This allows you to see all the programs that are currently running.

3. ___ In the space provided, list the names of the programs that are currently running. This will help you in the future when determining what is normally running and what might be a new program.

_____

_____

_____

_____

_____

_____

4. ___ Now close the dialog box by clicking the **Cancel** button.

5. ___ Open the WordPad, Notepad, and Paintbrush programs one-by-one followed by opening the Close Program dialog box. Observe the order of the list of active programs. Repeat this portion of the lab activity, opening the applications in different orders, until you can correlate the opening of a program to its effect on the list of programs in the Close Program dialog box.

6. ___ Close all of the programs and cancel the **Close Program** dialog box.

7. ___ Run the program called EndlessLoop.exe. To run the program, double click on the filename in Windows Explorer, or select the **Run** option from the **Start** menu.

8. ___ Before you press the **Start Endless Loop** button, try to minimize the window by clicking the **Minimize** button at the top right of the screen. It should reduce the program to a taskbar program icon.

9. ___ Return the program window to full-size by clicking on the taskbar icon.

10. ___ Now, press the **Start Endless Loop** button and try to minimize the program window again. This time the program should not respond. The program window should remain full-sized.

11. ___ Press the [Ctrl], [Alt], [Delete] key combination to display the Close Program dialog box. Inside the dialog box you will see the list of the programs currently running. Verify that the program called EndlessLoop is listed. Close the EndlessLoop program by clicking the **End Task** button located in the window. You may need to click the **End Task** button several times.

◼ Note:

*Simply clicking the **End Task** button may not terminate the EndlessLoop program. It may also be necessary to terminate the driver program for the floppy drive. If so, it will also be listed in the dialog box. In addition, certain anti-crash programs, such as Norton Crash Guard, can affect the way the dialog box appears and operates to a certain extent.*

12. ___ When you are satisfied that you understand the operation of the Close Program dialog box, shut down the system and return the EndlessLoop program disk to your instructor.

Review Questions

In the space provided, indicate whether each statement is true or false. Use a "T" for true and an "F" for false.

1. ___ The last program activated will appear at the top of the list.

2. ___ There are three options to choose from in the Close Program dialog box: **End Task**, **Shut Down**, and **Cancel**.

3. ___ After the Close Program dialog box appears, pressing the key combination [Ctrl], [Alt], [Delete] will have no further effect on the PC.

4. ___ Pressing the key combination [Ctrl], [Alt], [Delete] produces the exact same results in Windows 2000 as it does in Windows 98.

Name _____ Date _____

Class/Instructor _____

Operating Systems

Lab Activity

21

Format

After completing this lab activity, you will be able to:

★ Format a floppy disk in Windows Explorer.

★ Explain when to use the quick-format option.

Introduction

All disks need to be formatted before they can store files. When a disk is formatted, the surface of the disk is divided into sections called sectors, or allocation units. The allocation units are arranged in concentric circles on the disk surface. These circles of allocation units are referred to as tracks. There are tracks on both sides of the disks used today.

When disks are purchased, they can be purchased preformatted or unformatted. If they are unformatted, the disks need to be formatted before they can store data files. Disks that contain files that are no longer needed can be reformatted and used again. Formatting removes all data on the disk. The **format** command must be used carefully, otherwise you may accidentally erase valuable data.

One format option is called quick format. Performing a quick format is quicker than performing a full format, however, the data is still recoverable. When security or privacy is a concern, the full format option should be chosen. If privacy and security are not concerns, a quick format may be chosen to save time.

When quick format is used, only the file allocation table is erased. A file allocation table (FAT) is similar to a database directory written in hexadecimal code. It is placed at the very first sector of a floppy disk. The file allocation table locates the first sector that stores a specific file. This is how the computer locates data saved on a disk. A quick format erases the file allocation table while leaving the actual file on the disk. When the disk is accessed, it appears to be blank. The data can be recovered by third-party utilities or some versions of DOS, such as the full version of DOS 5.0 or later. The limited DOS editions that come as part of Windows operating systems do not have this capability. When using a full version of DOS, check the **unformat** and **recovery** commands.

It is interesting to note that you cannot format a disk if the disk contains an open file. This is a safety feature to prevent deleting files by accident.

Equipment and Materials

★ Typical PC with Windows 95 (or later) operating system

★ Blank 3 1/2" floppy disk (you may use a disk containing data, but all data will be lost)

Procedure

1. ___ Boot the PC and wait for the Windows desktop to appear.

2. ___ Place the floppy disk in the floppy drive. Open Windows Explorer and inspect the floppy to see if it contains any files. You will be formatting this disk shortly, and that process will erase any data on the files.

3. ___ Right click in the area of Explorer that normally displays the files associated with the floppy disk and create a new folder. Save the new folder as FormatTestFolder.

4. ___ Right click on the 3 1/2" drive icon on the left side of Windows Explorer and select **Format...** from the drop-down menu. A window should appear similar to the one in the following screen capture.

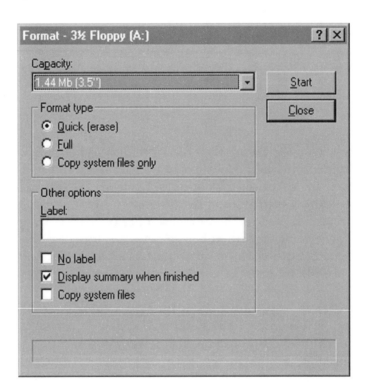

Look at the features of the **Format - 3 1/2" Floppy (A:)** dialog box. The Capacity: text window provides a means to select different media sizes such as 1.44MB and 720KB. In the Format type box, you can select either Quick (erase) or Full format. To use the quick format option, the disk must have been formatted previously. The Other options box provides a means of adding a label to the disk. Type a name in the text field to assign that name to the disk. The default option is no label. The **Display summary when finished** check box is located beneath the **No label** check box. When this option is checked, a summary dialog box will appear on the screen providing information about the success or failure of the disk formatting operation. A sample of the summary box is presented here.

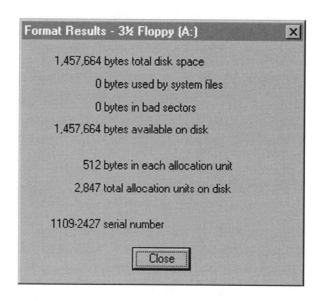

5. ___ Format the floppy disk. Select the **Quick (erase)** radio button in the **Format type** area, and do not assign the disk a label

6. ___ Inspect the disk to see if the saved file still exists. Also check the Recycle Bin to see if the file is present.

7. ___ Practice formatting a floppy disk with both quick format and full format types. When you are done, properly shut down the PC.

Review Questions

Answer the following questions with short, precise answers.

1. How is the **Format...** command accessed in Windows Explorer? _____
_____

2. Can data be recovered from a floppy disk that has been formatted? _____
_____

3. What two DOS commands can be used to recover data from a disk that has been formatted using the quick format option? _____
_____

Name _____ Date_____

Class/Instructor _____

Lab Activity

22

Copy Disk

Operating Systems

After completing this lab activity, you will be able to:

✶ Use the disk copying utility in Windows Explorer to copy a floppy disk.

Introduction

Copies of floppy disks are commonly made. Windows has expanded the **diskcopy** command associated with DOS and included it in Windows Explorer. To make a copy of the disk, insert the floppy disk into the drive, open Windows Explorer, and then right click on the floppy drive icon in the directory tree. Select **Copy Disk** from the menu that appears. The Copy Disk dialog box will appear, and should look similar to the one in the following screen capture.

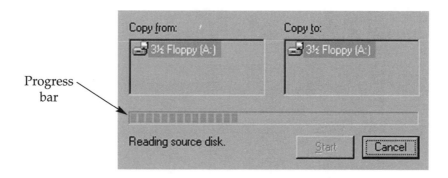

Notice the progress bar at the bottom of the dialog box. This bar shows the progress of the disk copying utility.

Equipment and Materials

✶ Typical PC with Windows 95 (or later) operating system

✶ (2) 3 1/2" floppy disks, one blank and the other may be blank but may also contain files

Procedure

1. ___ Boot the PC and wait for the Windows desktop to appear.

2. ___ Check both disks to see if they are blank or contain data that you do not wish to lose. Ideally, one disk will be blank and the other will contain some form of data. If both disks are blank, mark the labels "original" and "copy." The one that contains data should be marked original unless it is already labeled. The purpose of the labels is to prevent any confusion as you progress through the exercise. If you are comfortable with the labels presently on the disk, you need not mark them original and copy. If both disks are blank, open WordPad and type anything. Insert the disk labeled "original" into floppy drive and save the file as A:\testdisk. This is so you may be able to verify the transfer and copy of data.

3. ___ Now, with the disks ready, open Windows Explorer by right clicking on **My Computer** and selecting **Explore** from the drop-down menu.

4. ___ Right click on the **3 1/2" Floppy** icon to open the drop-down menu associated with the drive.

5. ___ Select **Disk Copy** from the drop-down menu and follow the instructions displayed on the screen.

6. ___ Verify that both disks contain the same information and then close all programs and shut down the PC. If the data does not match, call your instructor.

Review Questions

You may use the Help program from the Start menu to assist you in answering the following questions.

1. What key combination used with the mouse allows you to select multiple, consecutive files to copy at the same time? _____

   _____

2. What key combination used with the mouse can be used to select and copy multiple files that are not in consecutive order? _____

   _____

Name _____ Date_____

Class/Instructor _____

Lab Activity

23

Exposing the Hidden Files on a Typical DOS Boot Disk

After completing this lab activity, you will be able to:

✻   Change the Folder Options settings to expose hidden and system files for viewing and copying.

✻   Examine system files required to boot a PC.

Introduction

In this lab activity, you will apply the knowledge you have gained thus far about the Folder Options dialog box. First, you will use DOS to make a boot disk. You will then compare two views of the DOS boot disk. In the first view, you will look at the disk using Windows Explorer and record all the files that are visible. Then you will access the Folder Options dialog box and change the default settings to allow you to view all hidden and system files. Again you will view the boot disk in Windows Explorer and record all of the files that are visible.

Equipment and Materials

✻   Typical PC with Windows 98 operating system

✻   3 1/2″ floppy disk

Procedure

1. ___   Boot the PC and wait for the Windows desktop to appear.

2. ___   Access the DOS prompt (**Start | Programs | DOS Prompt**).

3. ___   At the DOS prompt, type **sys a:**. This command will copy system files to the floppy disk. The disk may need to be formatted first. If so, use the **format** command without the **/s** switch. Then, use the **sys** command to copy the system files to the floppy disk.

4. ___   To verify that the system files have been transferred to the floppy, use the **dir** command to view the contents of the floppy.

5. ___   In the following spaces, list the files you see and their size. Also, list the amount of free space indicated.

_____

_____

_____

What is the total free space left on the disk? _____

6. ___ Type **exit** at the DOS prompt. to close the DOS and return to Windows.

7. ___ Open Windows Explorer and look at the A: drive. What is the name of the file listed and its size?

8. ___ Right click on the **3 1/2 Floppy (A:)** icon on the left side of the Explorer window. This causes a drop-down menu to appear. Select **Properties** from the drop-down menu. Look at three things very carefully: the size of the used space, the size of the free space, and the size of the disk capacity. There should be a large discrepancy. Subtracting the amount of space used by the command.com file from the total disk capacity leaves a discrepancy of approximately 290KB. This discrepancy is caused by other files on the disk that do not appear. These files have their hidden attribute set. To reveal the files, select **View** from the Explorer menu bar at the top of the window. From the **View** drop-down menu, select **Folder Options**. A dialog box should appear similar to the following.

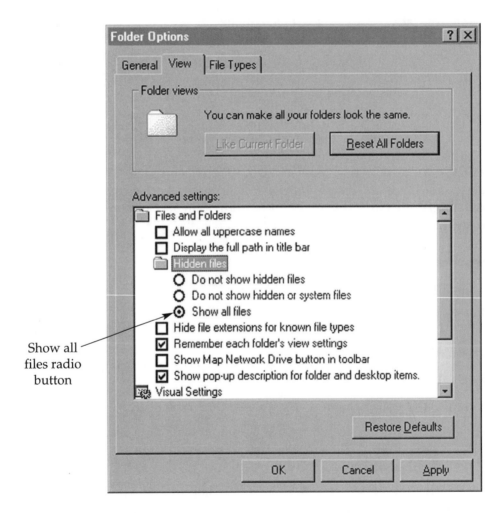

9. ___ Select the **View** tab at the top of the **Folder Options** dialog box. A list of check boxes and radio buttons is revealed. Notice the option category labeled **Hidden Files**. Click on the **Show All Files** radio button to activate it, and then click the **Apply** button at the bottom-right side of the dialog box. This allows you to view all hidden files on the floppy disk and hard drive.

10. ____ Close the dialog box and return to Windows Explorer to view the contents of the floppy disk. List all the hidden files that exist on the floppy disk in the following spaces. Notice that the hidden-file icons appear much lighter in color than the command.com icon.

_____

_____

_____

11. ____ Go back to the **Folder Options** dialog box once more. Click the **Restore Defaults** button, and then close the dialog box.

12. ____ Look at the Explorer window once more. The only file that should appear on the 3 1/2″ floppy is the command.com file.

13. ____ Return the PC to its original condition and then shut it down.

Review Questions

Answer the questions below with short, precise answers.

1. Explain how to reveal hidden and system files. _____

_____

2. Why do you think certain files are hidden by default? _____

_____

Name _____ Date_____

Class/Instructor _____

Lab Activity

24

Create a System Startup Disk

After completing this lab activity, you will be able to:

✴ Make a Windows 98 startup disk.

✴ Identify files contained on a startup disk.

✴ Reveal hidden files on the startup disk.

✴ Determine which files are necessary to start the computer system.

✴ Use the read-me file on the startup disk to become familiar with some common Windows 98 installation problems.

Introduction

A Windows 98 startup disk, or boot disk, helps you to gain access to the files on your hard drive if the system fails to boot. The startup disk is also used to run Setup. A Windows 98 startup disk is a must for your tool kit. Remember to label the disk and clearly indicate which version of operating system it was created from.

A Windows 98 startup disk uses a different collection of files than a Windows 95, Windows NT, Windows 2000, MS-DOS, or Linux startup disk. A typical startup disk includes many more than the three files generally associated with the DOS boot disk (io.sys, command.com, and config.sys). The Windows 98 startup disk also includes driver files for the CD drive of the machine it is made on.

However, the network driver for the network card is not included on the system startup disk. You may wish to copy it for later use. Booting the system from a startup disk presents you with certain options. One of these options allows you to choose to start the machine with or without CD support. There is also an option to abort the startup process.

■ Important!

A startup disk made with previous versions of Windows may not be compatible with Windows 98. Do not attempt to boot a Windows 98 or later system with a startup disk from a prior version.

Equipment and Materials

✴ Typical PC with the Windows 98 operating system installed

✴ Windows 98 Installation CD may be required

✴ 3 1/2" floppy disk

Procedure

1. ___ Boot the system and then run **Add/Remove Programs** from **Start | Settings | Control Panel**.

2. ___ Click on the **Startup Disk** tab and then click the **Create Disk** button. Follow the directions as they appear on the screen.

3. ___ Right click the **My Computer** icon and choose **Explore** from the menu. Open the A: drive, where the system startup disk you just made is located.

4. ___ Answer the following questions about the startup disk. You may need to adjust the view settings in order to see hidden and system files. To change the view settings, click **View** from the Windows Explorer menu bar. Next, pick **Folder Options** from the **View** menu. This opens the Folder Options dialog box. Select the **View** tab and then select the **Show all files** radio button in the Advanced settings: window. Click the **Apply** button to make the change.

Review Questions

1. What is the total number of files on the system disk? _____

Place a check mark in the appropriate column concerning the files listed below. If the file is on the startup disk, check the YES column. If the file does not exist on the startup disk, check the NO column. Some file extensions may not appear in the Explorer window. To see the extensions, right click on the filename. When the drop-down menu appears, select **Properties**.

YES NO

2. ___ ___ io.sys

3. ___ ___ command.com

4. ___ ___ msdos.sys

5. ___ ___ drvspace.bin

6. ___ ___ fdisk.exe

7. ___ ___ nologo.exe

8. ___ ___ readme.txt

9. ___ ___ review.txt

10. ___ ___ autoexec.bat

Part Two

Close all windows and open Notepad, found in **Start | Programs | Accessories | Notepad**. You may also use WordPad if you desire.

A PC-repair technician is always working with the cutting edge of PC technology. Because you will be installing the latest software or hardware on the market, there will be no textbooks available to teach you the very latest in technology. Consequently, many skills will be self-taught. A prime example is learning about new software. Often, there is only a read-me file to provide instruction and details about the software. As a technician, you must learn to read and study read-me files when they are provided.

This work sheet is a practice sheet based on the read-me file that is created with the startup disk, not the files on the Windows 98 Installation CD. The work sheet serves two purposes. First, it helps you to develop the habit of reading information files that come with new software. Second, it teaches you some special information concerning Windows 98 installation and the Windows 98 startup disk.

Review Questions

Open the readme.txt *file on the startup disk and read the contents. After you have read the file, answer the following questions. The* readme.txt *files can vary in content depending on the source of the Windows 98 CD.*

For Questions 1–3, indicate whether each item is true or false. Use a "T" for true and an "F" for false.

1. ___ The ebd.cab file is new with Windows 98.

2. ___ RAMDrive will change the letter designation of your CD-ROM drive by two letters. For example, if your CD-ROM drive is designated as the D: drive, RAMDrive will cause it to become the F: drive.

3. ___ The startup disk includes support for CD-ROM drives.

Answer the following questions with short, precise answers.

4. What is the size of the RAMDrive file used for startup? _____

5. Will Windows 98 installation support all CD-ROM drive types? _____

6. What is RAMDrive used for? _____

    _____

7. How does RAMDrive affect the CD-ROM drive letter assignment? _____

    _____

8. If Windows 98 fails to start properly, what does the Windows 98 readme file recommend you do first? _____

    _____

9. What two methods are used to start the Windows 98 operating system in Safe Mode?

    _____

    _____

10. Before installing Windows 98 on a PC, what should you do about any antivirus program that may be installed on the system? _____

    _____

11. What should you do if the Windows setup program stops responding during the hardware detection portion of the installation? _____

    _____

    _____

12. What command is used to check all your hard drives for errors? _____

13. What does **sys.com** do? _____

    _____

14. Which two utilities are used to prepare a new hard disk drive for use after physically installing the drive? _____

15. What does the command **format c: /s** do? _____

    _____

Name _____ Date _____

Class/Instructor _____

Lab Activity

25

Device Manager

After completing this lab activity, you will be able to:

✳ Access the PC's Device Manager.

✳ Identify hardware installed on a PC.

✳ Identify system resources typically assigned to system hardware.

✳ Identify IRQ assignments.

✳ Identify DMA assignments.

✳ Identify I/O and memory assignments.

Introduction

Device Manager can be opened by right clicking the **My Computer** icon, selecting **Properties** from the shortcut menu, and then selecting the **Device Manager** tab in the System Properties dialog box. The Device Manager can also be accessed through **My Computer | Control Panel | System | Device Manager**.

Device Manager is one of the dialog boxes most frequently used by PC technicians. It contains information about the type of hardware installed, IRQ and DMA settings, and I/O and memory assignments. The devices, or hardware, installed in the PC can be viewed in Device Manager in one of two ways: by type or by connection.

Students are confused at times when viewing the I/O and memory information displayed in the Device Manager dialog box. System I/O port addresses are expressed in hexadecimal form, similar to memory addresses. The I/O port is used in communications between devices and software programs. Devices and software programs must know where to send and receive information. The I/O port address is the location of the device's communication doorway, and is used to find the location of the device on the bus structure.

The memory address is the location of the RAM that the device uses to store information for transmitting and receiving. It can span a single range of one byte or span a very large range of memory addresses, depending on the function of a device. Not every device requires both an I/O port assignment and a range of memory. For example, most keyboards have only an I/O port assignment, not memory. Keyboards usually have their own buffer that serves as a memory area. A chip used as a bus bridge will have both, an I/O port assignment and a range of memory used to store data until it is transmitted across the bus.

Problems with assigned resources are usually indicated in Device Manager by an exclamation mark. If a device cannot be identified, a question mark usually appears in the list where the device has been assigned. These are good indications of a problem with a device.

System conflicts may arise when two devices share the same IRQ. However, some devices are compatible when using the same IRQ. For example, chipsets that control the bus communications commonly share an IRQ with devices assigned to that bus. In this case, the two devices work well together.Other devices may not function properly when sharing an IRQ assignment.

When two devices share the same IRQ assignment and one of the devices has a problem communicating with the CPU, it is referred to as an IRQ conflict. For example, when a scanner and a sound card are assigned the same IRQ setting, the system may lockup when the user attempts to use the scanner. When an IRQ conflict exists, one of the two devices must be reassigned to different IRQ.

With Plug and Play, most system resource assignments are managed automatically. Occasionally a conflict still arises. In these cases, you may need to disable the Plug and Play option in the system BIOS settings, and manually set a new IRQ for the affected hardware.

Equipment and Materials

✳   Typical PC with Windows 95 (or later) operating system

Procedure

1. ___ Boot the PC and wait for the desktop display.

2. Right click on the **My Computer** icon and then select the **Properties** option from the shortcut menu. You should see the System Properties dialog box.

3. Select the **Device Manager** tab. This will reveal a dialog box similar to the one shown here.

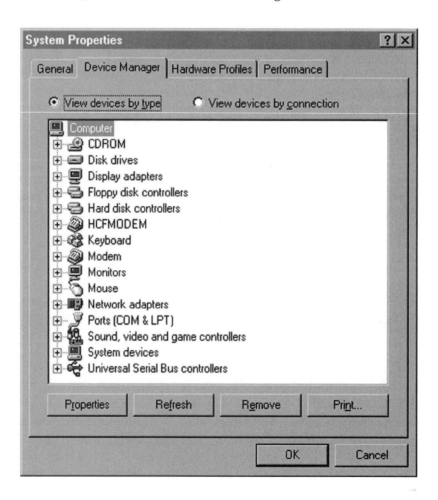

4. ___ Close the System Properties dialog box.

5. ___ Open the Device Manager through the Control Panel. Use **Start | Settings | Control Panel | System**.

6. ___ Again, select the **Device Manager** tab.

The Device Manager can be viewed in two ways: by device and by connection. Change the view several times by alternately clicking the **View device by type** and **View device by connection** radio buttons. Pay particular attention to how the devices are arranged in each view. Notice how the structure is similar in design to the Windows Explorer directory structure. Now, with the **View devices by type** radio button selected, click on the plus sign to the left of **Disk drives**. This expands the device tree and reveals the two types of disks installed on the PC. (There may be more devices depending on the PC used for the lab.)

7. ___ Now, click on the plus sign left of **Keyboard** to expand the device tree. Highlight the keyboard model that is identified, and then select the **Properties** button at the bottom of the window. This opens a dialog box that displays general information about the keyboard, the driver, and system resources used. Remember, the term *system resources* refers to I/O, IRQ, memory, and DMA assignments.

8. ___ Fill in the blanks in the following chart. Information for the chart can be found using the Device Manager. Not every block will be used. For example, if the device does not use a DMA channel, write "NA" (not applicable) inside the box.

Device	IRQ	I/O range	DMA channel
Mouse			
Keyboard			
Floppy drive			
Display adapter			
Monitor			
System timer			
CMOS real time clock			
Hard drive			
Modem			

9. ___ With the Device Manager open, locate the resources of the mouse. Attempt to reassign the mouse to interrupt request (IRQ) 11. Write a brief explanation what happens in the space provided.

_____

_____

10. ___ Select **Keyboard** from the Device Manager list to view the exact identification of the keyboard. (Click on the plus sign to the left of **Keyboard** in the Device Manager list.) Write the type of keyboard identified in the space provided.

_____

11. ___ After you have revealed the type of keyboard, select the **Properties** button, and then click the **Driver** tab.

12. ___ The Driver tab identifies the name and location of the driver file for that particular device. It also allows you to update the driver for the device.

13. ___ Leave the Device Manager dialog box on the screen while you answer the review questions. After you complete the review questions, return the PC to its original state before properly shutting it down.

Review Questions

1. What are system resources? _____

_____

2. How do you access the Device Manager dialog box? _____

_____

_____

3. How does Plug and Play affect system resources? _____

_____

_____

4. How can the device driver files and location of the driver files be viewed? _____

_____

5. How are problems concerning a device indicated in Device Manager? _____

_____

6. Do all devices have a direct memory access (DMA) assignment? _____

7. Can two or more devices share the same IRQ? _____

8. What is an IRQ conflict? _____

_____

9. How are IRQ conflicts resolved? _____

_____

_____

Name _____ Date_____

Class/Instructor _____

Lab Activity

26

Identifying PC BIOS and Operating Systems

Motherboards

After completing this lab activity, you will be able to:

✻ Identify the BIOS manufacturer and version.

✻ Identify the Windows operating system.

✻ Access and modify the BIOS CMOS settings.

Introduction

In this lab activity, you will learn to identify the manufacturer and version of the BIOS, Windows operating system, and browser.

The BIOS (Basic Input/Output System) translates commands given by the operating system into actions carried out by the PC's hardware. The type of hardware that makes up the PC system must be identified before the BIOS program can carry out commands that affect the system hardware. When the hardware is identified, the BIOS program stores the data in a CMOS (Complimentary Metal-Oxide Semiconductor). The CMOS must use a small battery to retain the settings after power to the computer is turned off.

The PC's hardware is usually identified automatically through Plug and Play technology. The Plug and Play technology automatically detects the hardware and records the settings on the CMOS. For the Plug and Play technology to work, three things are required. The hardware being installed, the BIOS, and the operating system must all be Plug and Play. All three requirements must be met for Plug and Play technology to work properly. For example, you may attach a Plug and Play device to a PC that is using a Plug and Play operating system, such as Windows 98. However, if the BIOS is not Plug and Play, the device will need to be installed manually. You may also upgrade the BIOS to a Plug and Play BIOS.

Typically, when the PC first boots, BIOS information is flashed across the screen. For example, a message similar to the following may appear in the upper-left quadrant of the screen.

    AMIBIOS 1992 C American Megatrends, Inc.
    BIOS Version 1.00.07
    0032 MB memory
    Press F1 to enter setup

This information displays the BIOS manufacture and version. The amount of RAM is displayed, and then instructions are given for accessing the BIOS setup program. The exact method of accessing the BIOS setup program is not standardized and is not always displayed on the screen. You may need to consult the PC or BIOS manufacturer's web site to identify the exact steps necessary to access the BIOS setup program.

Equipment and Materials

✻   Typical PC with a Windows 95 (or later) operating system

Procedure

1. ___ Turn on the PC and closely watch for instructions for accessing the BIOS setup program. If the information is not displayed, you may need to ask the instructor. In the space provided, write down the instructions for accessing the BIOS setup program.

   _____

2. ___ After accessing the BIOS setup screen, look for information to fill in the blanks that follow. You will not be familiar with much of the information recorded. This is normal. The information displayed in the BIOS settings will become clear to you as you progress through the course. What is important for you to understand is the type of information contained in the BIOS settings and what can be changed. There are many different BIOS-settings programs available and not all will display the information being requested, or display it in the same order. Answer all questions to the best of your ability.

   Is the system date and time displayed? _____

   Can the system time and date be changed? _____

   Is the BIOS version displayed? _____

   Is the amount of extended memory displayed and if so, how much memory does the PC have? _____

   What information can be viewed about the floppy drives?

   What information about the hard drive is present?

   _____

   Are there any security features present and if so, describe them.

   _____

   _____

   What information about the monitor is displayed?

   What are the Boot Options?

   _____

   What information is provided about the serial ports?

   _____

   What information is provided about the CPU?

3. ___ Now that you have found the information listed above, make special note of how the BIOS settings program is exited. You usually must exit by choosing an option such as: **Use default settings, Save Changes**, or **Do not retain changes to settings**. It is important to realize that changes are not automatically retained by the CMOS.

4. ___ If time permits and you have your instructor's approval, change the system time and date in the BIOS setup. Again, make sure you have instructor approval first.

5. ___ Return the system time and date settings to the correct settings and then shut down the PC system.

Review Questions

1. How did you access the BIOS setup program? _____

   _____

   _____

2. Why aren't the CMOS settings lost after the power is turned off to the PC? _____

   _____

3. Where is the manufacturer of the BIOS and the version displayed? _____

   _____

4. If instructions for accessing the BIOS setup program are not displayed on the screen, how could you find the information needed to determine the proper keystroke sequence for accessing the BIOS setup program? _____

   _____

   _____

Motherboards

Name _____ Date_____

Class/Instructor _____

Lab Activity

27

BIOS

Motherboards

After completing this lab activity, you will be able to:

* Explain the actions taken by the PC up to the point of loading the operating system.
* Acquire experience relating to diagnosing a bad hard drive.
* Acquire experience related to diagnosing a BIOS problem.

Introduction

BIOS stands for basic input/output system and is often referred to as firmware. Firmware is a combination of software (the program) and hardware (the chip) developed as a proprietary device. The BIOS allows the PC hardware to communicate with the operating system. This allows almost any operating system to be used on almost any PC. If it were not for BIOS, operating systems would have to be written for specific hardware systems. The BIOS program is stored on a chip located on the motherboard. When power is applied to a PC, the BIOS starts the POST. The POST is the acronym for power-on self-test. The power-on self-test does a quick check of the PC major components, including the monitor, keyboard, and RAM. It is not a detailed check, but rather a basic check of required devices.

The operating system is stored on the hard drive. In this lab activity, you will disconnect the ribbon connector from the hard drive. This will mean that the PC has no operating system, only the BIOS. You will boot the PC and closely watch the activity on the PC's monitor. You will record all activity observed from the boot-up until failure.

Equipment and Materials

* Typical PC loaded with a Windows 95 (or later) operating system

Procedure

1. ___ Boot the PC and watch the monitor closely. See if you can identify major changes in the screen presentation and read the messages on the display. You may want to reboot several times.

2. ___ Properly shut down the PC after each boot.

3. ___ Open the PC case carefully and identify the hard drive. Make a sketch showing the position of the hard drive and the orientation of the flat ribbon cable that plugs into it. There should be a colored line on one side of the ribbon cable. This colored line is used to correctly connect the cable to the drive. The colored line must line up with pin 1 on the drive's connector. Depending on the way the drive is mounted, it can be difficult to determine pin 1. This is why you need to make a sketch.

4. ___ With the power to the PC turned off, gently remove the cable from the hard drive by pulling on the ends of the connector, *not* the ribbon. Pulling on the ribbon can damage the integrity of the ribbon connection.

5. ___ With the flat ribbon connector removed, turn on the PC and watch the boot operation carefully. Record your observations in the following spaces.

_____

_____

_____

_____

_____

_____

_____

6. ___ Turn off all power to the PC.

7. ___ Reinstall the flat ribbon cable to the hard drive.

8. ___ Turn on the power to reboot the system. Be sure the PC is working properly before ending the lab activity. If there is a problem, please call your instructor.

Review Questions

1. What is the colored line on the side of the flat ribbon cable used for? _____

_____

2. What is the error message displayed when the system fails to load the operating system or locate the hard drive? _____

3. What does the acronym POST stand for? _____

4. Is the POST controlled by BIOS or by the operating system? _____

Replace or Upgrade a ZIF Socket–Type CPU

Motherboards

After completing this lab activity, you will be able to:

✳ Replace a ZIF socket–type CPU.

✳ Install heat sink or cooling fan as appropriate.

Introduction

This lab serves as a guide for the replacement or upgrade of a ZIF socket–type CPU. It is a set of generic instructions that may be followed. When replacing or upgrading a CPU, it is strongly advised that you obtain the manufacturer's technical documents or visit its web site for the exact installation procedures.

The original socket design used for CPUs required a great deal of force to install the CPU. The pins had to be perfectly aligned with the holes in the socket, and then sufficient force had to be used to insert the CPU pins into the socket holes.

The force required to insert the CPU could be as high as forty pounds. This caused many damaged CPU pins. Once a pin is bent on a chip, it is easily broken. Attempts to straighten the pin and reinsert the CPU into the socket often led to broken pins, which are not repairable. In this manner, a very expensive CPU can be permanently damaged.

A zero insertion-force (ZIF) socket requires no force (aside from the unit's own weight) to insert the CPU into the socket. Each socket hole acts like a tiny vise, gripping the CPU pins. A lever mounted on the side of the socket controls the clamping action. Lifting the lever to the up position releases the viselike connections to the CPU pins, allowing the CPU to be easily extracted.

Inserting a CPU into the socket requires no external force to be applied to the unit. The CPU drops into place if it is properly aligned. The socket pins must align with the pin pattern on the CPU before insertion. The socket is keyed to indicate proper CPU-to-socket alignment. Usually pin one on the CPU and hole one on the socket are identified. Once the CPU is placed into the socket, the lever is closed, which causes a physical as well as electrical connection between each pin of the CPU and the socket.

As speed of the CPUs increased, CPU cooling became a major concern. Excessive heat damages the sensitive electronic structure inside CPUs. To prevent overheating, heat sinks, fans, or combinations of both are installed on many CPUs. The heat sinks and fans come in a variety of shapes and sizes, but they are all designed to transfer heat away from the CPU.

It is important to note here that the expansion slot holes in the back of the computer case should not be left open. If a hole is not filled with an expansion card, it should be covered. A missing slot cover may hinder the proper air circulation inside the case, leading to the over-heating of computer components such as the CPU and RAM. A computer case is designed so the airflow from the case's fan cools the system board and vital components. A missing expansion slot cover could prevent proper cooling. When a slot cover is missing, a fan mounted in the back of the case draws in fresh air from the slot rather than from across the components. It also allows an excessive amount of dust to enter the system. A case cooling fan often has a screen or filter to reduce dust.

In this lab activity, you will remove and then replace the CPU of the assigned computer. There is no real need to change out the CPU. You will simply remove the existing CPU, try to boot the system, observe the effect of a missing CPU, and then reinstall the same CPU.

Equipment and Materials

* Typical PC with a ZIF socket–type CPU (a heat sink or fan should be included)
* Anti-static materials as required by the instructor (you will need an anti-static bag used to ship electronic parts or an anti-static pad on which to rest the CPU after removal)
* Web site access will be of great benefit to obtain technical information about the procedures for removing and installing the CPU

Procedure

1. ___ Boot the PC and wait for the Windows desktop to appear. This verifies the system is working properly.

2. ___ Properly shut down the system.

3. ___ Turn the power off and open the PC, exposing the inside of the chassis. Locate the CPU. Be careful not to touch the CPU. If the computer system has been on for a while, the CPU can be hot to the touch.

4. ___ Make a sketch of the position and connection point of any wiring from the CPU fan, if one exists. If a fan is used, be careful to note the exact location of the fan's power cable connection.

5. ___ Study the heat sink and/or fan assembly closely to determine how the fan and/or heat sink are retained. Heat sinks are usually stuck to a CPU unit using a heat-conducting paste. The paste not only ensures a tight fit between the heat sink and CPU but also transmits the heat generated by the CPU to the metallic heat sink. The fan may also be pasted into position as part of the heat sink assembly or held in place by a metallic retaining clip. Use the following illustration as an aid. The fan arrangement shown may not match the one you are using for your assignment.

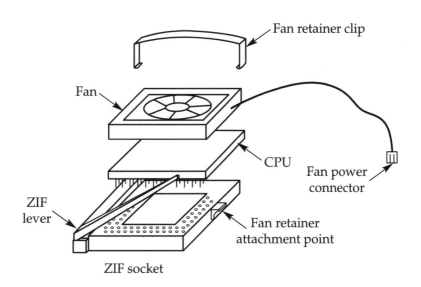

6. ___ Carefully remove any fan or heat sink retaining devices. There may not be any, depending on the equipment assigned. If a retaining clip is used to hold the fan in place, a light downward pressure will spring it. Some clips are equipped with small slots for inserting a small flat tip screwdriver. The screwdriver can be used to spring the clip away from the retaining clip attachment point on the socket. Always consult the web site of the manufacturer. Most have online information for assembly and disassembly of the major computer components.

7. ___ Locate the ZIF socket lever and move it into the upright position. This should release the CPU pins.

8. ___ Carefully remove the CPU and set the CPU on a foam anti-static mat or inside an anti-static bag. There should not be any force required to remove the CPU assembly. When the ZIF socket lever is in the release position, the CPU is held in place only by its own weight and the weight of the heat sink. Lift the CPU straight up; do not use a rocking motion.

9. ___ With the CPU removed from the motherboard, power up the system. Closely observe the monitor as the system boots and record your observations in the space provided.

_____

_____

_____

_____

10. ___ After you have observed the attempted boot sequence, turn off the power to the PC.

11. ___ Now, reinsert the CPU into the socket. Reverse the removal procedure to reinstall it. Be sure to line the pins up correctly with the socket. The socket and CPU should have some sort of pin identification used to properly position the CPU into the socket. Usually one of the corners of the socket is designed differently or the pin arrangement is such that the CPU can only go into the socket in the correct orientation. Look at Chapter 4 in your textbook to see the different socket styles.

12. ___ After the CPU, fan assembly, and heat sink have been reinstalled, power up the PC to see whether it will boot properly. After the PC boots, make sure the fan is running.

Review Questions

1. What is the function of the heat sink? _____

   _____

2. Why should expansion slot covers in the case not be left open? _____

   _____

3. How do you properly position the CPU when inserting it into the socket? _____

   _____

4. How much force is required to insert or remove a CPU from a ZIF socket? _____

   _____

Using a Meter to Check Continuity

After completing this lab activity, you will be able to:

* Define the term *continuity*.
* Explain how to test conductors for continuity.
* Explain the meaning of the term *ohms*.
* Explain the difference between infinity and zero ohms.

Introduction

In this lab activity, you will use a multimeter to measure resistance in a conductor. Checking resistance in a conductor is also referred to as a continuity test. Continuity is the term for a continuous path for the flow of electricity. A good fuse has continuity. A typical fuse found in most electronic equipment is nothing more than a small wire enclosed in a glass tube. The wire is designed to melt when the electrical energy reaches a specific current level. When the current level is exceeded, the wire melts, thus opening the electrical path. When the electrical path is opened, there is said to be no electrical continuity.

During the last part of the lab activity, you will take voltage readings of various batteries. This is not a check to determine if the battery is good or bad, but rather a simple exercise to learn how to properly take voltage readings. To check if a battery is good or bad, the voltage level must be checked while the battery is still installed in the equipment and the equipment is turned on. A bad battery can produce sufficient levels of voltage to appear as a good battery once it is removed from the equipment.

Equipment and Materials

* Digital multimeter
* 9-volt battery
* 6-volt battery
* 1 1/2-volt battery (common "D" or "C" cell)
* 12" of CAT-5 cable (any multiple conductor cable will do)
* Good fuse (any available size and style)

Procedure

1. ___ First, familiarize yourself with the digital multimeter you are provided with for this series of experiments. Look at the available selections, such as voltage, resistance, and current. Look at the various places on the meter where the test leads may be attached.

2. ___ Set the meter dial(s) and install the test leads into the correct input sockets to take a resistance reading. When you think the meter is set up properly to take a resistance reading, call the instructor or raise your hand. Do not continue until the instructor has given approval.

3. ___ Once the meter settings have been approved by the instructor, hold the test leads together and look at the meter display. The following illustration should assist you.

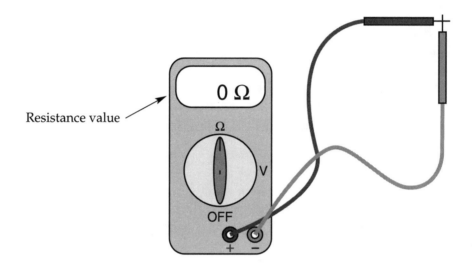

4. ___ Record the amount of resistance indicated on the display in the area provided below.
   _____

5. ___ Now, hold the leads apart and once again look at the meter display. Record the amount of resistance indicated on the display. _____

6. ___ Take the good fuse that you have been issued and take a resistance reading of the fuse. The following illustration may be used as a reference.

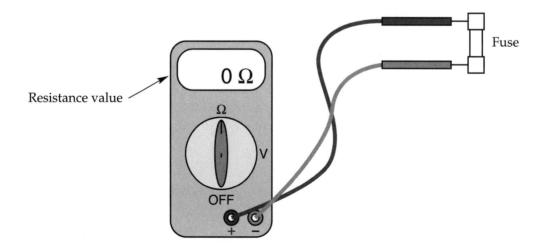

Name_____

7. ___ Write the amount of resistance in the good fuse. _____

8. ___ Take the segment of wire that you have been issued. Connect the leads to each end of the wire and check the amount of resistance. This type of check is often referred to as a continuity check. An indication of little resistance from one end to the other means the conductor has continuity. A reading of extremely high resistance or infinity means there is no continuity. No continuity is caused by a break in a conductor path. Take readings from one end of the conductor to the other end. There should be continuity between the ends of the wires with matching color. There will not be continuity between ends of the wire with different colors. Test all possible combinations of the wire strands and record your observations in the space provided. _____

_____

_____

_____

_____

_____

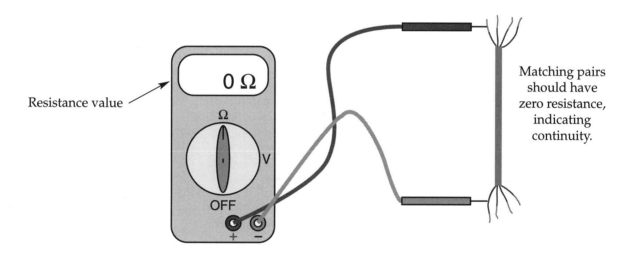

Resistance value

0 Ω

Ω

V

OFF

+   −

Matching pairs should have zero resistance, indicating continuity.

9. ___ Now, set the meter to read dc voltage. Once you have set the selector switch and are sure the leads are plugged into the appropriate jacks, call the instructor over to check the meter settings before you test the batteries. Be absolutely sure the meter is set to read voltage. If a meter is set to read resistance and is connected to an electrical source, such as a battery, the meter can be permanently damaged. Remember, never connect a meter to an electrical source when the selector switch is set to take a resistance reading.

10. ___ You will now read the voltage level of the three batteries provided. The following illustration may be used to assist you. Indicate the voltage of the batteries in the spaces provided.

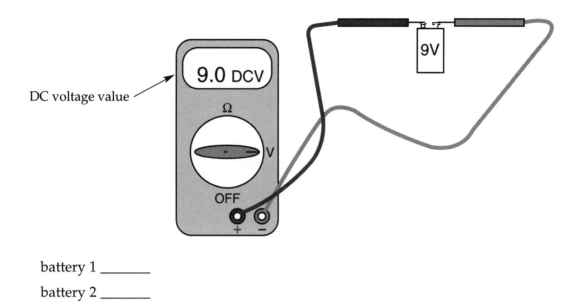

DC voltage value

battery 1 _____

battery 2 _____

battery 3 _____

11. ___ Turn off the power on the multimeter and return the meter and the supplies.

Review Questions

1. When the test leads of the meter are touched together and the meter is set to measure resistance, what should the resistance reading be? _____

2. A good fuse will have how much resistance? _____

3. A blown fuse will have how much resistance? _____

4. A good continuous conductor will have how much resistance? _____

5. A conductor that is broken in two will produce what resistance value? _____

6. When checking a multi-conductor wire, how much resistance should there be between wires of different coloring? _____

7. Define *continuity*. _____

_____

8. What can happen if a meter is set up to read resistance and is then connected to electrical energy?_____

_____

Lab Activity

30

Exploring and Replacing the Power Supply

After completing this lab activity, you will be able to:

✱ Replace a PC power supply unit.

✱ Determine if a power supply is defective.

✱ Check the voltage input and output of a power supply unit.

Introduction

One of the most common PC problems encountered is a defective power supply unit. The power supply unit is considered a field replacement unit. A field replacement unit is any module in a PC system that is commonly changed in the field, and does not need to be brought back to the repair shop to be replaced or upgraded. The power supply converts 120-volt ac input into 12-, 5-, and 3.3-volt dc outputs. It supplies the correct dc voltage to the PC's modules and devices, such as the motherboard, disk drive, and CD-ROM drive. Some of the dc voltages are positive, while others are negative. Some of the connections have no voltage indicated at all. These usually indicate a ground used by system components. Power supplies come in a variety of styles and arrangements. Their physical appearance depends on the motherboard and case style, referred to as the form factor.

Power supplies are classified by their wattage ratings. The wattage rating is an indication of how much electrical energy can be safely supplied to the PC's devices. In general, a higher wattage rating means that more devices can be connected to the power supply. In a typical repair scenario, you would replace a power supply with one having the same wattage rating. However, if additional devices have been added to the machine, then the power supply may need to be upgraded to a higher wattage rating.

In this lab activity, you will remove the existing power supply and then reinstall it in the same PC. After reinstalling the power supply, you will record the voltage output of the connectors. Note that not all power supplies supply the same voltage levels.

Equipment and Materials

✱ Typical PC with a 486 (or later) processor

✱ Digital multimeter to take voltage readings

Procedure

1. ___ Power up the assigned PC and make sure it is working properly. If all is well, properly shut down the unit.

2. ___ Remove the cover from the PC's case.

3. ___ Before removing any of the wiring or attempting to physically remove the power supply unit, *unplug the power cord* that runs from the power supply to the 120-volt outlet.

4. ___ Once the power cord has been removed, make a drawing of the power cables, noting their orientation to the various components. For example, draw the position of the black wires running from the power supply to the motherboard. The connector's orientation can be recorded by the color of the wiring as well as the connector identification marks. The following illustration shows how two power cables connect to the motherboard. The power cable connection to the motherboard may consist of one or two separate power cables, depending on the age of the technology.

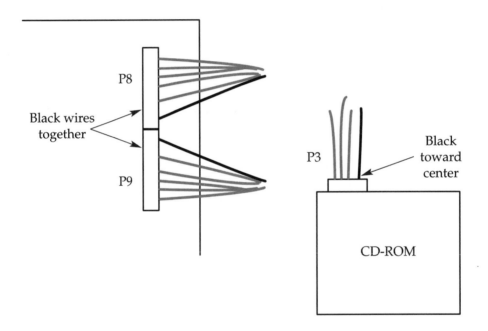

In the drawing, the connector identification marks have been labeled P8, P9, and P3. The orientations of the black wires to the physical devices have also been recorded. It is not necessary to indicate each color wire in the harness. The wiring in the drawing shown here will not necessarily match the wiring in the PC you are working on.

5. ___ Carefully remove each of the power cables from the various devices. As you remove the cables, be careful not to loosen any other connections or adapter cards installed on the PC.

6. ___ After all of the wiring from the power supply has been disconnected, locate the screws that connect the power supply to the case. Carefully remove the screws, being careful not to confuse the power supply mounting screws with the screws used to mount the fan to the power supply. You should not need to remove the power supply fan. Also, do not remove any screws used to fasten the cover to the power supply.

7. ___ After the power supply has been completely removed, call your instructor to inspect your work.

8. ___ Reverse the process to reinstall the power supply. Reconnect all the devices according to your drawing. Do not plug the power cord into the power supply or the outlet until your instructor has inspected your work.

9. ___ After the instructor has approved your reinstallation of the power supply, connect the power cord and boot up the PC.

10. ___ Check all devices to make sure that they have power. If they do not, call your instructor.

11. ___ Now, take voltage readings at each of the different connectors running from the power supply. You need to turn the power off, disconnect the power cables to the devices, and then reapply power to the power supply. Finally, measure the voltages at each terminal in the various connectors. On the following page, record your findings in the appropriate spaces of the worksheet. Follow the example shown.

Warning:

Disconnecting a power connector from any device while the device is energized could result in permanent damage to the device. This is especially true for the motherboard.

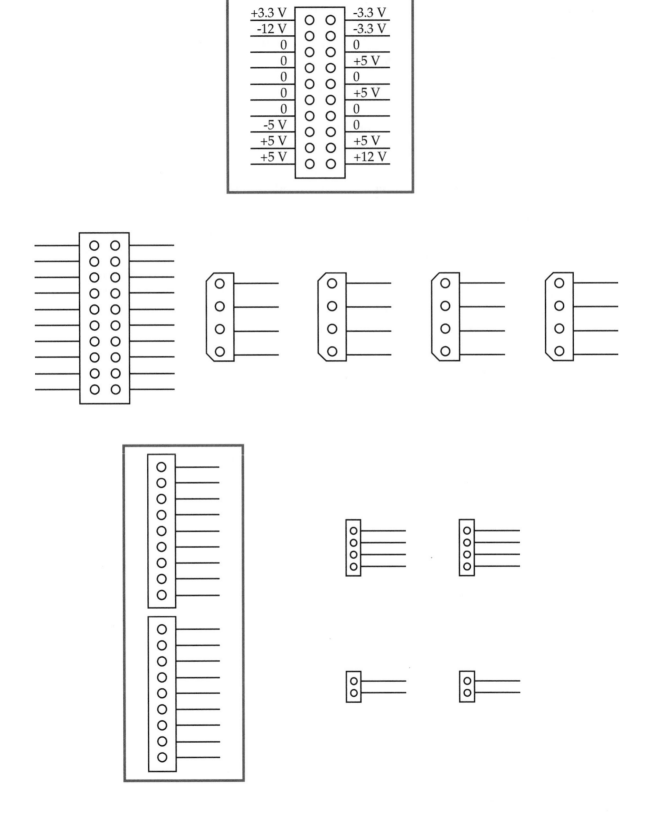

Example:

+3.3 V		-3.3 V
-12 V		-3.3 V
0		0
0		+5 V
0		0
0		+5 V
0		0
-5 V		0
+5 V		+5 V
+5 V		+12 V

12. ___ After recording all voltages at each power connection, return the PC to its original condition.

Review Questions

1. What other components of the PC affect the power supply's appearance? _____

   _____

2. Do all power supplies supply the same voltages? _____

3. What is the power supply's function in the PC? _____

   _____

4. What is the wattage rating of the power supply in your test unit? _____

5. Look on the power supply. What is the rated input voltage and frequency? _____

Power Supplies

Name _____ Date_____

Class/Instructor _____

Determine Amount of RAM

After completing this lab activity, you will be able to:

★ Identify the amount of memory installed on a PC.

Introduction

There are several different ways to identify the amount of memory installed on a typical PC. The amount of memory is revealed to the user when the PC runs the power-on self-test (POST). The RAM is tested and the amount of memory is displayed on the screen during the POST. The amount of memory can also be determined by looking in the System Properties dialog box, which can be opened by clicking the **System** icon in the Control Panel. You can receive a detailed accounting of the total amount of memory, and where it is allocated, by going to the DOS prompt and typing the command **mem**. The System Monitor utility, a very sophisticated diagnostic and monitoring tool, can monitor memory activity and give a good indication if the memory needs to be upgraded.

Equipment and Materials

★ Typical PC with 8MB or more of SIMM or DIMM memory and Windows 95 (or later) operating system installed

Procedure

1. ___ Boot the PC and watch the display closely for the POST RAM test and the amount of RAM installed. Write the amount installed below. If you missed it, shut down the PC and reboot. _____

The PC may not display the POST stages. This occurs when the option to show the POST process is disabled in the BIOS setup. This setting can be changed by running the BIOS setup program and enabling the POST display. The display is usually disabled for security reasons. By blanking out the display during the POST, the key combination to access BIOS is hidden from view, as is the memory information. Hiding this information limits unauthorized access to the setup program.

2. ___ Once the desktop is displayed, open the System Properties dialog box. This dialog box is opened through **Start | Settings | Control Panel | System**. Look under the **Performance** and **General** tabs. Write down the memory information in the space provided. The amount of information will be limited, compared to the amount of information provided by the DOS **mem** command.

_____

_____

3. ___ A quick way to access the System Properties dialog box is to right click on the **My Computer** icon, and select **Properties** from the short cut menu. Do so now.

4. ___ Close the System Properties dialog box.

5. ___ To access the Microsoft System Information dialog box, select the **Run** option from the **Start** menu and enter **msinfo32**. The Microsoft System Information dialog box should appear. This is a very detailed box concerning all system information, hardware and software alike. The default screen should display memory information in the System Information window.

6. ___ Another way to access the Microsoft System Information dialog box is to access it through **Start | Programs | Accessories | System Tools | System Information**. Try it now to see if you obtain the same results. The System Monitor utility may or may not be installed on your PC. It is not installed during a normal operating system installation. To run it, select **Start | Programs | Accessories | System Tools | System Monitor**. A screen similar to the one shown should appear.

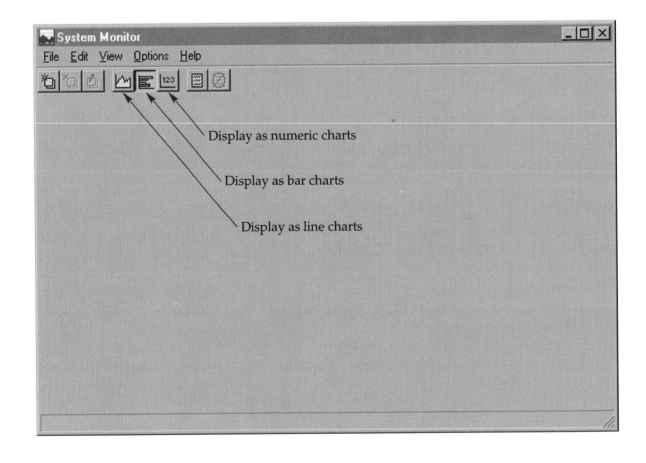

7. ___ If System Monitor is not installed, install it using **Add Remove Programs** in the **Control Panel**. Select the **Windows Setup** tab in the Add/Remove Programs Properties dialog box. Scroll through the **Components:** list, select **System Tools**, and click the **Details** button. Scroll through the **Components:** list, check the box next to **System Monitor**, and click **OK**. Finally, pick the **Apply** button, and follow the directions on the screen. Be sure to have the Windows 98 Installation CD available, although you may not need it. If System Monitor is not already installed on your machine, install it now.

8. ___ After you successfully install the System Monitor utility, select **Start | Programs | Accessories | System Tools | System Monitor**. This will run the System Monitor.

9. ___ Now, select **Allocated memory** and **Other memory** for monitoring. You select them by opening the **Edit** menu and selecting **Add item**. A list of categories appears in the Add Item dialog box. Choose **Memory Manager** and then select **Allocated memory** from the window on the right. Hold down the [Ctrl] key and select **Other Memory**. Both options should now be highlighted. Click the **OK** button.

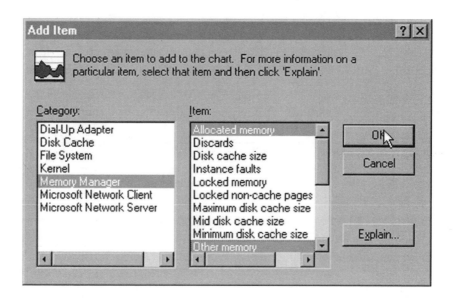

10. ___ The default display will be a line chart form. The data can also be displayed in bar chart and numeric chart forms. The chart styles are changed by selecting a new style from the **View** menu of the System Monitor window. Try the options for **Bar Charts** and **Numeric Charts** now.

11. ___ To find out more about the options available, highlight a system device you wish to monitor in the Add Item dialog box. Next, click the **Explain** button. A dialog box appears with a brief description of the selected item. Try it now. Remember, you must select **Edit | Add Item** from the System Monitor window, select a category from the **Components:** list, and then select an item from the **Item:** list before the **Explain** button becomes available.

12. ___ Now, answer the review questions. You may leave the PC on, and access **Help** while you answer the following questions. After you complete all of the questions, return everything to its original condition. If your PC did not have System Manager installed when you started, use the **Add/Remove Programs** feature in the **Control Panel** to remove it before shutting down the system.

Review Questions

1. List two ways to access the Microsoft System Information dialog box. _____

_____

_____

_____

2. What memory-related items can be monitored using System Monitor? _____

_____

_____

_____

_____

_____

_____

_____

3. At the DOS prompt, run **mem/?**, and list the option switches that can be used with the **mem** command. _____

4. What is the effect of using the **/d** and **/p** switches together in the **mem** command? _____

_____

_____

Name _____ Date_____

Class/Instructor _____

Lab Activity 32

Memory Diagnostics and Upgrade

After completing this lab activity, you will be able to:

✶ Describe the symptoms of a defective memory module.

✶ Determine the amount of memory installed on a PC.

✶ Determine the technical characteristics of the memory installed on the PC.

Introduction

One of the most common jobs of a PC technician is upgrading memory. The identification and selection of the correct type of memory can often be the most challenging part of the upgrade. Before additional memory can be added, the current memory must be identified. Additional memory should match the existing memory in the PC. The following is a list from the textbook describing the concerns that need to be addressed when upgrading memory:

✶ Physical Shape: Are you replacing or upgrading SIMMs or DIMMs?

✶ Quantity of RAM: What is the total amount of RAM desired? Are you adding to existing RAM or replacing?

✶ Parity or Non-parity: Does the current memory have parity checking or not? Does the current system support parity checking?

✶ Voltage: At what voltage do the memory chips operate, 5 or 3.3 volts?

✶ Type: What type of memory chip are you going to install, DRAM, SRAM, etc.?

✶ Speed: Are you going to match the existing chip speed or replace with higher speed?

To answer these questions correctly, you must cover all the material in the textbook and correctly identify the type of memory installed in the PC. The physical design of the memory can be misleading. For example, DIMMs may all appear identical, but some proprietary memory modules have nonstandard keys. In such cases, attempting to add additional memory or replace existing memory with a nonproprietary memory module could be disastrous.

Some signs of a need to upgrade or add additional RAM are as follows:

✶ Constant hard drive activity caused by the system using part of the hard drive as virtual RAM

✶ Slow screen updates, especially ones with intensive graphics

✶ Slow program performance, especially when opening new programs or switching between programs

Windows comes with some system tools that can help you look at the RAM performance objectively. The tools are System Monitor and System Resource Meter. These tools are not installed during a normal Windows installation and setup. To install these tools, you have to use the **Add/Remove Programs** icon in the **Control Panel**. A lab activity for installing and using these two tools is covered in this manual.

There are three major parts to this lab activity. First, you will simulate a defective memory module by removing memory from a PC and observing the error messages and the boot sequence. Second, you will remove and reinstall a pair of SIMM modules. Third, you will remove and reinstall a single DIMM module.

The machine assigned to you by the instructor will determine the order in which you complete this lab. Usually one-half of the class will use a PC containing SIMMs while the other half use machines equipped with DIMMs. After completing the lab procedures for one type of memory, you will repeat the lab using the PC with the other type of memory. Remember that SIMMs are usually installed as pairs, while DIMMs can be installed as single units.

Equipment and Materials

✱ (2) PCs with 486 or later processors (one PC with SIMM and the other with DIMM memory modules installed)

✱ Anti-static bag, or other type of anti-static container, for storing the removed memory module

✱ Internet access is also required for assistance in memory identification

Procedure

1. ___ Boot the PC to be sure it is in proper working order before you begin the lab activity. If the PC is in good working order, properly shut it down and prepare to remove the case. Be sure to follow all anti-static procedures as outlined by your instructor.

2. ___ With the electrical power shut off to the PC, remove the PC case.

3. ___ Locate the RAM on the motherboard. It is either a SIMM or DIMM module.

4. ___ Remove all RAM memory from the PC.

To remove a DIMM, simply locate the release levers on each end of the memory socket and move them into a downward direction as shown in the following illustration. DIMMs are inserted and removed vertically. There is no need to tilt a DIMM.

To remove a SIMM, release the memory-board retaining clips by gently pressing them away from the SIMM and then rotate the SIMM to a 30°–40° angle. The SIMM should automatically tilt when released. Place the memory unit on an anti-static surface.

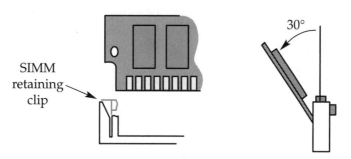

SIMM
retaining
clip

30°

The SIMM retaining clip is pulled to release the SIMM memory module. It is then tilted to approximately at 30° angle before it is removed. Installation is the reverse procedure.

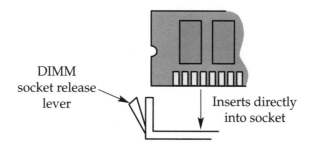

DIMM
socket release
lever

Inserts directly
into socket

The DIMM is inserted directly into the socket. There is no need to tilt the DIMM. Simply move the DIMM socket release lever outward.

5. ___ Look closely at the memory module for identification marks and a manufacturer's name. Copy down any information found on the memory module. All numbers are important. Go to the Internet and attempt to find the manufacturer of the memory unit. If the exact manufacturer cannot be determined, look up information on the PC at the PC manufacturer's web site. You may also identify the motherboard, and then go to the motherboard manufacturer's web site for memory information. List the information about the memory, such as speed, type, and parity issues, in the space provided. _____

_____

_____

_____

6. ___ Before replacing the memory unit, apply power to the PC and boot the system. Observe the sequence of messages on the screen. Write down, in general terms, what is observed and any error messages that may appear. _____

_____

_____

_____

Memory

7. ___ Power down the PC and then replace the RAM memory module(s). Be sure to properly align the notches at the bottom of the memory module with the notches in the memory socket on the motherboard. This will ensure that you do not install the memory modules backward.

To insert a DIMM, align the memory module with its socket. When the module and socket are perfectly aligned, gently push straight down on the module. When the module is as far down in the socket as it will go, locate the levers on each end of the socket. Move each lever into the upright position. This should seat the memory module at the bottom of the socket and lock it in place.

To insert a SIMM, lean the SIMM 30°–40°, and insert it into the socket. Make sure the bottom of the SIMM is in contact with the bottom of the socket. The SIMM must seat properly in order to establish good electrical contact. Gently rotate the SIMM to an upright position. You should feel the retaining clips snap into place when the SIMM is completely upright in the socket.

8. ___ After the memory has been replaced, boot the PC to be sure you have properly installed the memory and that the system is working properly. If it is not, call your instructor.

9. ___ Now repeat the lab steps using the PC that has the other type of memory modules.

10. ___ After removing and reinstalling both types of memory modules, boot the PC and watch the screen to see if the amount of memory installed is displayed on the screen during the POST. The memory should be displayed, unless the BIOS is set up to hide the display during a system boot.

Another way to quickly identify the amount of memory installed on a PC is to right click on the **My Computer** icon and then select **Properties**. The amount of RAM installed is displayed under the General tab in the System Properties dialog box.

11. ___ Close the System Properties dialog box, and return the PCs to their original conditions before leaving the lab area.

Review Questions

1. _____ are usually installed in pairs while _____ can be installed as single modules. _____
_____

2. Where can you find specific technical information about the memory modules installed in the PC? _____
_____

3. What precautions should be taken when removing and replacing memory? _____
_____
_____
_____

4. What are three signs that a PC needs more memory? _____
_____
_____
_____

5. What two software tools can be used to analyze memory performance? _____
_____

Name _____ Date_____

Class/Instructor _____

Lab Activity

33

System Monitor

After completing this lab activity, you will be able to:

✶ Use System Monitor to evaluate the CPU.

✶ Use System Monitor to evaluate the memory.

✶ Change the appearance of the data presented by System Monitor.

Introduction

The System Monitor tool can monitor the activity of many PC items, such as the CPU, memory utilization, disk cache. In this lab activity, you will become familiar with the abilities and applications for the System Monitor program. The System Monitor is not installed during a typical Windows 98 installation. You must load it from the Windows 98 installation disk. When placing the Windows 98 CD into the CD drive you can prevent the CD from automatically running if you hold down the [Shift] key while inserting the CD.

The System Monitor is a good tool for objectively determining if a PC needs a memory upgrade or CPU replacement. It also helps determine if more disk cache space is required. After System Monitor is added, it will be located at **Start | Programs | Accessories | System Tools | System Monitor**.

In the System Monitor, data can be displayed in several ways. It can be presented as a bar chart, line chart, or as strictly numerical data. A sample chart of processor usage, allocated memory, unused physical memory, and the read speed of the file system are all shown here. Note that all of the readings are displayed as line charts.

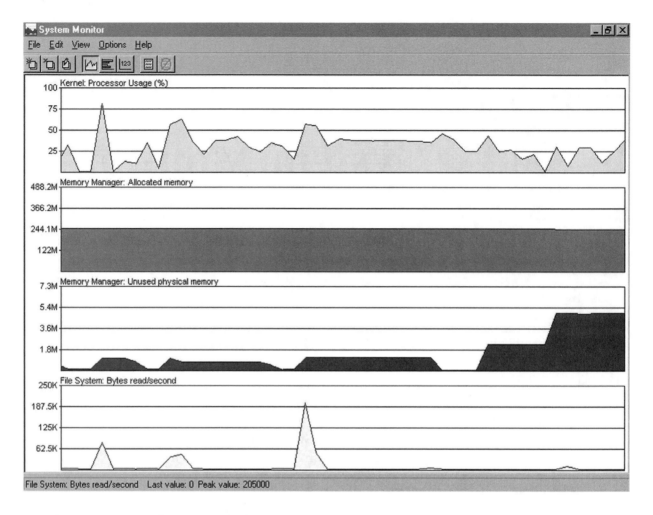

Equipment and Materials

* Typical PC with Windows 98 operating system installed
* Windows 98 Installation CD

Procedure

1. ___ Boot the PC. After the Windows desktop is displayed, insert the installation CD while holding down the [Shift] key.

2. ___ Open the **Add/Remove Programs** icon in the Control Panel. Select the **Windows Setup** tab. In the Components: window, scroll down to System Tools. Select **System Tools**, and then click the **Details** button to reveal the list of components available. Select **System Monitor** from the list and then click **OK**. The System Monitor program will be loaded.

3. ___ Open System Monitor through the Start menu by selecting the following: **Start | Programs | Accessories | System Tools | System Monitor**. If you are unable to locate the System Monitor, call your instructor for assistance.

4. ___ Once System Monitor is loaded, you can select the items you wish to load from the **Edit** menu. Select **Add Item** to reveal a list of categories that can be monitored. Selecting a category reveals all of the specific items within that category that you may monitor. Select an item and then click on the **Explain** button to view information about the item selected.

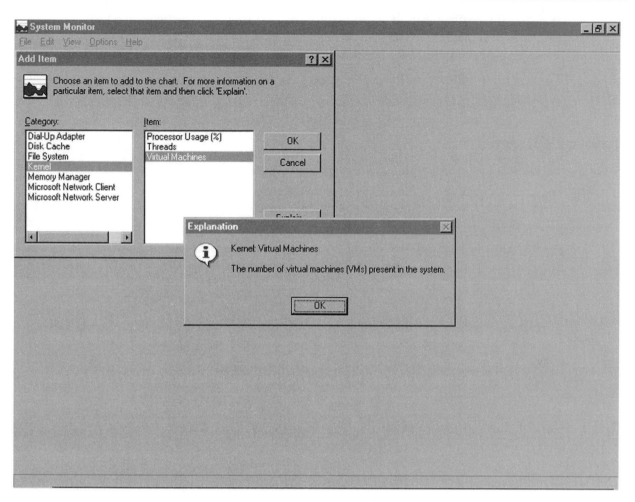

5. ___ Select three items to monitor and add them to System Monitor. The three items are **Kernel/Processor Usage**, **Memory Manager/Allocated memory**, and **Memory Manager/Unused physical memory**. Select the line chart to display information.

6. ___ After selecting the items, view the line chart and allow it to scroll for approximately two minutes without touching a key or moving the mouse. This establishes a baseline reading for those features.

7. ___ Now, open the calculator located at **Start I Programs I Accessories I Calculator**. Do some calculations with the calculator, such as seven divided by 22, and click the equal sign approximately twenty times.

8. ___ Observe the effect on the resources being charted by System Monitor.

9. ___ Now, open the Paint program. Open the largest drawing area you can, create a doodle, and save it. Next, open **Help** from the **Start** menu, and search for the subject "memory." Note the effects of each of these programs on the resources being monitored.

10. ___ Now, display the System Monitor data as bar graphs. Next, display the data as numeric values. The display types are indicated by icons located directly below Options heading in the menu bar at the top of the dialog box. Simply hold the cursor over the icon and the name of the chart type will be displayed.

11. ___ Try using the **Explain** button to find out more about an item selected for monitoring. The Explain button becomes available by selecting **Edit | Add Item** from the **System Monitor** dialog box, and then highlighting an item in the **Item:** window.

12. ___ Before using **Add/Remove Programs** to remove System Monitor from the PC, answer the review questions below.

Review Questions

You will need to leave System Monitor on the desktop to answer some of these questions.

1. What three types of charts can be used to display data? _____

_____

2. What does a chart of Disk Cache/Cache hits reveal? _____

_____

_____

3. What are the seven categories of items that can be monitored by the System Monitor program? _____

_____

_____

*After completing the review questions or before you leave the lab area, remove the System Monitor program and restore the PC to its original condition. Use **Add/Remove Programs** in the **Control Panel** to remove System Monitor.*

Name _____ Date_____

Class/Instructor _____

Virtual Memory

After completing this lab activity, you will be able to:

✴   Access and change the settings in the Virtual Memory Device Manager.

Introduction

System memory is always in demand. It seems there is never enough memory available for program use, especially when using graphic-intensive programs. The use of a swap file, virtual memory set up on the hard drive to assist RAM, offers one solution to this problem. The swap file is named win386.swp. If Windows manages the size of the swap file, it can grow and shrink dynamically. You can check the swap file's size from Windows Explorer.

When dealing with computer technologies, the term "virtual" always means a simulation, something not real. Consequently, virtual memory is simulated memory, not real memory. An area on the hard drive can be reserved to assist and emulate RAM. When this is done, it is referred to as virtual memory. Virtual memory can be set up manually or automatically. Microsoft recommends leaving the virtual memory size in automatic mode.

Equipment and Materials

✴   Typical PC with Windows 95 (or later) operating system

Procedure

1. ___ Boot the PC and wait for the Windows desktop to appear.

2. ___ Right click on **My Computer** icon and select **Properties**.

3. ___ When the System Properties dialog box appears, select the **Performance** tab. The current performance status will be displayed. It lists the amount of RAM installed, the type of file system, the present condition of the system resources, and disk compression status.

4. ___ Look at the bottom right side of the dialog box and you will see a button labeled **Virtual Memory**. Click the button to access the Virtual Memory dialog box.

5. ___ Take special note of the warning at the top of the box. The default setting for virtual memory is **Let Windows manage my virtual memory settings**. This is the preferred choice, although it can be changed. Usually, increasing the size of the virtual memory block does not pose a problem. However, decreasing the virtual memory size could cause a system memory error when attempting to open certain programs. Such an error occurs when there is not sufficient memory to run the program. Do not select **Disable virtual memory**. This should only be done as a last resort while troubleshooting a suspected bad memory module. Selecting the **Disable virtual memory** could prevent Windows from starting.

6. ___ Click the option **Let me specify my own virtual memory settings**. Once selected, the other options will appear such as the **Maximum:** and **Minimum:** spinners, which set the maximum and minimum size of the swap file.

7. ___ Select **Let Windows manage my virtual memory settings**. This should restore the virtual memory's original settings. Pick **OK** to accept the settings.

8. ___ Close the System Properties dialog box.

9. ___ Open **Help** from the **Start** menu, select the **Index** tab, select **Virtual Memory** from the topics list, and click the **Display** button. This should provide more information on how to access the virtual memory settings. Read the file before answering the review questions.

Review Questions

1. How can you access the virtual memory settings without using the My Computer icon?

_____

_____

2. Where is virtual memory physically located? _____

_____

3. What is the name of the system swap file? _____

4. What is the default setting for virtual memory? _____

_____

Name _____ Date_____

Class/Instructor _____

Lab Activity

35

Keyboard Properties

After completing this lab activity, you will be able to:

✶ Adjust the typing characteristics of a typical keyboard.

✶ Change the default language of the keyboard.

Introduction

As a PC technician, you may be called on to make certain adjustments to the keyboard. Many people, especially professional secretaries, are sensitive to such keyboard characteristics as the repeat rate of a key press. In this exercise, you will make adjustments to the keyboard's typing rate characteristics. You will also select a set of language characters, other than English, to be output by the keyboard. In addition, you will learn to adjust the English properties to change the layout of your keyboard, such as making it function as a Dvorak-style keyboard.

A Dvorak-style keyboard has a different physical arrangement, designed for use by the very fastest typists. The original keyboard layout was designed to limit the speed of the typist. This prevented the typist from typing too fast, which could jam the typewriter's mechanism. A Dvorak keyboard, named after the inventor, has a layout designed to maximize speed. It is not a very common keyboard style, but it does exist.

Equipment and Materials

✶ Typical PC with Windows 98 operating system and a typical keyboard

✶ Windows 98 Installation CD

Procedure

1. ___ Boot the PC and wait for the desktop to be displayed.

2. ___ Activate the Keyboard Properties dialog box by opening the **Control Panel**, right clicking on the **Keyboard** icon, and then selecting **Open** from the menu. (**Start | Settings | Control Panel | Keyboard**.)

3. ___ The Keyboard Properties dialog box will appear similar to the one shown here.

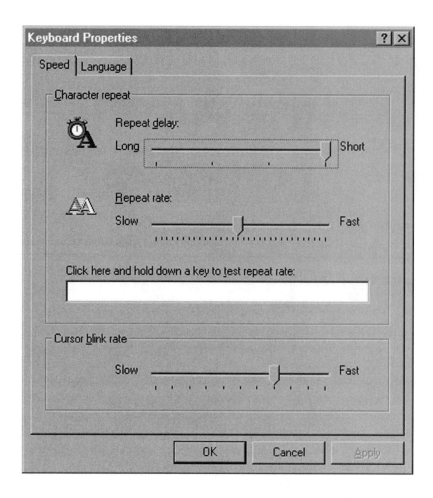

4. ___ Look at the two adjustment sliders, one labeled **Repeat delay** and the other labeled **Repeat rate**. Experiment with the two adjustments until you can answer the following questions.

When a key is held down, a character will be repeated rapidly across the screen. The rate at which the character repeats is controlled by the repeat _____.

When a key is held down, the time delay before the second character appears on the screen is controlled by the repeat _____.

5. ___ Select the **Language** tab at the top of the Keyboard Properties dialog box. The dialog box should appear similar to the one shown.

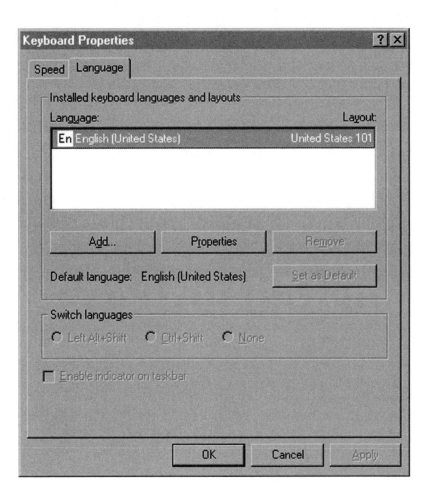

6. ___ Click on the **Properties** button to view the properties associated with the English language selection. This will open a new dialog box. Click in the **Keyboard layout:** field to see the additional selections available for the keyboard, such as Dvorak.

7. ___ Add a different language and set it as the default. To do this, click the **Add** button, click in the **Language:** field, select a language, and click **OK**. Finally, click the **Set as Default** button, and click the **Apply** button at the bottom of the dialog box.

8. ___ Open WordPad and try typing something; be sure to include the special character keys. Also take special note of the fact that the second language can be turned on and off by certain key combinations, such as [Alt][Shift]. You can change the key combination used to toggle between languages by selecting the appropriate radio button in the **Switch Language** area of the Keyboard Properties dialog box. You may need the Windows 98 Installation Disk for the language installation.

9. ___ Next you will remove the second language, and return the PC to its original settings. To remove the language, highlight the newly installed language in the Keyboard Properties dialog box, and click **Remove**. Click the **OK** button to remove the language and close the dialog box.

Review Questions

1. How does the Repeat delay setting differ from the Repeat rate setting? _____

   _____

   _____

2. Explain how to add a set of characters for a second language to the keyboard. _____

   _____

   _____

   _____

   _____

   _____

Name _____ Date_____

Class/Instructor _____

Lab Activity

36

Mouse Properties

After completing this lab activity, you will be able to:

✭ Adjust the double-click speed of the mouse.

✭ Change the pointer icon.

✭ Adjust the speed of the mouse movement.

✭ Change the appearance of the mouse-trail.

✭ Set the mouse for right- or left-handed use.

Introduction

In this lab activity, you will learn to adjust mouse properties. Mouse properties are the characteristics associated with the mouse, such as movement speed, click speed, and overall appearance of the onscreen pointer. The properties of the pointing device are set in the Mouse Properties dialog box located in the Control Panel. The path for opening the Mouse Properties dialog box is **Start | Settings | Control Panel | Mouse.**

Equipment and Materials

✭ Typical PC with Windows 98 operating system

✭ Typical two- or three-button mouse (variations in the lab may occur when using various mice and may not exactly match the lab content)

Procedure

1. ___ Boot the PC and wait for the Windows desktop to appear.

2. ___ Click the **Start** button and maneuver along the following path: **Start | Settings | Control Panel | Mouse**. This will open the Mouse Properties dialog box. The four most often used tabs in the Mouse Properties dialog box are shown here. Depending on the type of mouse that you have installed on your computer, your Mouse Properties dialog box may appear considerably different. However, the tools and basic layout should be similar in all cases.

Buttons tab active

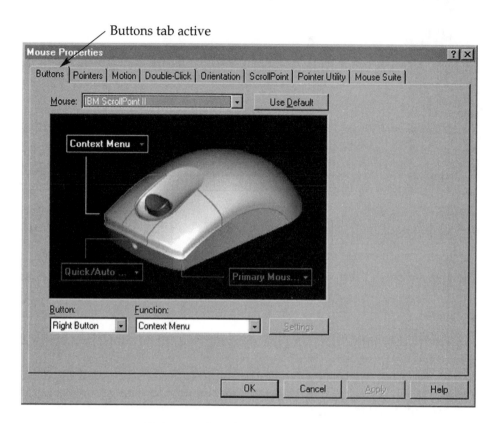

Pointers tab active

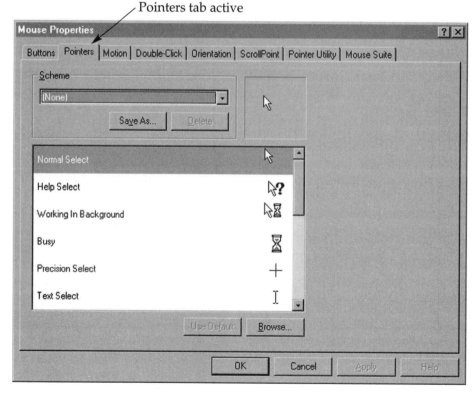

Motion tab active

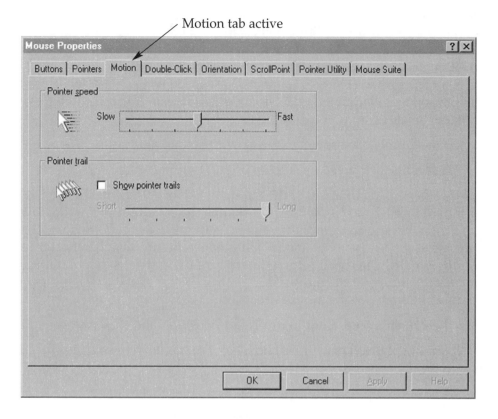

Double-Click tab active

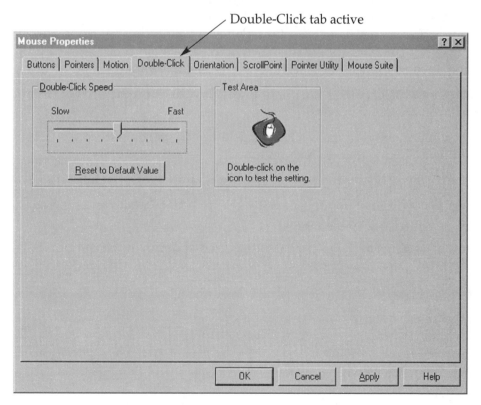

3. ___ There are many mouse properties that can be modified. By changing the settings, you can switch the right and left mouse buttons, change the speed required for a double click, or change the appearance of the mouse pointer.

Input/Output Devices

4. ___ First, find the double-click settings. These will usually be under the **Buttons** or **Double Click** tab. Note the setting for the double-click speed. Often, the double-click speed must be set to accommodate the user, especially with some of the high speed PCs available today. Usually the **Double-Click Speed** slider is set approximately halfway across the scale. Write down its position and then change it to the highest speed setting. Test the speed using the Jack-in-the-box, or a similar animated icon in the Test Area of the dialog box. Double clicking should activate the animation.

5. ___ Now, set the double-click speed to the slowest setting and test it.

6. ___ Reset the double-click speed back to its original setting.

7. ___ Select the **Motion** tab at the top of the dialog box. Now, you will change the speed at which the mouse pointer moves. Before you change the speed setting, write down the current setting. You will need to restore the original settings when you are done. Set the **Pointer speed** to the slowest speed setting, and pick the **Apply** button. Test the effect by moving the mouse pointer around. The speed setting determines the distance the pointer moves on screen for each revolution of the mouse ball. Set the **Pointer speed** to the highest setting and test it. Note the difference in the mouse's reaction.

8. ___ Return the **Pointer speed** slider to its original position and click **Apply**.

9. ___ Put a check in the **Show pointer trail** box. Now move the mouse and note the change in the display.

10. ___ Click the box once more to remove the **Show pointer trail** option.

11. ___ Select the **Pointers** tab at the top of the **Mouse Properties** dialog box. This area is used to modify the pointer's appearance. The default settings are listed in a window in the center of the dialog box. The names of the selection modes appear in the left-hand side of the window, and their assigned pointers appear on the right. Normal Select, Help Select, and Working in Background are just a few of the selection modes that have assigned pointers.

12. ___ Select **Normal Select** by clicking on it once. Now, click on the **Browse...** button. This reveals the available pointer icons.

13. ___ Select another pointer type, such as **Appstart** or **Globe**. You select the icon by clicking on it once and then clicking on the **Open** button.

14. ___ Next click the **Apply** button and observe the change in the pointer.

15. ___ Return to the original pointer shape by selecting **Use Default** and then clicking on **Apply**. This should restore the original pointer.

16. ___ Return all settings to their original values, and shut down the computer.

Review Questions

1. What mouse attributes or properties can be changed? _____

_____

2. Explain the difference between the Double-Click Speed and Pointer speed settings.

_____

_____

Name _____ Date_____

Class/Instructor _____

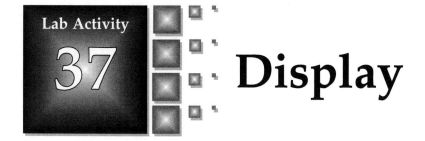

Lab Activity 37

Display

After completing this lab activity, you will be able to:

✶ Modify the appearance of the desktop area and screen saver.

✶ Adjust the screen size.

✶ Set password protection in the Display Properties dialog box.

✶ Change the monitor settings that affect display performance.

Introduction

This lab activity will familiarize you with the many setting options available for a standard display. You will change many of the display settings, and then restore the original settings. Throughout the lab activity, you will be prompted to write down the settings before you change or experiment with them. Please do so in the space provided. This will assist you when attempting to restore the system to its original configuration.

The Display Properties dialog box can be used to change the appearance of the desktop, screen saver, windows, and dialog boxes. The more advanced settings in the Display Properties dialog box, such as refresh rate and energy management, affect the technical performance of the monitor. The variety and effect of display-setting options depends on the display manufacturer's hardware and drivers. For example, not all monitors allow you to change the refresh rate. For some monitors, refresh rate is determined entirely by the hardware and the driver software.

Some of the settings will be viewed but not used. Do not make any permanent changes to the desktop area. If you follow the information in the lab activity, you will not permanently change any of the settings. The settings you change will only be temporary.

Equipment and Materials

✶ Typical PC with a SVGA monitor (a VGA monitor may be substituted) and Windows 98 installed

Procedure

1. ___ Boot the PC and wait for the desktop display.

2. ___ Click the **Display** icon, located at **Start | Settings | Control Panel | Display**.

3. ___ The Display Properties dialog box should appear similar to the one below.

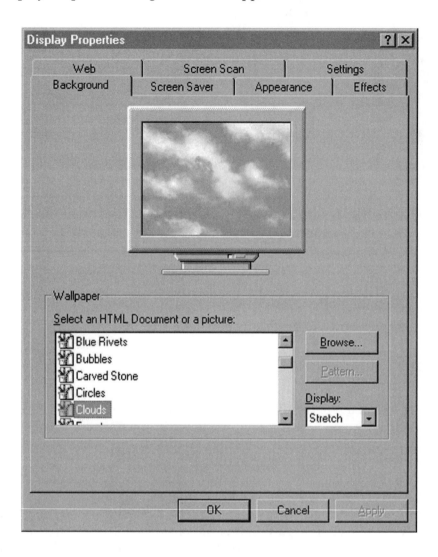

4. ___ In the space provided, list the tabs found in the Display Properties dialog box. For example, the first tab is Web. _____

_____

_____

5. ___ First, click on the **Settings** tab. Next, click on the **Advanced** button. This opens a dialog box that incorporates your video card name in its title bar. List the names of the tabs available in this dialog box. _____

_____

_____

6. ___ Compare the sets of tabs available in this dialog box and the Display Properties dialog box. Can you tell which set is used for cosmetic purposes and which set is used for the display's technical settings?

7. ___ Now go back to the Display Properties dialog box by clicking the **Cancel** button in the new dialog box.

8. ___ Select the tab marked **Background**. This is where the screen's background can be changed. Another name for the background is wallpaper. A window in the center of the dialog box lists all of the files in the selected directory that can be used as wallpaper. The currently selected wallpaper is highlighted in the list. In the space provided, write down the name of the current wallpaper so that you can restore it when you are finished.

_____

9. ___ Scroll through the list and select **Pinstripe**. After Pinstripe is selected, click in the **Display:** field and select **Tile** from the menu. Click **Apply** and watch the effect on the monitor.

10. ___ Select several other types of wallpaper and watch their effect on the display.

11. ___ Restore the original wallpaper selection.

12. ___ Next, select the **Screen Saver** tab at the top of the Display Properties dialog box. This screen is where different screen savers can be selected and installed. Write down the name of the screen saver that is displayed in the Screen Saver text box so you can restore it after your experiment. _____

13. ___ Try selecting some different screen savers, and then clicking the **Preview** button to see their effect on the display.

14. ___ Next, select the **Appearance** tab at the top of the Display Properties dialog box. Look at the text box labeled Scheme. This is the title of the screen appearance now selected. Write it in the space provided. _____

15. ___ After the scheme title has been recorded, experiment by selecting different schemes. *Do not* change any of the settings in the text box titled Item. This is used to change the settings of various individual items that compose all the different parts of the Windows desktop themes. Do not alter them at this time.

16. ___ Next, restore the original scheme.

17. ___ Select the **Effects** tab at the top of the dialog box. This tab is used to change many of the icons used to represent functions. For example, the Network Neighborhood icon can be changed to a number of different icons. Select the **Network Neighborhood** icon, click the **Change Icon...** button, and then view some of the other icons available. Do not apply the new selection, simply look. Other students may need to use this PC and changing the icons could confuse and frustrate them.

18. ___ Next, select the tab labeled **Web**. This screen is where you modify your desktop to work with your web browser. For example, you can add access to a weather map, stock ticker, news reports, etc. You must be connected to the Internet to fully apply modifications.

19. ___ The last tab is **Settings**. This tab allows you to change the technical properties of the display, such as refresh rate. Click the button labeled **Advanced** to open a video card properties dialog box. You should recognize this dialog box from step 5. This dialog box is where you can select or identify your video card (also referred to as video adapter) and your monitor. From this dialog box, you can also change your refresh rate, and accelerate the graphic display.

■ **Special Note:**

The refresh rate can be changed to a higher setting to help relieve eyestrain. The optimal setting is usually fine, but at times it may need to be faster to prevent eyestrain. The eye can perceive the raster moving across the screen even though the brain allows us to see only the image presented. Nevertheless, the action of the raster can cause eyestrain and headaches after a long period. A screen that has an apparent flicker usually needs a higher refresh rate.

Input/Output Devices

20. ___ Take the rest of the time allocated for this lab activity to experiment with the settings available in the Display Properties dialog box. Before changing any settings, write the current setting down. After you have experimented with a new setting, immediately restore the original setting before changing the next setting. Change only one option at a time. Changing several options at the same time can lead to confusion when trying to return the display to its original settings. For your first experiment, change the **Screen area** setting, which is listed under the **Settings** tab. See how this affects the screen display area.

21. ___ You may leave the PC on and the Display Properties dialog box open while answering the review questions. After you have answered all the questions, return all display properties to their original settings and properly shut down the PC.

Review Questions

1. How do you add access to the weather information on your desktop? _____
_____
_____

2. Where can you access the options to change to a higher contrast for the Windows display?
_____

3. How can the icon for My Computer be changed? _____
_____
_____

4. Where can you adjust the resolution of the screen display? _____
_____
_____

5. What happens to the size of the screen icons when you select a higher resolution on the Screen area slider control? Remember that the Screen area slider is located under the Settings tab of the Display Properties dialog box. _____
_____

After you answer the review questions, restore the original settings for the wallpaper and screen saver.

Name _____ Date_____

Class/Instructor _____

Floppy Drive Installation

After completing this lab activity, you will be able to:

✳   Install or replace a 3 1/2" floppy drive.

Introduction

At one time, adding an additional floppy drive was a common task. Today, adding a second floppy drive is almost unheard of. You will most likely replace an existing floppy drive. Because floppy drives have become very inexpensive, it is no longer practical to repair them. In this lab activity, you will replace an existing floppy drive. As part of the lab activity, you will also connect the data cable incorrectly to see the effect on the drive.

You will use a PC with a floppy drive already installed. In this exercise, you will simply remove the existing drive and then reinstall the same floppy drive. Look at the following drawing to become familiar with how a single floppy drive or a multiple floppy drive system is installed.

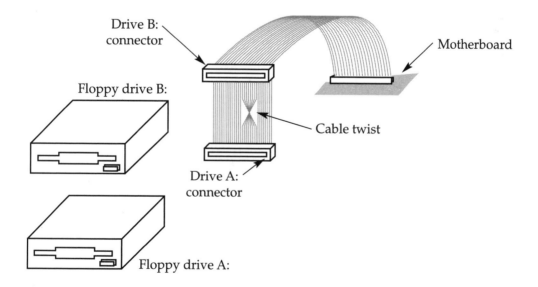

Floppy drive connections are similar to the cable connections between other devices and the motherboard. Pin 1 on the floppy drive is connected to pin 1 on the controller port of the mother-board. The ribbon cable has either a red or a blue line on one edge. The colored line is used to identify the pin-1 connection. The side of the ribbon cable with the colored line should always be installed at pin-1.

Magnetic Storage

Also take special note of the twist in the floppy drive's ribbon cable. The twist in the cable is used to identify the master and slave relationship between two floppy drives connected to the same ribbon cable. Floppy drives do not use jumpers to identify the master and slave units. Instead, the master and slave are identified by their position on the ribbon cable in relation to the twist. The master drive (A: drive) is attached at the end of the cable, after the twist. The slave drive (B: drive) is attached before the twist in the cable. This arrangement is referred to as the cable-select style of identification. Be sure to draw the relationship of the drive and the position of the twist in the ribbon cable during disassembly and installation.

Equipment and Materials

✳   Typical PC with a 3 1/2" floppy drive installed

Procedure

1. ___ Boot the PC to be sure it is working properly. Test the floppy drive unit before you begin disassembly. After you are sure the PC is in good working order, properly power down the PC.

2. ___ Remove the case cover and look at the orientation of the 3 1/2" floppy drive. Make a sketch in the area provided here. Sketch the floppy drive, the motherboard, and the ribbon cable that connects them. In the sketch, use a heavier line or different color to denote the colored edge of the ribbon cable. Be sure to note the twist in the cable and its position relative to the floppy drive.

Sketch area:

3. ___ When the sketch is complete, disconnect the power and data cables from the floppy drive. Remove the floppy drive from the drive bay and rest it on a static-free bag for protection.

4. ___ Remove the data cable from the motherboard's controller port. Call the instructor to inspect your work before proceeding to the next step.

5. ___ Now, reverse the procedure to reinstall the floppy drive. Be sure to line up the colored line on the ribbon cable to pin-1 on the floppy drive and the controller port.

6. ___ Connect the power cable to the floppy drive.

7. ___ Do not replace the case cover yet. Boot the system to be sure that the floppy drive works correctly. Insert a floppy disk into the drive and list the contents to be sure the floppy drive is functioning properly.

8. ___ Now, power down the PC and remove the floppy drive's ribbon cable.

9. ___ Next, connect the ribbon cable to the floppy drive incorrectly. Simply reverse one end of the ribbon cable so that the colored stripe does not connect to pin-1.

10. ___ Reboot the PC and observe the activity of the drive closely. Record what you observe in the space provided. _____

_____

_____

11. ___ Power down the PC and reconnect the ribbon cable correctly to the floppy drive.

12. ___ Power up the PC again, and test the floppy drive with a disk to be sure it is working correctly.

13. ___ Now, open Device Manager and fill in the missing information below.

Floppy drive IRQ _____

DMA assignment _____

I/O port range _____

_____

14. ___ Properly shut down the PC, and replace the case cover.

Review Questions

1. What does the colored stripe running along the edge of the ribbon cable signify?

_____

_____

2. Generally speaking, where along the length of the ribbon cable is floppy drive A: connected in relation to the twist in the cable? _____

_____

3. What is a sure sign that the ribbon cable is incorrectly connected to either the floppy drive or to the motherboard? _____

_____

_____

Name _____ Date_____

Class/Instructor _____

ScanDisk

After completing this lab activity, you will be able to:

✶ Run the ScanDisk program to inspect disk media.

✶ Explain what ScanDisk is used for.

✶ Describe the type of repairs ScanDisk can be expected to make.

Introduction

ScanDisk is a general disk diagnostic and repair program. It can be used to inspect and repair floppy disks, hard disks, and RAM drives (virtual drives in RAM). Some of ScanDisk's functions are as follows:

✶ Check the disk surface for bad sectors and mark them so they cannot be used

✶ Check and repair the file allocation table (FAT)

✶ Check and repair the file directory tree structure

✶ Check and repair cross-linked files and lost clusters

✶ Check and repair files compressed with DriveSpace or Doublespace

✶ Check and repair long names

The disk area is divided into sectors to be used as storage compartments for data. The sectors are formed when the disk is formatted. When data is stored on a disk, it is usually broken into small units and stored in a string of sectors. A string of sectors is called a cluster. The file allocation table (FAT) records the clusters' locations on the disk.

At times, this information can become corrupted and result in a lost cluster. A lost cluster, also called a lost file fragment, is a cluster, or string of sectors, that is recorded by the FAT as being in use, but is not associated with any file. Lost clusters may contain important data, or they may be empty. Either way, the clusters are inaccessible; any data stored there cannot be recalled, nor can the clusters be overwritten. ScanDisk attempts to recover lost clusters from the disk, either by freeing the clusters, or by converting them into files.

If the cluster is not recoverable, it is marked as unusable in the file allocation table so that it will not be used to store data in the future. If the data is recoverable, it is saved as a separate file. The separate file can later be opened and a cut and paste technique can be used to rejoin the data in the cluster to the original file where it belongs. Again, the bad cluster is marked in the file allocation table not to be used in the future for storage.

Another common problem is cross-linked files. Files are composed of data stored in a string of sectors. Each sector contains information about the location of the next sector used to store data for the file. At times, the information can become corrupt and result in two files claiming the same sector. One sector that is identified as part of two different files is known as a cross-linked file.

Magnetic Storage

ScanDisk attempts to fix cross-linked files by making a copy of the sector in question and assigning one copy of the cross-linked sector to each file. This provides the user with a chance to recover the file.

ScanDisk offers the option to ignore cross-linked files. System files may become cross-linked as easily as data files. In an instance when a system file has become cross-linked, an attempt to repair the file may result in the system crashing on the next reboot. This is one more reason to have a backup of important data.

When running ScanDisk on a large drive, it is a good idea to turn off the screensaver program and any anti-virus programs that may be running. ScanDisk will work with these programs running, but it will run faster if they are turned off.

You start ScanDisk by clicking the **ScanDisk** icon located at **Start | Programs | Accessories | System Tools**. Once it is running, you should see a ScanDisk dialog box similar to the one shown.

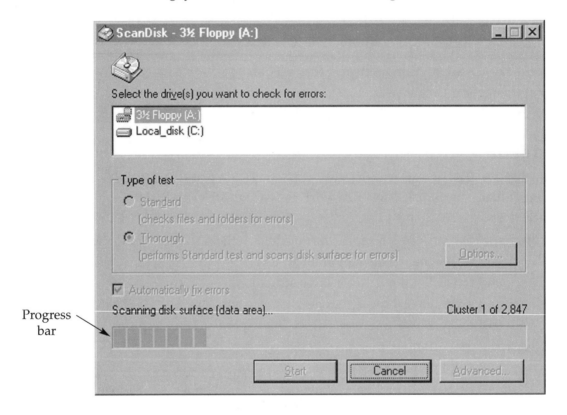

Progress bar

There are two types of scans that can be run, standard and thorough. The standard scan checks files and folders for problems such as crossed links and lost clusters, but it does not test the physical disk surface for flaws. The thorough scan checks files, folders, and the physical disk surface. When checking the disk surface, the utility reads each disk sector, copies the information into another sector, and then compares the two. If the two do not match, the second sector is flagged as a bad sector. Because each sector inspected is copied, rewritten, and then compared, this option takes a long time to run. It can take hours sometimes.

This exercise will be much shorter because you will perform a scan on a floppy disk rather than a much larger hard disk system. Bad sectors are not repaired; they are flagged in the FAT so that they cannot be used to store data.

Equipment and Materials

✴ Typical PC with Windows 98 (or later) operating system

✴ 3 1/2" floppy disk with some files on the disk (do not use a blank floppy disk for this exercise)

Procedure

1. ___ Boot the PC and wait for the Windows desktop.

2. ___ Insert the floppy disk into the drive and then start **ScanDisk** by clicking its icon in **Start | Programs | Accessories | System Tools**.

3. ___ When the ScanDisk dialog box appears, select the 3 1/2" floppy drive for the choice of drives to scan. Do a standard scan and then do a thorough scan. At the bottom of the dialog box, a horizontal progress bar displays ScanDisk's progress. When the scan is complete, a summary box appears on the screen.

4. ___ The results of the scan are saved to a log file called scandisk.log, located in the root directory. The scandisk.log can be accessed and read using Notepad. Open the scandisk.log now.

5. ___ Close Notepad and return to the **ScanDisk - 3 1/2" Floppy (A:)** dialog box.

6. ___ Explore the other options made available by clicking the **Options** button. (The **Thorough** radio must be selected for this button to be available.) After you have explored the options in the Surface Scan Options dialog box, close it. Next, click on the **Advanced** button at the bottom of the **ScanDisk 3 1/2" Floppy (A:)** dialog box. Review the available options. The two dialog boxes should appear similar to the ones shown here.

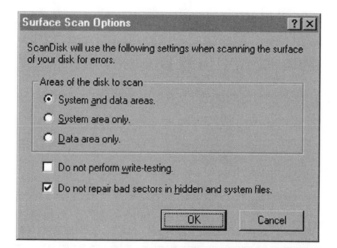

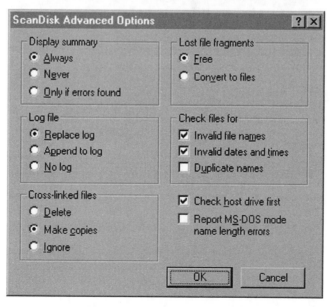

Magnetic Storage

As you can see, there are many options to choose from. For example, you can select the areas on the disk that will be scanned, and you can tell ScanDisk how to handle cross-linked files and lost clusters.

Note:

Before using ScanDisk, be sure all antivirus programs are disabled. Antivirus programs can hinder ScanDisk's performance.

Review Questions

1. What is ScanDisk? _____

   _____

   _____

2. What types of storage media can ScanDisk be used for? _____

   _____

3. What items can ScanDisk repair on a hard disk? _____

   _____

4. Explain what a cross-linked file is. _____

   _____

   _____

5. What is a cluster? _____

   _____

   _____

6. What is a lost cluster? _____

   _____

   _____

   _____

7. What is the difference between a thorough and a standard disk scan? _____

   _____

   _____

   _____

Name _____ Date_____

Class/Instructor _____

Defragmenting Disks

Magnetic Storage

After completing this lab activity, you will be able to:

✳ Defragment a disk.

✳ Explain the cause of file fragmentation.

✳ Explain the advantage of disk defragmentation.

Introduction

As a hard drive or any magnetic storage media is used in successive saves and deletions, a phenomenon known as file-structure fragmentation (or just fragmentation) takes place. When files are saved to disk, they are usually saved in a sequential series of sectors, or disk allocation units. When the next file is saved, it starts immediately after the previous file. The file structure continues to grow in size as more files are saved to disk. Each file starts in the allocation unit immediately following the end of the previous file.

However, the neatly structured file storage system can be disrupted as files are deleted or increased in size. In the normal operation of a PC, files are saved, deleted, and modified in size over time. As the file structure grows and changes, files that were previously written in sequential sectors can be broken up and scattered over the surface of the disk. The Disk Defragmenter utility rearranges the scattered segments of files and restructures them in sequential sectors. This process of rearranging the files into sequential order is known as defragmentation, commonly referred to as "defragging."

Disk defragmentation decreases the amount of time required to retrieve files from the disk. When files are written in sequential sectors, the read head of the hard drive doesn't need to change tracks as often as it does when the files are scattered across the hard drive. Also, the entire file structure is much easier to rebuild when all the file sectors are located together. Disk defragmentation is recommended as routine maintenance of hard drives.

In this lab activity, you will perform defragmentation on a floppy disk. The principle is the same for the hard disk, but the operation is much quicker on a floppy disk.

■ **Note:**

It is recommended that anti-virus and screen-saver programs be disabled while defragmenting a hard drive. The defragmentation operation will perform faster without these programs running.

The advantage of disabling these programs is negligible when formatting a floppy disk.

Equipment and Materials

✳ Typical PC with Windows 98 operating system

✳ (1) 3 1/2" floppy disk, preferably blank

Procedure

1. ___ Boot the PC and wait for the Windows desktop to appear.

2. ___ To perform this lab activity properly, you will need to fill the disk with a random rather than an orderly arrangement of files. Use Word or WordPad to create two different text files. The files can consist of random letters; they only need to take up disk space. However, the files must have different file sizes. Suggested sizes are approximately 800 bytes for the first file and approximately 2500 for the second size. The smallest sector on a floppy is 512 bytes. Saving two differently sized files ensures gaps when some of the files are removed. When the two files have been created, save each one to the floppy disk at least ten times. Rename the file each time it is saved. For example, save the file as File1, and then File2, and so on.

3. ___ Now, delete every third file from the disk.

4. ___ Next, copy one of the files and save it to disk at least seven times using a different file name each time: filetwo1, filetwo2, filetwo3, and so on.

5. ___ The files should now be in some random order, with some unused spaces and fragmented files.

6. ___ Open the Disk Defragmenter tool, located at **Start | Programs | Accessories | System Tools**.

7. ___ Be sure to select the A: drive for defragmentation, not the C: drive. Also, select the **Show Details** button located on the bottom right side of the **Defragmenting Drive A:** dialog box. This presents you with a graphic representation of the defragmentation process.

8. ___ After the disk has been defragmented, run the Disk Defragmenter program again and see how much faster it is this time. The program runs faster because the file structure has been reorganized to an optimum state.

9. ___ Now, start defragmenting the C: drive. This may take a long time, but you need not finish it. You can exit the defragmentation operation at any time. Be sure to click the **Show Details** and **Legend** buttons to watch the defragmentation operation as it progresses.

10. ___ Properly shut down the PC after answering the review questions.

Review Questions

1. What four options are available under the Settings button? _____

_____

_____

_____

2. What symbol represents free space? _____

_____

3. What symbol represents a bad area of the disk? _____

_____

4. What actions can you take to make the defragmentation operation run faster? _____

_____

_____

_____

_____

Name _____ Date_____

Class/Instructor _____

FDISK and Partitions (Part One)

After completing this lab activity, you will be able to:

✶ Use the **fdisk** command to prepare a hard drive for use.

✶ Create multiple partitions on a hard drive.

✶ Create logical partitions on a hard drive.

✶ Create a primary partition.

✶ Set a partition as active.

✶ Display partition information.

Introduction

The **fdisk** command is used routinely when replacing a hard drive or adding an additional hard drive to a PC. Partitioning is the act of dividing the hard disk surface into separate storage areas. While it is common to have multiple partitions on a single hard drive, every drive must have at least one partition before it can be formatted and used to store data.

Each partition area on the hard disk appears as a separate hard drive to the user. When a drive is divided into several partitions, each partition is referred to as a logical drive rather than a physical drive.

There are several reasons for partitioning a hard drive into multiple logical drives. By dividing a hard disk into several smaller areas, disk space is better utilized. When using FAT16, VFAT, or FAT32, cluster size is directly proportional to the size of the logical or physical drive. This can result in a lot of wasted storage space. For example, 20GB drive prepared as FAT32 has a cluster size of 16KB. A file consisting of only a few bytes of information uses the entire 16KB section of the disk to store the data. If the same 20GB drive is divided into two logical drives of 10GB each, the cluster size drops to 8KB. In this case, the same small file takes up only 8KB of space on the disk.

Another reason for partitioning a drive is to separate operating systems. You may install more than one operating system on a hard drive by creating a separate partition for each system. For example, you can install Linux and Windows 98 on the same physical drive using separate partitions.

Partitioning a drive can also be useful for backing up files. You could install the operating system on one partition and save data to a separate partition, making it much easier to back up the data files. When multiple users use the same PC station, multiple partitions are useful for separating files created or commonly accessed by the different users. In this case, a separate partition can be assigned to each user.

The **fdisk** command should not be used unless you fully understand its effect on the computer system. This command can wipe out all information on a hard drive in a matter of seconds.

As stated before, the **fdisk** command partitions a hard drive, preparing the drive for formatting and data storage. A hard disk must have a primary, or active partition, even if only one partition is created. After a partition has been created, it must be formatted before it can be used to store data, including the operating system and other programs. If you attempt to access an unformatted partition, an error is generated. Typical error messages are "Invalid media type" and "General failure reading drive." Failing to format or partition the hard drive is the most common mistake made during the installation of a new hard drive.

A typical startup disk created from Windows 95 or later contains the fdisk.exe and format.com programs. The **fdisk** command can be issued with two optional switches, **fdisk/status** and **fdisk/x**. **Fdisk/status** displays the status of any existing partitions on the hard disk. **Fdisk/x** ignores any error messages associated with extended disk partitions.

■ **Note:**

The **fdisk** *command is not recognized by Windows 2000 operating system.*

Special Precautions

✳ Do not attempt to install or remove a hard drive while the system is powered up. It can permanently damage the drive and motherboard.

✳ Do not move a hard drive while it is energized. Moving a hard drive while it is in read or write mode can permanently damage the disk surface and the read/write head. Students performing labs often damage hard drives because the drives are not securely mounted.

✳ Do not allow the hard drive's circuit board to touch any metal parts. This can cause a short circuit in the board, destroying the electronic components.

✳ Do not mix IDE and EIDE drives in the same system. However, ATA can be mixed with either IDE or EIDE. ATA can be mixed because it is similar to a SCSI design. It has its own BIOS, and does not have to rely entirely on the system's BIOS for communication.

✳ Backup your data before installing a new hard drive. When using **fdisk**, a simple mistake, such as typing the wrong drive letter, could lead to a loss of all data on the existing drive.

You may run across the term *LBA* when dealing with hard drive BIOS setup. LBA is an acronym for logical block addressing. It is a standard used by IDE and SCSI drives larger than 528M to translate cylinder, head, and sector specifications into addresses that can be accessed by enhanced BIOS systems. Most modern drive-setup software automatically enables LBA.

Some older systems may not be able to recognize disk drives larger than 2GB. The hard drive manufacturer can usually provide software that is loaded during the setup to allow a larger disk size to be recognized by the BIOS. One example is MaxBlast by Maxtor.

You will use a PC with a working hard drive for this exercise. You will disconnect the existing hard drive and connect the new hard disk using the same ribbon cable and power cable. Do not add the new hard drive as a second hard drive. When disconnecting data or power cables to the hard drive or motherboard, all power must be off.

During a normal workplace scenario, the first thing you would do before adding an additional hard drive is back up critical files. Things do go wrong from time to time, and data can be lost. However, for this exercise it will not be necessary to back up the existing hard drive.

Equipment and Materials

✳ Typical PC with working hard drive already installed

✳ New hard drive to be installed in the PC (any size drive can be used but at least 2GB is preferred)

✳ Windows 98 startup disk. You need to use the **fdisk** and **format** programs located on the disk. You can create a startup disk using **Add/Remove Program**, located in the **Start | Settings | Control Panel**

■ Note:

Handle a hard drive carefully. Do not drop or handle the drive roughly. The disk platters can be damaged from dropping and rough handling. Also, remember that disk drive units contain static-sensitive electronic components. Follow all precautionary procedures outlined by your instructor.

Procedure

1. ___ Boot the PC and wait for the Windows desktop to appear.

2. ___ Access the DOS prompt. From the DOS prompt, enter the command **fdisk/status**. This command reveals information about the existing hard drive partitions. In the area provided, write the information about the existing hard drive as it appears on the screen.

_____

_____

_____

_____

3. ___ **Exit** the DOS prompt.

4. ___ Open Windows Explorer, right click on the hard drive icon, and select **Properties** from the menu. This will reveal the hard drive properties such as size and file type. Write the size of the existing hard drive and the file system type (FAT16, FAT32) in the space provided.

_____

5. ___ Close all programs, and shut down the PC.

6. ___ Remove the cover from the PC case. Follow all antistatic practices outlined by your instructor.

7. ___ Locate the currently installed hard drive. The number one pin may be difficult to determine while the hard drive is installed. Before you remove the hard drive, sketch its position in the case, and the way the ribbon cable connects to it. Pay extra attention to the red line running along one edge of the ribbon cable. The red line on the cable must align with pin 1 on the drive when it is reinstalled.

8. ___ Remove the data cable and the power cable from the existing hard drive.

9. ___ Connect the power and data cables to the new hard drive. Place the new hard drive in a position where it will not be disturbed. It is not necessary to complete the physical mounting of the drive for this exercise, but the drive must be secure to prevent damage to the disk. Moving a disk during a read or write operation can damage the disk surface.

Magnetic Storage

10. ___ Boot the PC and observe the display. This is an ideal time to observe what a PC display looks like when the hard drive is totally unusable. Watch the stages of the POST and BIOS carefully. Everything that appears on the screen is controlled by the BIOS program. You should see a message telling you that the PC cannot boot, find system files, or something similar to that. The exact message will vary according to the BIOS manufacturer. The messages are telling you that the PC cannot find the files necessary to complete the boot sequence. No operating system exists at this point, only the BIOS program.

11. ___ Place the Windows startup disk in the floppy drive and reboot the system or follow the screen prompts. Depending on the system you are using, you may only need to press a key to have the system boot from the system disk.

12. ___ The Windows 98 Startup Menu should appear, allowing you to choose to start with CD support or to start without CD support. You can make a choice or simply allow the system to time out. When the system times out, it will select the CD support option automatically.

13. ___ Next, a series of messages should appear on the screen. The messages should confirm that there is a hard drive installed but does not contain a valid FAT or FAT32 partition. Next, three possible causes for no valid FAT or FAT32 partition being are listed. List the three reasons in the spaces provided. _____

_____

_____

14. ___ There is a remark on the screen in reference to the diagnostic tools. What is it? Write it in the space provided. _____

_____

_____

15. ___ Type **dir c:** at the A: prompt to see if there are files loaded on the hard drive. If there are files on the C: drive, list them in the spaces provided. _____

_____

_____

_____

_____

16. ___ Now, carefully type and enter the following command at the A: prompt: **fdisk/status**.

17. ___ What information was revealed by using the **fdisk/status** command?

18. ___ Now enter the **fdisk** command at the DOS prompt.

19. ___ There should be a message displayed on the screen. Read and record the entire message in the following spaces. _____

_____

_____

_____

20. ___ Press [N] for no large disk support. If you pressed [Y] by mistake, you will be able to correct the wrong choice by pressing [Esc]. If you make a mistake at any time, while in the **fdisk** program, you can use the [Esc] key.

21. ___ The next screen to come up should look similar to the one below.

Microsoft Windows 98
Fixed Disk Setup Program
©Copyright Microsoft Corp. 1983 – 1998

FDISK Options

Current fixed disk drive: 1

Choose one of the following:

1. Create DOS partition or Logical DOS Drive
2. Set active partition
3. Delete partition or Logical DOS Drive
4. Display partition information

Enter choice: [1]

Press Esc to exit FDISK

22. ___ Press the [Esc] key to exit the fdisk.exe program. This will show you what to expect when the [Esc] key is used.

23. ___ Now, run the fdisk.exe program again by using the **fdisk** command once more.

24. ___ When the **(Y/N)** choice for large disk support comes up, select **[N]** to display the menu choices once more.

25. ___ Select **4. Display partition information** from the **FDISK Options** menu and observe the information displayed. Write the information in the space provided. _____

_____

_____

_____

_____

26. ___ Press the [Esc] key to return to the main FDISK Options menu.

27. ___ Select **1. Create DOS partition or Logical DOS Drive** from the menu. This should display a new menu titled **Create DOS partition or Logical DOS Drive**. Write the three options listed for this menu in the spaces provided. _____

_____

_____

_____

28. ___ Select option **1. Create Primary DOS Partition** from the menu.

29. ___ The next screen will ask you if you wish to use the maximum available size for a Primary DOS Partition and make the partition active? Answer **N** and observe the next display. The display should give you information about the size of the hard drive and tell you the maximum available DOS partition size.

What is the maximum allowable partition size? _____

Magnetic Storage

30. ___ Press [Enter] to accept the default size. This selection should cause a new screen display to appear similar to the one below.

Create Primary DOS Partition Current fixed disk drive: 1						
Partition	Status	Type	Volume Label	Mbytes	System	Usage
C: 1		PRI DOS		2047	UNKNOWN	26%

The usage size will vary depending on the size of the hard drive used in the lab activity. Note that the drive is now the primary DOS partition, as noted by "PRI DOS" appearing in the Type column.

31. ___ Next, go back to the FDISK Options menu. Notice the warning at the bottom of the screen telling you that there are no partitions set to active at this time. Select **2. Set active partition** from the menu. The next display screen will prompt you to select the partition to make active. The active partition is the one that the system boots from. Select the only one that exists right now, number 1 the C: drive primary partition. Press [Esc] key to return to the FDISK Options menu.

32. ___ Now you will create another partition on the hard disk. From the FDISK Options menu, select **1. Create DOS partition or Logical DOS Drive** once more.

33. ___ Now the Create DOS Partitions or Logical DOS Drive menu should appear on the display screen. Choose **2. Create Extended DOS Partition** from the menu listing. The Create Extended DOS Partition screen lists the current drive information. At the bottom of the screen, you are asked to enter the size of logical drive you wish to create. You can choose the size in megabytes or by percentage. Enter 20%. The next screen should appear, the current drive information should show both the primary DOS partition and the extended DOS partition.

34. ___ Press the [Esc] key to go back to continue. You will now be prompted to enter the size for the logical disk drives. Again enter 50%. You will have created a logical drive using half of the extended drive area. The screen should prompt you once more asking about the remaining 50% of the extended drive area. Make it also 50%.

35. ___ Use the [Esc] key to go back to the FDISK Options menu.

36. ___ From the FDISK Options menu select **4. Display partition information**. The screen that appears displays information about the primary and extended DOS partitions. Study the screen carefully and notice how the primary, extended, and active partitions are identified. Also notice how the percentage of disk space is expressed for each. Looking in the System column, notice that the system is "UNKNOWN" at this time.

37. ___ Press the [Esc] key until a message appears on the screen telling you that you must restart the system before changes take effect. What does the message say you must do to the drives after restarting the computer? Write the answer in the space provided.

_____

38. ___ Press the [Esc] key again and you should be back at the A: DOS prompt. At the A: DOS prompt, enter the **fdisk** command. When the message appears asking if you wish to enable large drive support, answer with **N**. The next screen should display the FDISK Options menu. Choose **4. Display partition information**.

39. ___ The display screen will now prompt you to display logical drive information, choose the default **Y**. What drive letters have been assigned to the two logical drives?

_____

40. ___ Press the [Esc] key and keep pressing it until you arrive back at the DOS screen with the A: prompt displayed. Use the **dir** command to look at the C: drive and the two logical drives you created. What error message is displayed if any? Write the message in the space provided.

_____

41. ___ Reboot the PC using the Windows 98 startup disk. Choose CD support from the Windows 98 Startup menu.

42. ___ When the A: prompt appears attempt to access the C:, D:, and E: drives using the **dir** command.

43. ___ Use the **fdisk/status** command from the A: prompt and note the information displayed. It should be similar to the information below.

Fixed Disk Drive Status

Disk	Drv		Mbytes	Free	Usage
1			8025	4370	46%
	C:		2047		
	D:		808		
	E:		808		

44. ___ You can display the fixed disk status using **fdisk**, but you should not be able to access or display information about the C:, D:, and E: disks using the **dir** command. This is because the drives need to be formatted. They have not been formatted yet.

45. ___ Now type the drive letter at the DOS prompt to see if you can change to the various drives. For example, type **e:** at the prompt to see if the E: drive becomes the default drive. It should.

46. ___ Type the command **format c:** at the prompt and observe the action. Do not enter a volume label.

47. ___ After C: has been formatted, repeat the operation for D: drive.

48. ___ Now format the E: drive.

49. ___ Now use the **dir** command to look at the various drives once more. Is the error message displayed? _____

50. ___ Type **fdisk** to display the FDISK Options menu. Choose not to enable large disk access.

51. ___ When at the FDISK Options menu, choose to display the partition. Take note of the listing under the System column. It should now say FAT16.

52. ___ Select the option at the bottom of the screen to display **Logical DOS Drives**. Notice the information for drive D:, and E:. Both are now identified as FAT16 systems.

53. ___ Answer the review questions.

54. ___ Return the PC to its original condition. To return it to its original condition, shut down the PC and turn off the power. Remove the hard disk used for this exercise and reconnect the original hard drive. Use the sketch you made to ensure a proper connection of the data cable. Be sure to follow the antistatic procedures when reassembling the PC.

55. ___ Return the practice hard drive to your instructor.

Magnetic Storage

Review Questions

1. What does the **/status** switch do when added to the **fdisk** command? _____

   _____

   _____

   _____

2. After a hard drive is partitioned, what else must be done before you can store data or install an operating system on the drive? _____

3. What are the four choices listed under the FDISK Options menu? _____

   _____

   _____

   _____

   _____

4. How can you identify the primary DOS partition on the drive? _____

   _____

   _____

5. When creating an extended or logical partition, what two ways can the size of the partition be entered? _____

   _____

   _____

   _____

Name _____ Date_____

Class/Instructor _____

FDISK and Partitions (Part Two)

After completing this lab activity, you will be able to:

✱   Set up a multiple drive system to instructor specifications.

Introduction

In this lab activity, you will practice setting up and modifying hard drive partitions. You will create a primary DOS partition and an extended partition consisting of multiple logical drives. This is an exercise, not a performance examination. Below is a list of things to complete.

1. Remove the data and power cable from the PC's existing hard disk drive.

2. Install a practice hard drive.

3. Delete the existing partition structure on the practice drive.

4. Create a primary DOS partition and an extended partition. The extended partition will consist of 2 or more logical drives.

5. Set the size of the drives using both percentage and actual size in megabytes. You will need to practice the assignment and reassignment of the active partition.

6. Practice formatting the partitioned drives.

7. Repeat the set up and removal of the hard disk structure until you are comfortable with the procedure.

8. Enable large disk support and inspect the hard disk drive for the proper file system.

Notify your instructor when you are comfortable using FDISK.

Name _____ Date_____

Class/Instructor _____

Installing a Second Hard Drive

After completing this lab activity, you will be able to:

* Add a second hard drive to a PC.
* Prepare the second hard drive to store data.

Introduction

A PC technician is frequently asked to add an additional hard drive to an existing system. In this lab activity, you will add an additional hard drive to an existing PC. When more than one disk drive is installed on a PC, one of the drives must be made the master and the other, the slave. The designation is usually determined by jumper settings. Most often, the jumpers are located at the back end of the drive unit, usually beside the data cable and power connection. Look at the drawing shown here.

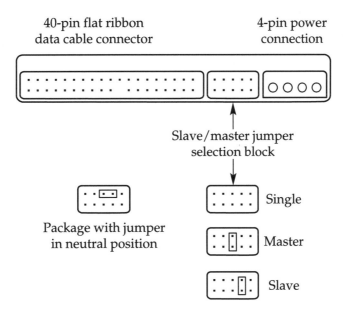

Jumper settings for a Western Digital Caviar 24300 EIDE drive.

The settings of the jumpers are not universal. You may need to consult the manufacturers' web sites to find the jumper settings for the drive you are installing and the drive already installed. When possible, the two drives should be mounted to the same IDE connection on the motherboard. See the following illustration.

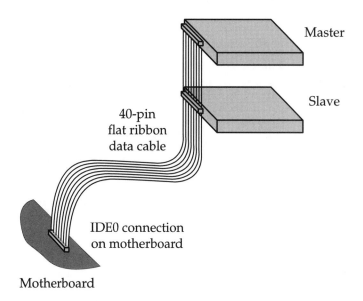

Master

Slave

40-pin
flat ribbon
data cable

IDE0 connection
on motherboard

Motherboard

The new hard drive must be prepared before it will store data. The process of preparing a hard disk—or any form of magnetic media—to store data is called formatting. In this lab activity, you will need to run fdisk.exe to identify and partition the new hard drive.

It is standard operating procedure to back up important data from the existing hard drive before installing the second hard drive. Otherwise, data could be permanently lost by accidentally formatting the wrong hard drive. Data could also be lost if the system crashes because of improper hard-drive installation or a change in the physical connections.

For example, while installing the second drive, the data cable can easily pull loose from the IDE controller on the motherboard. The cable could then be reattached incorrectly and damage not only the new drive but the original as well. The IDE connector is not keyed and can very easily be misaligned or even connected backward. Because things do go wrong, you should back up any important data on the existing hard drive before beginning the installation of the second drive.

You can use one of several pieces of equipment to back up the hard drive, such as a tape drive, a CD-R(W), or an Iomega Zip drive. The backup may consist of either everything on the hard disk drive or simply important data such as files or programs that are in addition to the operating system. A tape backup usually has a lot of storage space and can generally be used to back up the entire hard drive system, operating system and all files.

Because the second drive may not be the same make and model as the original drive, the specific jumper settings for each drive should be determined before beginning the installation. The two drives might very well require two different master/slave jumper-setting positions. Always be sure of the setting position; do not randomly try different jumper-setting positions.

Equipment and Materials

✳ Typical PC with only one hard drive

✳ Hard drive to install as the second disk drive

✳ A means of backing up important data (to be determined by the instructor)

Procedure

1. ___ Gather the necessary materials and report to your assigned station.

2. ___ Boot the PC to be sure it is in proper working order before you begin.

3. ___ Shut down the PC and remove the cover. Follow all anti-static procedures as outlined by your instructor. Many students mistakenly believe that static precautions do not apply to a hard drive. Look at a hard drive and you will see a circuit board that contains many static-sensitive components. That is the reason hard drives ship inside an anti-static bag.

4. ___ Inspect the existing hard drive and determine if the jumper has been set in the master position, the neutral position, or has been removed altogether. A single disk drive usually has the jumper in a neutral position, but this is not always the case. Look for a jumper-setting chart on the side of the hard drive. You may need to remove the drive for a close inspection, or go to the manufacture's web site to obtain the jumper setting information. In addition, some software, such as EZ Drive, contains jumper setting information for the most common drives.

   If you remove the drive, take pencil and paper and draw the orientation of the ribbon cable that connects the drive and the IDE controller. Look at the colored line running along the edge of the flat ribbon cable. The colored line (either red or blue) is used to identify which side of the cable connects pin-1 on the motherboard to pin-1 on the hard drive. Also, sketch the position of the jumper on the hard drive. The drawing will help you to put the PC back into its original condition when the lab is done.

5. ___ Inspect the hard drive that is to be installed as the slave. Determine the setting needed to designate the hard drive as a slave, and change the jumper setting accordingly.

6. ___ Install the second drive and connect it to the open connector on the existing hard drive ribbon cable. Remember, the original drive is set as master and the second drive needs to be set as the slave; otherwise the PC may not boot properly.

7. ___ As previously discussed, the colored line on the ribbon cable identifies the side of the ribbon cable that connects pin-1 on the hard drive to pin-1 on the IDE controller. Be sure to correctly align the colored edge of the ribbon cable to pin-1 on both, the motherboard and the hard drive.

8 ___ Mount the hard drive with the mounting screws provided. Do not overtighten the screws; a snug fit is fine for this exercise.

9. ___ After the second drive has been properly installed, boot the PC but leave the cover off. The new hardware should be automatically detected by the Windows operating system. You may need to access the BIOS setup program to verify the new hard drive has been detected. If the second drive is not automatically detected, you may need to set up the second hard drive manually, or through third-party software, such as EZ Drive. This is especially true for computers with older BIOS systems.

10. ___ After the second hard drive has been detected, open a DOS window and run the **fdisk** program to partition the new hard drive. You will also need to format it before attempting to store any data. Check with the instructor for the file system to use, such as FAT16.

11. ___ After the new drive has been partitioned and formatted, run **fdisk** once more and verify that the second hard drive has been formatted correctly. If the partition and formatting have been done correctly, the fdisk program will display the letter of the drive assigned and the type of file system format. If it does not identify the file system format, call the instructor.

12. ___ Exit the fdisk program and close the DOS window. Use the WordPad program to create a short file and then save it to the new hard disk drive.

13. ___ After saving the test file on the new hard disk drive, use Windows Explorer to view the contents of the newest hard disk drive. If the file does not exist, call the instructor.

14. ___ If everything has gone as instructed and you experienced no problems, call the instructor to view your finished project.

15. ___ Open the **Device Manager** tab in the System Properties dialog box. The System Properties dialog box is accessed by right clicking on the **My Computer** icon and then selecting **Properties**. Write in the requested information in the spaces provided.

   Master hard disk drive IRQ setting _____

   I/O memory assignments _____

   Slave hard disk drive IRQ setting _____

   I/O memory assignments _____

16. ___ After the instructor inspects your project, you may remove the second hard drive and restore the PC to its original condition. Remember to restore the original jumper setting on the original hard drive.

17. ___ Before replacing the case cover, reboot the PC to be sure it is in working order. If it is not, look for loose cable connections before calling the instructor. Do not reattach any loose cables while the power is on.

18. ___ Replace the case cover and reboot the PC once more to be sure it is in working order. Sometimes a cable will be pulled slightly while reinstalling the cover.

19. ___ If everything is in good working order, shut down the PC and return all materials. Be sure to place the second hard drive into the anti-static bag.

Review Questions

1. What is the purpose of the colored line that runs along one side of the IDE ribbon cable?

   _____

2. What names are used to identify the two hard drives connected to the same ribbon cable and controller port? _____

3. What should always be done before adding a second hard drive to a client's PC?

   _____

4. Why must you follow anti-static precautions when installing a second hard drive?

   _____

5. How do you access the Device Manager? _____

   _____

Name _____ Date_____

Class/Instructor _____

Disk Cleanup

After completing this lab activity, you will be able to:

✳ Apply the Disk Cleanup utility to remove unwanted files.
✳ Explain the various options available for the Disk Cleanup utility.

Introduction

The Disk Cleanup utility is located at **Start | Programs | Accessories | System Tools**. The utility can also be accessed by right clicking on the selected drive in Windows Explorer and choosing **Properties** from the menu. In the Properties dialog box for the selected drive, there is a button titled **Disk Cleanup**. Clicking this button accesses the Disk Cleanup utility also.

The Disk Cleanup utility is designed to remove certain types of files, creating additional free disk space. When Disk Cleanup is first accessed, the Select Drive dialog box allows you to select the drive you wish to clear of unwanted files. Once the drive has been selected, a Disk Cleanup dialog box appears, similar to the one shown.

Magnetic Storage

Disk Cleanup for LOCAL_DISK (C:)	? X

Disk Cleanup | More Options | Settings |

You can use Disk Cleanup to free up to 3.93 MB of disk space on LOCAL_DISK (C:).

Files to delete:

☑ 🔒 Temporary Internet Files		2.50 MB
☑ 📄 Downloaded Program Files		0.00 MB
☐ 🗑 Recycle Bin		0.22 MB
☐ 📄 Temporary files		1.21 MB

Total amount of disk space you gain: 2.50 MB

Description

The Temporary Internet Files folder contains Web pages stored on your hard disk for quick viewing. Your personalized settings for Web pages will be left intact.

View Files

OK   Cancel

The dialog box allows you to select various file types for deletion, such as Temporary Internet Files, Downloaded Program Files, Recycle Bin (deleted files), and Temporary Files. As each category is highlighted by the cursor, the description box provides information about the selected option.

The **More Options** tab allows you to choose two more ways to free up disk space. You can remove programs that are no longer used, or Windows components that are no longer used. These two options take the user to the Add/Remove Program dialog box. This is the proper place to remove program files installed on the Windows system. A third option, called Drive Conversion (FAT32), may also be available. If your hard drive is already set up as a FAT32, the option will not be available. Converting your file system to FAT32 can save disk space. When the **Convert** button is selected, the wizard will walk you through the FAT32 conversion.

■ **Important:**

You can convert the file system from FAT16 to FAT32 but you cannot change the file system from FAT32 back to FAT16.

There are some negative points to using FAT32. First, you cannot use the standard Windows 98 compression tool, DriveSpace. Also, most disk utilities designed for FAT16 cannot be used on a FAT32 system. Lastly, if you install a dual boot system on the hard drive and use a system other than Microsoft Windows 95B, 98, or 2000, you may not be able to see or access the files on the FAT32 structure. However, you may find third-party software that overcomes FAT32's restrictions.

In addition, there is a check box under the **Settings** tab that will allow the Disk Cleanup utility to run automatically when disk space is low. The types of files deleted by Disk Cleanup are generally considered the most disposable types. By automating Disk Cleanup, you may avoid more extreme solutions, such as deleting more important files, when hard drive space gets low.

Equipment and Materials

✳ Typical PC with Windows 98 (or later) operating system

Procedure

1. ___ Boot the PC and wait for the Windows desktop to appear.

2. ___ Open **Start | Programs | Accessories | System Tools | Disk Cleanup**. This opens the Select Drive dialog box.

3. ___ Select the C: drive for cleanup. This opens the Disk Cleanup dialog box.

4. ___ Look at the Disk Cleanup dialog box. The dialog box should list how much space can be gained. How much space can be gained? _____

5. ___ Select **Temporary Internet Files**.

6. ___ Select the **More Options** tab at the top of the dialog box. List the options available in the space provided. _____

_____

_____

7. ___ Now, select the **Settings** tab from the top of the dialog box. What option is made available through the **Settings** tab? _____

8. ___ Properly shut down the system after answering the review questions.

Review Questions

1. What two ways can you access the Disk Cleanup utility? _____

   _____

   _____

2. What four types of files can Disk Cleanup delete in order to free up more disk space?

   _____

3. In order to save space, what type of file system can the disk be converted to?

   _____

Magnetic Storage

Name _____ Date_____

Class/Instructor _____

Lab Activity

45

Disk Compression

After completing this lab activity, you will be able to:

✷   Compress data stored on a disk.

✷   Decompress data stored on a disk.

✷   Explain how to set up automatic disk compression based on remaining free disk space.

✷   Explain the options available using DriveSpace 3.

Introduction

In this lab activity, you will use DriveSpace to compress the files stored on a floppy disk. Disk compression is a way to increase the amount of drive space available on hard drives and floppy disks. A compression program can reduce the size of files by as much as fifty percent.

Windows 98 contains the DriveSpace 3 utility. DriveSpace is a descendant of DoubleSpace, the original Microsoft disk-compression utility. Starting with MS-DOS 6.22, DoubleSpace was renamed DriveSpace because of legal issues. Any files compressed with the earlier version can be accessed by the Windows 98 version. There are several options available with DriveSpace 3.

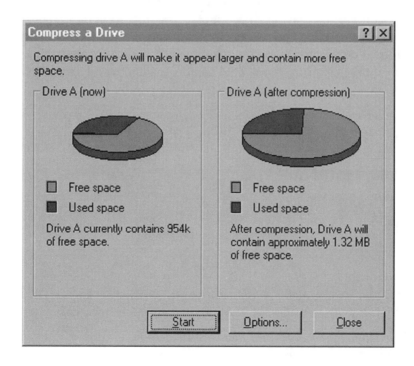

As you can see in the screen capture of the Compress a Drive dialog box, the A: drive currently contains 954 KB of free space, which can be expanded to 1.32 MB after standard disk compression. You can create even more space by using the HiPack compression option but at the cost of speed, as it will take longer to compress and decompress files. Look at the screen capture of Disk Compression Settings dialog box. In this dialog box, the user indicates the type of compression and whether compression should take place automatically, based on the amount of free disk space.

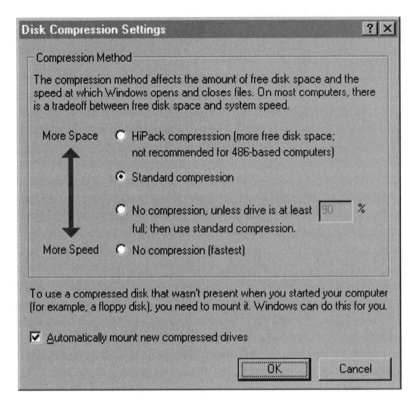

The decision to compress a drive or leave it uncompressed boils down to a choice between optimizing system speed and increasing disk space. Disk compression can be quite useful when you are running low on hard drive space. You can gain needed space until you have the opportunity to add an additional drive or replace the existing drive with a bigger one. However, you should be aware that it takes slightly more time to access files from a compressed drive.

◼ Note:

You may need to check the Microsoft technical support web site if you are having difficulty with DriveSpace 3. There are several known problems associated with this utility.

Equipment and Materials

✳   Typical PC with Windows 98 operating system
✳   Windows 98 Installation CD
✳   3 1/2″ floppy disk

◼ Note:

Because DriveSpace 3 is an optional installation program and is not installed during a typical Windows 98 installation, the Windows 98 Installation CD may be required.

Also, some of the following procedures and their results may vary slightly, depending on the version of Windows 98 being used in the activity.

Procedure

1. ___ Boot the PC and wait for the Windows desktop to appear.

2. ___ Prepare the floppy disk to be compressed. For this exercise, you should use a floppy disk that is either blank, or contains no important files. Using Windows Explorer, select files totaling approximately 500 KB from C:\Windows directory. Do not select any files with a .cab extension because these files are already compressed. Copy the selected files to the floppy disk. Leave at least 512 KB of free space on the floppy disk (it would be 2 MB if you were compressing a hard drive). The compression program needs this free space to operate.

3. ___ See if the DriveSpace program is installed on your computer. Look in **Start | Programs | Accessories | System Tools**. If the program is already installed, go on to step 4. If the program is not installed, you will need to install it using the **Add/Remove Program** utility located at **Start | Settings | Control Panel**. Double click the **Add/Remove Programs** icon, and then select the **Windows Setup** tab in the Add/Remove Programs Properties dialog box. Next, highlight **System Tools** and click on the **Details** button. The System Tools dialog box should appear. Place a check in the box next to **DriveSpace 3** and click **OK**.

4. ___ Now start the DriveSpace 3 program by selecting the **DriveSpace** icon located in **Start | Programs | Accessories | System Tools**, or typing **drvspace** in the **Run** dialog box accessed from the **Start** menu. When the DriveSpace 3 dialog box appears on the screen, select the A: drive and then select **Compress** from the **Drive** menu.

5. ___ Before you perform a standard compression of the floppy disk, record the current amount of free space on the disk and the amount of free space expected after compression.

   Space before compression _____

   Space after compression _____

   After the disk is compressed, Windows Explorer will only display the file size as the uncompressed value.

6. ___ Next, click on the **Options** button at the bottom of the Compress a Drive dialog box. This should activate a dialog similar to the one shown here.

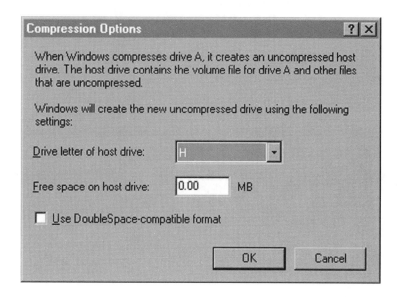

The DriveSpace program automatically assigns the next available drive letter to the new compressed drive. For example, if a PC only has drive letters A:, B:, and C:, the next drive letter would be D:. The drive letter assigned to the uncompressed (host) drive, which contains the newly created compressed drive, can be changed in this dialog box. This feature is useful when it is necessary to resolve a conflict with another drive letter.

7. ___ Click the **Cancel** button to close the Compression Options dialog box.

8. ___ Click the **Start** button to begin compressing the floppy disk. The Are you sure? dialog box appears next, confirming your desire to compress the floppy disk. You have the option of making a backup of the files at this point. This is not necessary for this exercise. However, if you were compressing an entire hard drive, it would be a prudent step, since files can be corrupted during disk compression operations.

Click the **Compress Now** button to continue with the compression.

9. ___ A progress window appears on the screen, showing the progress of the disk compression utility. The length of the process depends on the number of files being compressed.

10. ___ The results of the compression should appear now in the Compress a Drive dialog box. Click the **Close** button, which should bring the DriveSpace 3 dialog box to the foreground. The dialog box will be similar to the one shown here. Take note of the new drive letter in the window area of the DriveSpace 3 dialog box. The new drive letter represents the host drive, or the drive that contains the compressed files.

The compressed files are stored in a file named DRVSPACE.000 on the host drive. If this file is deleted or corrupted, the compressed files cannot be recovered, and all data is lost. Remember to back up your data.

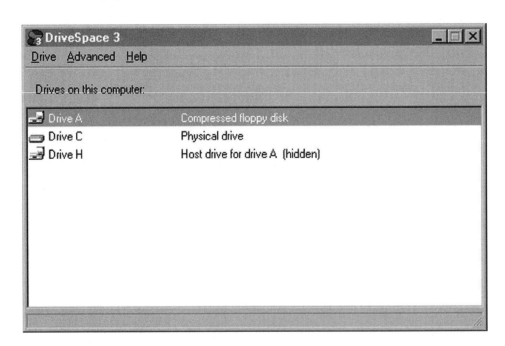

11. ___ Open Windows Explorer and look at the floppy disk. Do you see the host drive letter? If it is not apparent, it should appear after an attempt is made to open it, such as double clicking on the icon.

12. ___ Right click on the 3 1/2" drive icon and then select **Properties** from the drop-down menu. When the **3 1/2" Floppy (A:) Properties** dialog box appears, select the **Compression** tab. The screen should display assorted information about the compressed disk, such as the type of compression and available disk space.

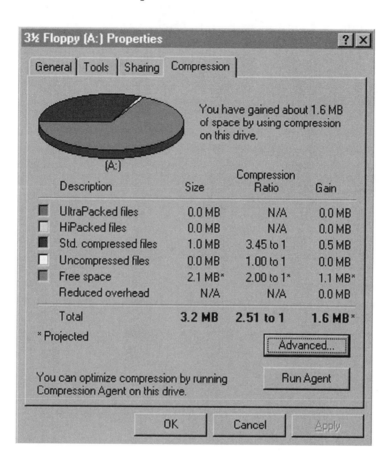

You have the option to run Compression Agent from here. Compression Agent is started by selecting the **Run Agent** button in the bottom right corner of the dialog box. The Compression Agent can also be launched through the **Start | Programs | Accessories | System Tools**. The Compression Agent is an enhanced feature of Windows 98. It allows the compression of individual files rather than the entire disk. It also uses a technique called UltraPack, which offers a higher compression ratio.

13. ___ Put the compressed disk into the drive of another computer and see how it appears in the Windows Explorer. If the host drive does not appear, try accessing the A: drive. This should cause the host drive to appear.

14. ___ Now place the disk back into the original PC and uncompress it. In the Drive Space 3 dialog box, highlight the A: drive, select **Uncompress** from the **Drive** menu, and click the **Start** button to begin the decompression process. Follow the onscreen directions to complete the process.

15. ___ Experiment with DriveSpace, but restrict the experimentation to the floppy disk. Do not compress the system's hard drive.

16. ___ Experiment with the Compression Agent utility. Like DriveSpace, it is located in the System Tools menu. Compression Agent is an advanced feature introduced in Windows 98. It allows you to compress specific files rather than the entire disk.

17. ___ When you have finished experimenting with the disk-compression programs, answer the review questions. You may use Windows Help to assist you. There is a lot of information about DriveSpace and disk compression in the Help files.

18. ___ Return the PC to its original configuration before shutting down the system.

Review Questions

1. What was the previous name of the DriveSpace utility? _____

2. DriveSpace is incompatible with which Windows file system structure? _____

3. Where is DriveSpace located? Write the answer in **Folder1 | Folder2 | Folder3** form.

_____

4. If DriveSpace cannot be found under System Tools, what is the most likely explanation?

_____

_____

5. What is the name of the file that stores the compressed files on the host drive?

_____

6. What amount of free disk space is required to compress a hard drive using DriveSpace?

_____

Name _____ Date_____

Class/Instructor _____

CD Drive Installation (IDE)

After completing this lab activity, you will be able to:

* Install any type of IDE CD drive.
* Identify common problems associated with CD-drive installation.
* Identify the major parts required for CD-drive installation.

Introduction

In this lab activity, you will either be installing a new drive in a PC that didn't previously have one, or you will be replacing or upgrading an existing CD drive. The exact type of procedure will be assigned by your instructor. The installation process is similar for both types of installation.

Installing a CD drive is a simple task. The installation can be more complicated when a sound card is used in combination with the CD drive. When a sound card is incorporated with the CD drive for enhanced audio, some problems may develop. Usually the sound card and CD will share the same IRQ assignment.

Another common problem is Plug and Play's failure to properly identify the new drive. If the CD drive is not identified automatically, or is incorrectly identified by the Plug and Play feature, the CD drive will not operate properly. In this case, you may need to disable the Plug and Play feature. The Plug and Play feature can usually be disabled in the BIOS setup program.

Loading the proper driver can be another problem when installing a CD drive. New drives are placed on the market daily. The operating system you are using may not contain the very latest drivers needed for the installation. The driver is usually included when the CD drive is purchased. It is a good idea to check the manufacturer's web site for the latest driver for the unit as well as information about known problems. Checking the web site can save many frustrating hours during an installation.

Proper connection of the CD drive can be another troublesome area during the installation. When installing a CD drive, avoid sharing the IDE connection with the hard drive. Sharing the same IDE connection can create compatibility problems between the CD drive and the hard drive.

The following illustration is of a typical CD-drive unit and shows the connection points on the end of the drive. Take special note of the master/slave jumper selection area. The master/slave jumper setup is similar to that found on hard drives. When more than one device is connected to an IDE or EIDE connection, one device must be designated the master and the other, the slave.

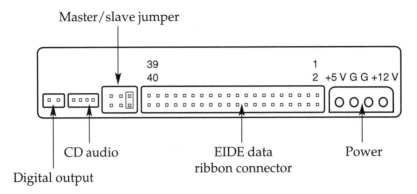

Typical connections on a CD-drive.

The mechanics of installing a CD drive are quite simple. The only real concern is the possibility of loosening a connection to one of the other cables while installing the CD-drive cables.

Equipment and Materials

* Typical PC with a 486 (or later) CPU

* CD drive, such as a CD-RW

* *Instructor note: For this lab, students may install a CD drive into a PC that does not currently have one. However, it is recommended they replace an existing CD drive. For example, you may choose to have the students replace an older CD-R drive with a newer CD-RW drive.*

Procedure

1. ___ Boot the PC to be sure it is working before you begin the installation procedure.

2. ___ Once you have verified that the assigned PC is in good working order, properly shut it down and turn off the power.

3. ___ Remove the PC cover and select the bay in which the new CD drive will be installed. If you are replacing an existing drive, sketch the drive and its cable connections. Take care to mark the proper orientation of the cables, as you will most likely have to reinstall the original drive at the end of the lab. Once you have sketched the drive setup, disconnect the cables and remove the mounting screws from the mounting rails. Slide the CD drive out of its bay. This procedure will vary based on the make and model of the drive and the case.

4. ___ If you are performing a new installation, install the mounting rails to the bay now. For a unit replacement, check the existing mounting rails for compatibility with the new CD drive. You may need to remove the existing mounting rails and replace them with a set of rails compatible with the new CD drive. Before securing the CD drive, check the master/slave jumper settings. Be sure to choose the correct setting for the installation. Check the documentation or look on the side of the drive for a chart of jumper settings.

5. ___ Mount the CD drive into the bay using the mounting rails. Be careful not to overtighten the mounting screws. Use only the mounting screws that were provided with the drive. Screws that did not come with the drive may be too long and damage the CD drive during installation.

6. ___ Attach the power cable to the CD drive.

7. ___ Attach the ribbon cable between the CD drive and the IDE-controller port on the mother-board. As with other drives, the colored strip on the cable indicates the side of the cable that must align with pin 1 on the controller.

8. ___ Next, attach the audio cable to the sound card, if the computer is equipped with one. You may need to read the sound card documentation to locate the correct connection for the audio cable. The audio cable may connect to the motherboard if the sound system is integrated into the motherboard.

9. ___ Have the instructor inspect your installation now.

10. ___ After the instructor has checked your installation, you may power up and boot the PC. Watch the screen for the detection of the new CD drive. If the new drive is not correctly identified, you may need to manually install the driver software. The manual installation begins by clicking the **Add New Hardware** icon in the Control Panel. The Add New Hardware icon is located at **Start | Settings | Control Panel | Add New Hardware**. After opening the Add New Hardware program, simply follow the instructions prompted on the display. You will need to have the floppy disk containing the driver for the CD-drive, because the CD probably will not work with the generic drivers provided by the operating system.

11. ___ After the CD-drive installation is complete, test the CD drive to be sure it is functioning properly. Either access a CD or burn a CD depending on the type of drive installed.

12. ___ Open Device Manager and record the resource assignment for the CD drive in the spaces provided. The exact resource assignments will vary. You may need to open the sound card assignments to obtain the CD-drive assignments. When a CD-ROM is tied to the sound card, it shares the same resources as the sound card. They work together as a single unit. Look in both places if a sound card is installed. _____

_____

_____

_____

13. ___ Have the instructor once more check your project to verify it is working properly. Once inspected, the instructor will advise you to either leave the existing device mounted in the PC, or reverse the operation and place the original device back into the unit.

14. ___ If you removed the newer drive and reinstalled the original unit, test the system to be sure it is working properly before answering the following review questions.

Review Questions

1. What problems might arise during a CD-drive installation? _____

_____

_____

_____

CDs

2. How do you correct a wrong IRQ assignment by the Plug and Play feature?

_____

_____

3. How is Plug and Play usually disabled? _____

_____

_____

4. What does the stripe running along the ribbon cable indicate? _____

_____

5. Where could you locate the latest driver for the CD drive you are installing?

_____

6. Why should you use only the screws designed for the mounting of the drive unit?

_____

Name _____ Date_____

Class/Instructor _____

Lab Activity

47

Printer Configuration (Part One)

After completing this lab activity, you will be able to:

✷   Install and set up a typical printer.

✷   Explain the various printer options available.

Introduction

The installation of a new printer is a common procedure. During the early years of personal computers, printer installation could be quite difficult. Now, in the era of Plug and Play and wizard programs, printer installation is much easier. In this exercise, you will install a printer driver. For the purpose of lab instruction, an HP laser printer is used, although the exact model will not be specified. You should substitute the manufacturer and model of your own printer in its place.

A printer driver is necessary for communications between the software that uses a printer and the printer hardware. The driver translates the communications between processor and printer. The processor communicates in hexadecimal or binary codes. The printer driver translates those and reissues them as commands that the printer can understand. In turn, the printer starts a new page, changes font size or style, copies an image from RAM, or prints a line.

If the correct driver is not selected, many things go wrong. An endless stream of paper may be ejected from the printer, completely blank or filled with unintelligible symbols. The printer may simply sit there and appear dead.

To install a printer, access the printer installation program located at **Start | Settings | Printers**. The printer installation program can also be accessed by double clicking the **Printers** icon located at **Start | Settings | Control Panel**. Once the Printers window is open, double click the **Add Printer** icon and follow the instructions in the Add Printer Wizard dialog box to install the printer.

Equipment and Materials

✷   Typical PC with Windows 98 (or later) operating system

✷   Windows 98 Installation CD

✷   HP laser printer or any equivalent printer

◼ **Note:**

The lab is compatible with most printers. Simply substitute the brand and model you are using in place of references made to the HP laser printer.

Printers

Procedure

1. ___ Boot the PC and wait for the Windows desktop to appear.

2. ___ Access the Printers dialog box located at **Start I Settings I Printers**.

3. ___ Double click the **Add Printer** icon. The Add Printer Wizard dialog box should appear, similar to the one shown.

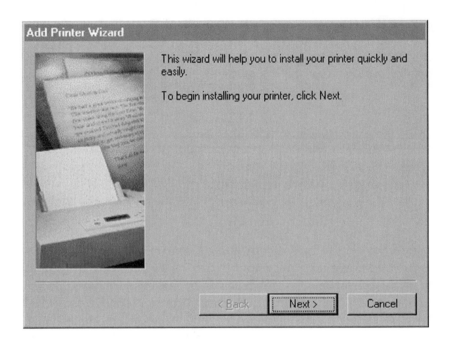

4. ___ Next, click on the **Next >** button and follow the onscreen prompts.

5. ___ The Add Printer Wizard dialog box should now appear similar to the following illustration. You must make a choice of printer connection, by selecting either the **Local printer** or **Network printer** radio button.

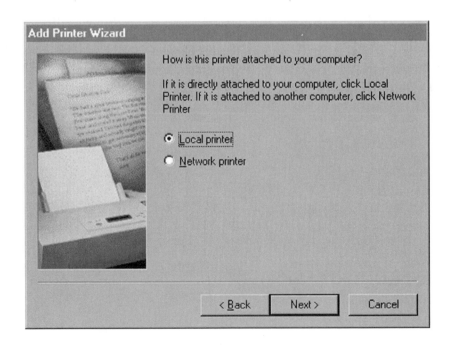

A local printer is one that is directly connected to the PC while a network printer is one that is accessed via a network. In this lab activity, you should select the **Local printer** radio button.

6. ___ When installing a local printer, the Add Printer Wizard dialog box then asks you to identify the manufacturer and model of the printer you are installing. The list of manufacturers is on the left side of the dialog box, and the models from the selected manufacturer are listed on the right. Use the scroll bar to locate the printer manufacturer and then select the manufacturer by clicking on its name. The screen should appear similar to the following illustration.

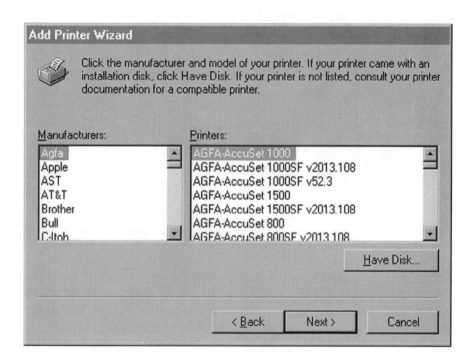

7. ___ Locate the model in the right panel by using the scroll bar on the right side listings. Select the model by clicking on it. After the manufacturer and model have been selected, click on the button labeled **Next**. Once this is done, Windows will automatically load the correct software driver for the printer. At times, the exact model will not be listed, and you will need to have a disk containing the correct printer driver for your printer.

8. ___Next, the dialog box asks you to identify a port for the printer to connect to. See the following screen capture.

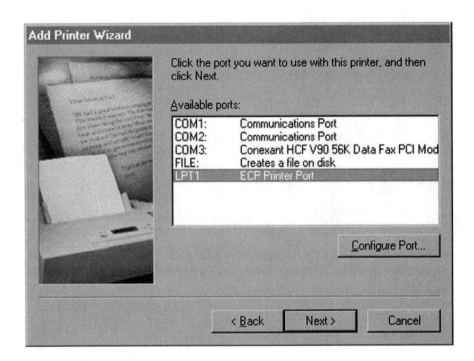

The usual choices are **COM1:**, **COM2:**, **FILE:**, and **LPT1:**. COM1 and LPT1 are commonly associated as printer ports. When the serial ports of COM1 or COM2 are selected, you will need additional information such as type of parity, number of data bits, number of stop bits, etc. This information can usually be found in the printer manual. Most modern printers can use USB ports as well. It is also common to purchase printers that have an RJ-45 port, commonly used for networking a printer. For this exercise, select **LPT1: Printer Port**.

9. ___ The next screen in the Add Printer Wizard dialog box contains a Printer Name: text box. A new name can be typed in this field if you wish to rename the printer. This option is designed to assist you and others in identifying the printer. The ability to rename the printer is especially useful when several printers can be accessed, such as in a network environment.

10. ___ Below the Printer Name: text box is a prompt that asks if you wish to use the new printer as the Windows default printer. Select the **Yes** radio button.

11. ___ Next, the dialog box asks if you wish to print a test page after installation. Select the **Yes (recommended)** radio button. If everything prints correctly, you are finished. If the printer does not print correctly, you can enter the Windows Troubleshooters program by simply replying **No** when prompted.

12. ___ If everything is correct with the printer, you may close all Windows programs and shut down the PC. If things are not correct or if you have questions, please call your instructor.

Review Questions

1. Which two physical ports types are typically used to connect to older printers? _____

   _____

2. What does the printer driver do? _____

   _____

   _____

3. If a printer prints unintelligible characters or symbols when first installed, what is most likely the problem? _____

   _____

Printers

Name _____ Date_____

Class/Instructor _____

Printer Configuration (Part Two)

After completing this lab activity, you will be able to:

* Select paper orientation, such as landscape and portrait.
* Adjust settings, such as Not selected: and Transmission retry:.
* Capture a printer port.
* Explain printer spooling.
* Explain EMF, RAW, and PostScript printing images.

Introduction

Printer installation consists of connecting the printer to the computer and installing the driver needed to establish communications between the PC and the printer. When you configure a printer, you specify settings that produce desired results from the printing process. For example, you must configure the printer to print on the paper in horizontal fashion (landscape) rather than vertical (portrait).

In this lab activity, you will become familiar with the various configuration options for a printer. To change the printer configuration, open the Printers window located at **Start | Settings | Printers**. Right click on the printer's icon and select **Properties** from the drop-down menu. The options available and the layout of the Properties dialog box depend on the exact printer that is selected for this lab activity.

Equipment and Materials

* Typical PC with Windows 98 (or later) operating system
* HP LaserJet printer or equivalent

Procedure

1. ___ Boot the PC and wait for the Windows desktop to be displayed.

2. ___ Access the Printers window by going through **Start | Settings | Printers**. You should see a dialog box similar to the one shown here.

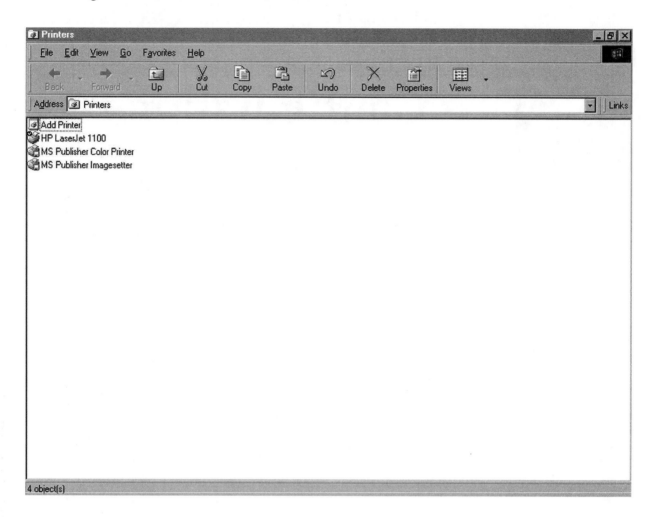

3. ___ To configure a printer, you must access the printer's Properties dialog box. To access this dialog box, right click on the printer's icon and then select **Properties** from the drop-down menu. You should see a Properties dialog box similar to the one shown. The exact details of the dialog box may vary according to the manufacturer and type of printer installed.

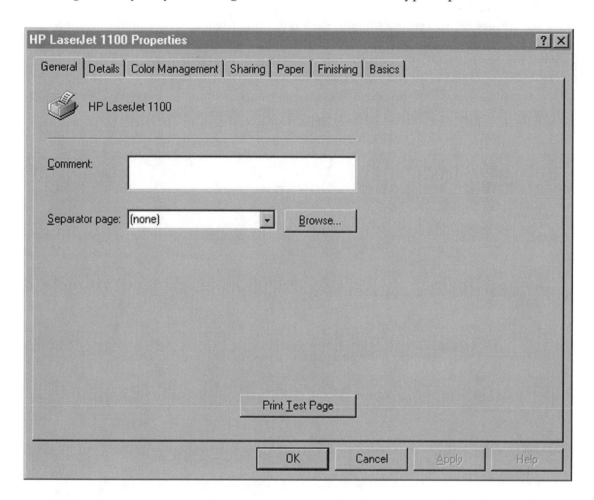

4. ___ Under the **General** tab there are two text boxes labeled Comment: and Separator page:. The Comment: text box is used to write a short comment about the printer. This is particularly useful when there are multiple printers available to the user. The comment can include the type of paper that is typically loaded into the printer, where the printer is located, and whether it is a black-and-white printer or a color printer. The second text box, labeled Separator page:, provides the option of printing a separator page after print jobs. For example, if a printer is shared by several different users, as an expensive graphics printer would be, the separator page can be used to identify the print job's originator.

The options for the separator page are (none), Full, and Simple. The function of the (none) option is obvious; no separator page is printed. This is the default setting. The Simple option prints the document file name, which PC ordered the print job, and the date and time it was printed. The Full option prints everything included under the Simple option and more. It can be customized to suit your needs. When this option is selected, you can add graphics and additional text information to the separator page.

Printers

5. ___ Clicking the **Details** tab reveals information and allows selection of the printer port and printer driver to use. After a printer is installed, you may need to modify these settings if the printer is not working correctly. Printer drivers can be updated to correct known bugs or improve performance. You may need to change the communication port after installing additional equipment.

Users sometimes change the settings in the dialog box to attempt to correct a problem, but end up creating additional problems for the support technician to correct. A classic example occurs when the network goes down and a user tries to print a report on a networked printer. The printer fails to print the report, so the user changes settings in the dialog box in a futile attempt to solve the problem. When the network problem is corrected, the printer still will not work correctly because all the properties have been changed.

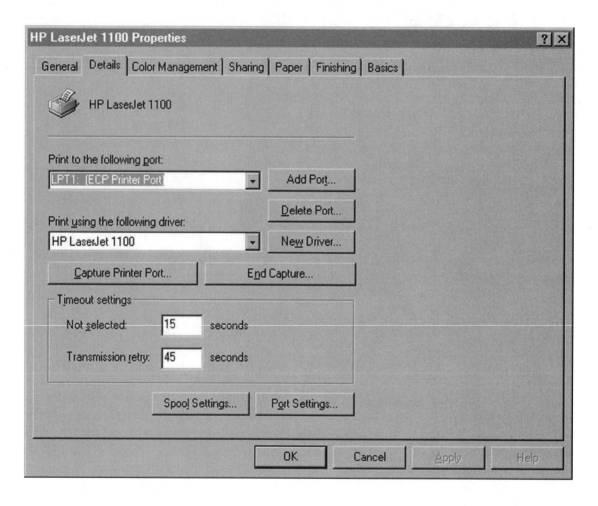

6. ___ Look at the screen capture to see some of the settings that can be adjusted from the Details tab. The options such as Add Port, Delete Port, Capture Printer Port, and End Capture are used on network systems to add or release connections to network printers. COM ports are serial ports and the LPT ports are parallel ports. A serial port transmits data one bit at a time while a parallel port transmits data in bytes. LPT ports are used to connect a computer to a printer.

An LPT port can also be identified as a printer port on a network. To connect to a network printer, called capturing a printer port, click the **Capture Printer Port** button in the Properties dialog box. When the Capture Printer Port dialog box appears, type the exact path for the printer in the **Path:** text box. A sample of a network path to a printer is as follows: \\Station5\HPLJ4. The path name indicates the PC and the printer. The path is to a computer named Station5 and the printer connected to Station5 is HPLJ4 for Hewlett Packard LaserJet 5.

To disconnect from the network printer, click the **End Capture** button displayed on the dialog box. There will be more about network printers in the network lab activities. There is also an option to create a file on disk or even to a fax. The time-out settings are used to control the period of time to use before notifying the user of a problem with the printer. The Not selected: setting is usually a relatively short period of time. It controls the delay before the user is notified that the printer is not ready. A printer may generate a message after the Not selected: time expires if the printer is not turned on, turned on but not on line, or not plugged in. The second time setting, Transmission retry:, controls the time period for transmitting the data to the printer and the printer to accept the entire transmission. This setting is usually a longer time span than the Not selected: setting. If a long document is not completely printed before the printing process ends, the total time needs to be increased. In the space provided, write the default values for the Not selected: and the Transmission retry: periods.

Not selected: = _____ seconds

Transmission retry: = _____ seconds

7. ___ The **Spool Settings...** button accesses the Spool Settings dialog box. Print spooling is similar to multitasking. Print spooling is a technique that allows the user to do other things on the PC while a file is printed on the printer. There are options such as Start printing after last page is spooled and Start printing after first page is spooled. Choosing **Start printing after last page is spooled** allows you to return to another application faster, but causes the actual print job to take longer. Usually the default settings do not need adjustment. The Enable bi-directional support for this printer option allows communication back and forth between the PC and the printer. This causes messages to appear on the screen display about the condition of the printer and the print job.

8. ___ There are usually two choices for the Spool data format: setting, RAW and EMF. The acronym EMF stands for enhanced metafiles. The default for Windows 98 is EMF, which is faster than RAW. EMF is faster because it takes full advantage of Window's 32-bit architecture. RAW is similar to PostScript. PostScript is a printer language developed by Adobe. If you experience problems with printing relating to scaling the image or what seems to be interpretation of fonts, you may wish to switch the setting from RAW to EMF or vice versa.

9. ___ Under the **Paper** tab, you can select the size of paper, the type of paper tray, and the EconoMode to use. Pay particular attention to the paper orientation selection radio buttons. They are marked Portrait and Landscape. These two settings are used to change the way the image is printed on the paper, either horizontally (Portrait) or vertically (Landscape) across the paper.

Printers

10. ___ The **Graphics** tab contains the settings used for images rather than text. The resolution and dithering options can be set in this tab. The term *dithering* refers to how the small printed dots of an image are formed to represent the original image. Note the position of the dithering selection at present. Feel free to experiment with the dithering settings. When you are done, restore the setting to default. There is no need to print to paper to see the effects of dithering. There should be a cube displayed in a window in the dithering area that will illustrate the effects of the different settings.

11. ___ The **Fonts** tab is used to access and change the font properties. A font is a classification of a style of lettering, numbers, and symbols.

12. ___ Under the **Device Options** tab you can select the print quality and the amount of memory to allocate to the printer.

13. ___ In the upper-right corner of the HP LaserJet Properties dialog box is a small question mark inside a box. You can click on the question mark and then position the cursor over an item to find out more about that particular item. Try it now. Click on the question mark and then click on dithering.

14. ___ Close the Properties dialog box and go back to the original Printer dialog box. Select the **File** menu and look closely at two of the choices in the drop-down menu, **Pause Printing** and **Purge Print Documents**. If these choices are not available, you may need to click on the printer icon to make them accessible. These two selections will be used often. When a user develops a problem with a printer, they often attempt to solve the problem by clicking repeatedly on the print icon or selecting print from the file menu. This causes the print spool to fill with print jobs. Even if the problem is corrected, the print errors can continue until all the print jobs up to the point of correction have been completed. You may need to pause the printer and purge all print jobs before troubleshooting a printer.

15. ___ You may now experiment with the settings. Make sure you write down the default settings and restore all original settings before shutting down the system.

Review Questions

1. How do you access the Printers dialog box? _____

_____

2. How do you access printer's Properties dialog box? _____

_____

3. Is COM1 a serial port or a parallel port? _____

4. Is LPT1 a serial or parallel port? _____

5. How are serial ports and printer ports different? _____

_____

6. What do landscape and portrait paper orientation settings affect? _____

_____

7. What must you do when you determine the user has tried to print a document numerous times without any success? _____

_____

_____

Name _____ Date_____

Class/Instructor _____

Direct Cable Connection

After completing this laboratory activity, you will be able to:

* Describe the various ways to transfer data from a laptop to a desktop PC.
* Define the host and guest as it applies to direct cable connections.
* Explain how to install the Direct Cable Connection utility.
* Set up a share on a resource located on one PC to be accessed by another PC.

Introduction

This lab activity introduces you to the various ways to directly connect a laptop to a desktop PC and then access or transfer files. You can transfer data between two PCs by using a special parallel cable, a special serial cable, or an infrared port. Files can also be transferred by connecting the laptop and the desktop to a network. This networking option is covered in later chapters.

What makes the direct connection cable special is the way the cable is wired from end to end. With a normal cable, all the individual wires connect straight through. Each pin is connected to an exact matching pin number on the opposite end. The cable used to make a direct connection between two PCs is referred to as an *interlink cable* or a *null-modem cable*.

The direct connection cable comes in two main styles, serial and parallel. The parallel cable connection is much faster than the serial cable connection. Examine the drawing that follows to view the pin connections of a typical serial cable and a typical parallel cable used for direct connection between two PCs. When a straight-through cable is used between, for example, a PC and a printer, the transmit signal is sent to the receive pin on the printer. There is no need to switch the pin assignments around. However, when connecting a PC directly to another PC, a special cable is required so that the send and receive pins are correctly connected. If a straight-through cable was used, the transmit pin on one PC would be connected to the transmit pin on the other PC. No communications would take place.

pin 5 ——————— pin 5	pin 2 ——————— pin 15
pin 3 ——————— pin 2	pin 3 ——————— pin 13
pin 7 ——————— pin 8	pin 4 ——————— pin 12
pin 1+6 ——————— pin 4	pin 5 ——————— pin 10
pin 2 ——————— pin 3	pin 6 ——————— pin 11
pin 8 ——————— pin 4	pin 15 ——————— pin 2
	pin 13 ——————— pin 3
	pin 12 ——————— pin 4
	pin 10 ——————— pin 5
	pin 11 ——————— pin 6
	pin 25 ——————— pin 25

9-pin serial cable

25-pin parallel cable

Portable PCs

Before you can establish a communication between two PCs, you will most likely need to install the software that allows direct cable communications. When a typical Windows operating system installation has been performed, not all of the programs are installed. There are a number of programs that you might find useful listed under the **Windows Setup** tab of the Add/Remove Programs dialog box. Direct Cable Connection is one of the programs usually not installed during a typical Windows desktop installation, although it is standard for a portable installation. To install the Direct Cable Connection program, you will need to use a Windows installation CD. After you obtain the Windows installation CD, open the Control Panel and click on **Add/Remove Programs**. You should see the following:

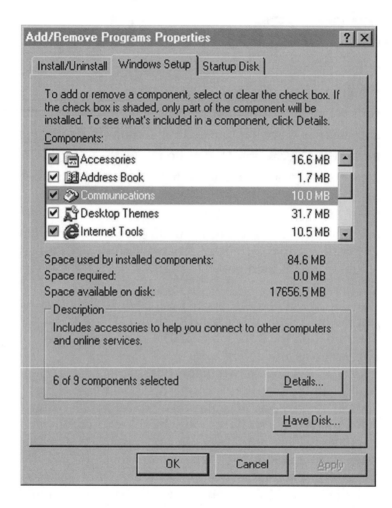

The **Windows Setup** tab needs to be selected. Place a check mark in the **Communications** check box and then select **OK**.

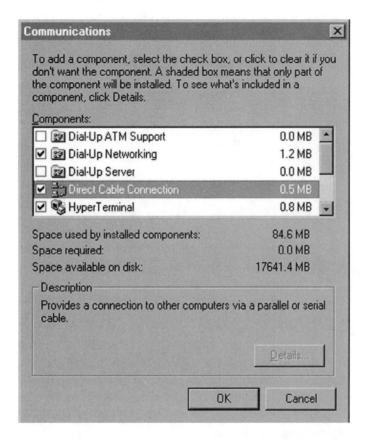

After the Communications dialog box appears on the screen, place a check mark in the **Direct Cable Connection** box. Follow the screen prompts and the Direct Cable Connection program will be successfully installed. Once the program has been installed, you can access it through **Start |** **Programs | Accessories | Communications | Direct Cable Connection**.

When the program activates, you will see a series of windows as the cable connection wizard walks you through the setup. In the first window, you must choose Host or Guest. A short definition of each appears beside the choice.

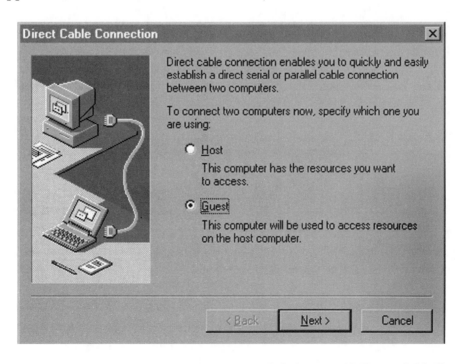

Portable PCs

The next window asks what type of port you plan to use, serial or parallel.

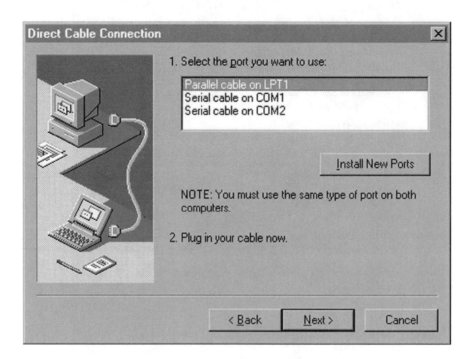

The final window verifies the completion of the wizard setup. You are now ready to verify your connection between the host and guest.

You use the same program to transfer files between the guest and host when an infrared port is available. When using an infrared port, no cables are necessary. The infrared port can also be used to transfer files to a printer that is equipped with an infrared receiver. An infrared receiver can be adapted to a printer through the parallel printer port located on the printer.

Equipment and Materials

✻ Typical PC with Windows 98 (or later) operating system

✻ Portable PC with same operating system

✻ Windows Installation CD

✻ One of the following: a parallel PC-to-PC cable or a null-modem serial cable

Procedure

1. ___ Gather the materials required for the laboratory exercise. Your instructor will identify the type of cable to use.

2. ___ Boot both the laptop and the desktop. Be sure the operating systems are working.

3. ___ If it has not already been installed, install the Direct Cable Connection program on the desktop PC. Review the instructions in the introduction to locate the file.

4. ___ Activate the Direct Cable Connection program through **Start I Programs I Accessories I Communications I Direct Cable Connection**.

Name_____

5. ___ When the program starts, follow the directions as they appear on the screen.

6. ___ After the cable connection wizard is complete, try viewing the contents of the text file from the host to the guest. If there is a problem, look at the following notes. If there are no problems, move on to Step 7.

If the Direct Cable Connection program does not work, check to see that **File and Print Sharing...** has been activated on the host computer; it is located under the **Network** icon in the Control Panel. Activate the Network icon and a dialog box will appear with a button on it labeled **File and Print Sharing...**. The dialog box should look similar to:

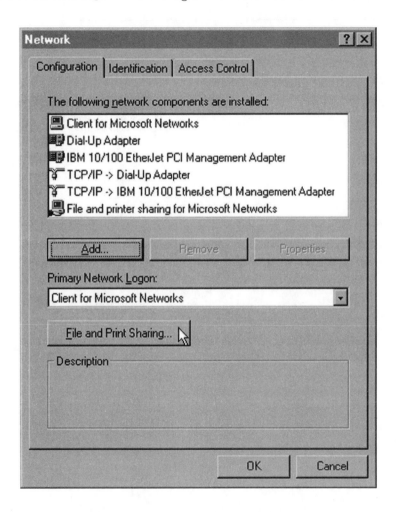

Press the **File and Print Sharing...** button and activate file and print sharing capabilities. Attempt to access the files once more.

You also may want to check to see if the access is controlled by a password. If so, this could be the reason that you cannot make a successful connection. Try changing the role of host and guest to see if this clears the problem. Also be sure you are using a PC-to-PC parallel cable and not a regular printer cable.

If none of this helps, check the system IRQ settings for a conflict.

7. ___ After you have successfully connected the two PCs, experiment with setting up different shares and using passwords to protect the files being shared. Use the word "password" as the password. Do not use any other password unless instructed to do so by the instructor.

8. ___ After successfully experimenting with Direct Cable Connection, return the system to its original condition and return all materials to the instructor.

9. ___ Answer the following review questions.

Review Questions

1. Which transfers data faster, a serial cable or a parallel cable? _____

2. How do you access the direct cable program starting with the **Start** button?_____

   _____

3. The PC that permits files to be accessed is called the _____ (host, guest).

4. When a PC is used to access files on a portable PC, the portable PC is called the _____ (host, guest).

5. Why do you think using a password is an option to accessing the files rather than a must do requirement? _____

   _____

Name _____ Date_____

Class/Instructor _____

Modem Installation

After completing this lab activity, you will be able to:

✶ Configure a dialing location.

✶ Explain the purpose of a UART.

✶ Explain how a modem operates.

✶ Identify various communication utilities.

Introduction

In this lab activity, you will not only install a modem but also access the Internet. The term "modem" is a contraction of the two electronics terms, "modulation" and "demodulation." Modulation is the process of modifying an electrical signal or electronic waveform. A modem allows a PC to access the Internet as well as connect to an office network or another PC.

A PC outputs information as a digital signal; a modem converts that high-speed digital signal into an analog waveform that can be carried over a typical telephone line. A typical telephone line is not designed to transport a high-speed digital signal. Therefore, the signal generated by a computer must be converted into an analog signal before it can be transmitted over the phone lines. When the signal reaches the destination, such as another PC, the modem on the receiving end converts the signal from analog back into digital, and it can then be processed by the receiving PC system.

The main electronic component of a modem is a chip called a Universal Asynchronous Receiver-Transmitter or UART. The UART converts the parallel digital signal into a serial digital signal. The digital signal is then converted into an analog signal, a series of waves of varying height and width. See the illustration below.

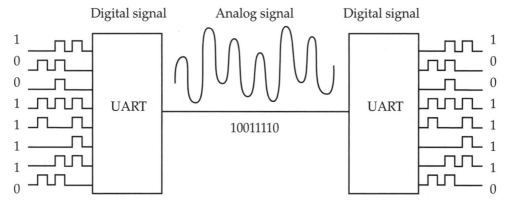

The digital signal of one PC is converted to an analog signal, transmitted on telephone lines, and then converted back into a digital signal at the other PC.

The modem can be integrated into the motherboard (onboard modem), installed as a separate unit outside the PC (external modem), or installed inside the PC as an adapter card (internal modem). In this lab activity, you will install an internal modem (expansion card) into the appropriate expansion slot. Once installed into the slot, the card is easily set up by Plug and Play technology.

After installing the modem card, you will need to configure the settings to make a connection over a telephone line. Connecting via phone lines to a network that has a file server is often referred to as dial-up networking (DUN) or remote access service (RAS). You can also connect to the Internet using an Internet service provider (ISP).

Equipment and Materials

*   Typical PC with Windows 98 operating system installed
*   56K modem
*   Access to an active telephone line
*   Telephone number to be used by your PC modem is _____ (provided by instructor)
*   Telephone number of destination is _____ (provided by instructor)

Procedure

1. ___ Boot the PC and wait for the Windows desktop.

2. ___ Turn the power off to the PC and remove the cover. Be sure to follow all anti-static precautions outlined by your instructor.

3. ___ Insert the new modem into the appropriate expansion slot.

4. ___ Power up the PC and watch as the modem is automatically detected and installed by the Plug and Play system. If it is not automatically detected or if a system resource conflict should appear, contact your instructor.

5. ___ Next, access the Control Panel and double click the **Modem** icon. The Install New Modem dialog box should open.

6. ___ Click on the button labeled **Don't detect my modem; I will select it from a list,** and then click the **Next** button. The Install New Modem dialog box will appear. It will contain a list of modem manufacturers on the left and the models of selected manufacturers on the right. Select the appropriate manufacturer and model. Click the **Have Disk** button if your exact manufacturer and model are not listed. Make sure the modem's driver disk is handy, and follow the onscreen prompts.

7. ___ After selecting the appropriate make and model, you must select the port the modem will use, typically COM1.

8. ___ Now, click **Finished** and the Location Information dialog box will appear. Enter your country, area code, and the number to access an outside line. You must also indicate if it is a pulse or tone type connection.

9. ___ After entering the appropriate information, select **Finished** once again.

10. ___ Now, double click the **Modem** icon in the Control Panel. Click the **Properties** button under the **General** tab to inspect the settings of the modem. In the dialog box that is opened, you can change such values as the maximum speed and port used by the modem. Usually you will not need to change the properties of the modem after it has been successfully installed except for troubleshooting purposes.

11. ___ Double click the **Add/Remove Programs** icon in the Control Panel, select the **Windows Setup** tab, highlight **Communications**, and then click the **Details** button. You will see a number of options listed such as Dial-Up Networking, Dial-Up Server, Direct Cable Connection, Hyper Terminal, Microsoft Chat, NetMeeting, Phone Dialer, and Virtual Private Networking. Highlight each one and write a summary of its description in the spaces provided.

Dial-Up Networking _____

_____

Dial-Up Server _____

_____

Direct Cable Connection _____

_____

Hyper Terminal _____

_____

Microsoft Chat _____

_____

NetMeeting _____

_____

_____

Phone Dialer _____

_____

Virtual Private Networking _____

_____

Review Questions

Use Windows Help to answer the following questions.

1. What protocol is used for a virtual private network? _____

2. Can you use your personal computer as a dial-up server? _____

3. What is a virtual private network (VPN)? _____

_____

4. What is dial-up networking? _____

_____

5. What does the acronym UART represent? _____

_____

6. Does a modem convert analog signals to digital or digital signals to analog? _____

_____

Modems

Name _____ Date_____

Class/Instructor _____

Lab Activity

51

Accessing the Startup Menu

After completing this lab activity, you will be able to:

✱   Access the Startup Menu using [F8] during the system boot.

✱   Identify and explain the Startup Menu options.

Introduction

One of the most common steps in troubleshooting a PC system is accessing the Windows Startup Menu. This menu is accessed by holding the [F8] key or the [Ctrl] key while booting. A menu listing various startup options should appear on the screen. You simply highlight the appropriate option and press [Enter] to select your startup choice.

The typical choices are listed below.

> Normal
> Logged (\BOOTLOG.TXT)
> Safe Mode
> Safe mode with network support
> Step-by-step confirmation
> Command prompt only
> Safe mode command prompt only
> Previous version of MSDOS

Selecting **Normal** boots the PC as it would under ordinary conditions. You would use this option if you have accessed the menu accidentally.

Selecting the **Logged (\BOOTLOG.TXT)** option creates a file named bootlog.txt, which records the boot process. Choose this option if you wish to create a log of the boot activities. The boot log can be opened later in Safe Mode using Notepad. This is a valuable aid for determining the point at which the system locks up during the boot process. The bootlog.txt file is saved in the root directory of the C: drive.

Selecting the **Safe Mode** option prevents the loading of many drivers and disconnects peripherals. Safe Mode bypasses many of the things that commonly cause system startup problems. If a PC is not properly shut down or fails to boot properly, Safe Mode will be automatically activated.

Selecting the **Safe mode with network support** option allows the necessary drivers that are used with a network system to load.

Selecting the **Step-by-step confirmation** option steps you through the typical startup process. This is a valuable aid for determining the point at which the system locks up during the boot process.

Troubleshooting

Choosing the **Command prompt only** option loads all the standard components of the operating system except for the Windows graphical interface. Windows graphical interface can be started from the command prompt by entering the **win** command.

Selecting the **Safe mode command prompt only** option boots the computer using the bare requirements. It does not load Windows.

The **Previous version of DOS** option uses the files that were backed up during the upgrade of Windows. This option is usually used when a problem develops after upgrading to Windows 95.

Depending on the computer's hardware and operating system, some of these options may not appear in the Startup Menu. For example, you will not see the network options unless the PC is setup to work with a network system.

Equipment and Materials

✳   Typical PC with Windows 95 or 98 operating system

Procedure

1. ___ Boot the computer and wait for Windows desktop to be displayed. This step is to ensure that your system is working properly.

2. ___ Look in the root directory to see if the bootlog.txt file exists. Does it? (The boot log is a hidden file) _____.

3. ___ Shut down the PC, and then restart the computer using [F8] function key to access the Startup Menu. If this method fails, hold the [Ctrl] key while booting. If this also fails to access the Startup Menu, call your instructor.

4. ___ List the Startup Menu options in the following spaces.

_____

_____

_____

_____

_____

_____

_____

_____

5. ___ After listing the options, select the **Safe Mode** option.

6. ___ Describe the screen display when the computer is in Safe Mode. _____

_____

_____

7. ___ Try opening Windows Explorer by right clicking on **My Computer** and choosing **Explore** from the drop-down menu. Did it work? _____

8. ___ Try opening the Paint program in **Start | Programs | Accessories | Paint**. Can it be accessed? _____

9. ___ Try opening the Device Manager from Safe Mode. Can it be accessed? _____

10. ___ After opening the Device Manager, open up some of the devices such as COM1, COM2, and LPT1. Write down which system resources, such as the IRQ settings and the memory assignments, that each is using._____

_____

_____

_____

11. ___ Use the **Run** option of the **Start** menu to run the program named **msinfo32.exe** located in the Program Files\Common Files\Microsoft Shared\MSINFO directory. A window labeled Microsoft System Information will appear. The left side of the window displays system information in hierarchical (tree) form, similar to the way Explorer displays directory structures. Expand the **Hardware Resources** branch by clicking on the box to its left. Next, click on the **IRQs** branch. Examine the list of IRQs on the right side of the window. Which ones are listed as free? _____

_____

12. ___ Now select the **I/O** branch. Are any I/O ranges assigned? _____

13. ___ Now select **Memory** to see the memory assignments. Which memory ranges are assigned? _____

_____

Take special note of the information you have just gathered. System resources are not assigned in Safe Mode.

14. ___ Shut down the system.

15. ___ Reboot the system, and this time select the **Step-by-step confirmation** startup option.

16. ___ What is the first item to confirm? _____

17. ___ What is the second item to confirm? _____

18. ___ Continue through the rest of the step-by-step startup process. It may take a few minutes before the Windows screen appears. Be patient.

19. ___ Now, try experimenting with the other options from the Startup Menu.

20. ___ When you are finished, return the PC system to its original condition.

Troubleshooting

Review Questions

1. Can the Device Manager be accessed when in Safe Mode? _____

2. Can Windows be loaded from the command prompt when the **Command prompt only** option has been chosen? _____

3. Must the PC be rebooted after completing the step-by-step confirmation? _____

4. What happens to IRQ settings in Safe Mode? _____

   _____

5. How might the step-by-step confirmation be used when troubleshooting a boot problem?

   _____

   _____

6. What does the boot log tell you? _____

   _____

7. What is the difference between the **Command prompt only** and the **Safe mode command prompt only** startup options? _____

   _____

Name _____ Date_____

Class/Instructor _____

Lab Activity

52

A Close Look at the Windows 98 Startup Process

After completing this lab activity, you will be able to:

✳ Explain the step-by-step details of the Windows 98 startup process.

Introduction

In this lab activity, you will use the Step-by-step confirmation option from the Microsoft Windows 98 Startup menu. To access the startup menu try holding the [Ctrl] key during the boot process. You may need to boot the PC several times to answer the questions listed in the lab activity.

Equipment and Materials

✳ Typical PC with Windows 95 (or later) operating system

🔲 **Note:**

The PC should be a stand-alone system, not a workstation logging on to a network system

Procedure

1. ___ Boot the computer and hold down the [Ctrl] key or [F8] key to access the Windows 98 startup menu. Select the **Step-by-step confirmation** option.

2. ___ As you respond to the step-by-step confirmation prompts, load all commands in the list except **Load the graphical user interface** and **WIN**.

3. ___ After you decline to load WIN by pressing [N] or [Esc], a default prompt should appear. At the default prompt, enter the command **set**, and observe the display.

4. ___ Complete the following text that appears on the screen.

```
TMP=C:\WINDOWS\TEMP
TEMP=C:\WINDOWS\TEMP
PROMPT=$p$g
Winbootdir=C:\WINDOWS
PATH=C:\WINDOWS;C:\WINDOWS\COMMAND
COMSPEC=C:\WINDOWS\COMMAND.COM
```

_____

_____

_____

Troubleshooting

5. ___ After completing the above text lines, simply type **win** at the command line prompt followed by [Enter]. The system should finish booting after confirming the loading of the device drivers.

Review Questions

Answer the following questions by selecting the best choice. You may need to reboot the computer several times to answer all the questions. Remember to hold down the [Ctrl] key while the system boots in order to access the startup menu.

1. When is the system registry processed?

   (A) It is the last item in the confirmation process.

   (B) After the win.com file.

   (C) After the autoexec.bat.

   (D) It is the first item in the confirmation process.

2. What is bootlog.txt used for?

   (A) It is a log of startup activities.

   (B) It is a reference file to follow during a normal boot operation.

   (C) It is used only by legacy programs.

   (D) It is a log file used to record boot options using notepad.

3. When is the config.sys file processed? Choose all that apply.

   (A) After the system registry.

   (B) After the bootlog.txt file.

   (C) After the WIN file.

   (D) After the autoexec.bat.

4. Where is the ifshelp.sys file loaded?

   (A) Into conventional memory.

   (B) Into extended memory.

   (C) Into expanded memory.

   (D) Into upper memory.

5. What is the last file to load during the step-by-step confirmation process?

   (A) gdi.exe

   (B) WIN

   (C) Msmouse

   (D) himem.sys

After selecting the correct answers to the questions above, return your PC to its original condition and properly shut it down.

Name _____ Date_____

Class/Instructor _____

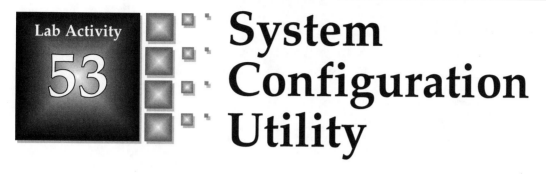

Lab Activity

53

System Configuration Utility

After completing this lab activity, you will be able to:

✲ Activate the System Configuration Utility.

✲ Explain the reason for using the System Configuration Utility rather than modifying the original files to test the system.

✲ Explain the various functions and options associated with the System Configuration Utility.

✲ Modify and test a typical PC system configuration.

✲ Restore a PC's original configuration.

Introduction

In this lab activity, you will activate, explore, and set options for the System Configuration Utility (msconfig.exe). This utility is a valuable configuration-troubleshooting tool. Traditionally, configuration settings were changed by making a backup of the original configuration file and giving it a different name or file extension. Changes were then made to the original to alter the configuration settings. For example, to make changes in the win.ini file, you would make a copy of the win.ini file and save it as winbkup.ini or a similar name. The backup copy could later be renamed to restore the original configuration.

The System Configuration Utility allows a user to troubleshoot the system configuration without making changes directly in the file or a copy of the file. Check marks are added or removed next to specific items to change the configuration. This prevents a user from accidentally making a typo when modifying files or lines in the file.

Troubleshooting

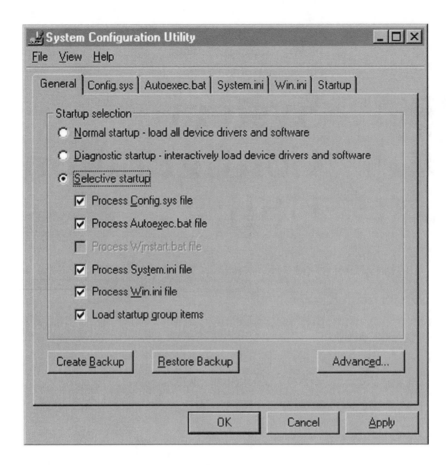

This is a screen capture of a typical System Configuration Utility dialog box. In this lab activity, you will access various areas of the utility to become familiar with the many options available. Let's get started exploring the System Configuration Utility.

Equipment and Materials

✳ Typical PC loaded with Windows 98 or Windows Me operating system

Procedure

1. ___ Boot the PC and verify that the system is operating properly.

2. ___ Open the following path: **Start | Programs | Accessories | System Tools | System Information**. This opens the Microsoft System Information window. Select **System Configuration Utility** from the **Tools** menu. The System Configuration Utility dialog box should appear similar to the one shown in the previous illustration.

3. ___ Now, you will access the System Configuration Utility another way. Close the dialog box. Click the **Start** button and select the **Run...** option. In the Run dialog box, enter **msconfig** in the **Open:** text field. This runs the System Configuration Utility once again.

4. ___ Take special notice of the three radio buttons in the Startup selection area of the dialog box. These radio buttons are labeled Normal startup, Diagnostic startup, and Selective start-up. Selecting the Normal startup causes the PC to start normally. This radio button should be selected when you are done testing the system. Selecting the Diagnostic startup radio button loads the device drivers and software programs interactively, similarly to the Step-by-step confirmation option available in the Windows Startup Menu. The last option, Selective Startup, allows you to select the options that you want to bypass during the next startup of the PC. A check mark in the box indicates that the item will be processed during the next startup. Simply click inside the box to select or deselect an item. If the check box is grayed out, the item is not installed or is not available.

5. ___ In the screen capture, which item is not available? _____

6. ___ Referring to the screen capture, which items are available to be removed from the startup process? _____

_____

7. ___ On your own PC, select the **System.ini** tab and view its contents.

8. ___ Select **Run...** from the **Start** menu and enter **sysedit** in the Run dialog box. Do not close the System Configuration Utility. After the System Configuration Editor (sysedit.exe) is open, select the system.ini file and compare its contents to the view in the **System.ini** tab of the System Configuration Utility. Are the listings similar? Yes or No.

■ **Note:**

Read these directions carefully. Notice that the names of the programs are very similar. The program activated by running sysedit.exe is named System Configuration Editor. The program activated by running msconfig.exe is named System Configuration Utility.

9. ___ Now select the win.ini file in the System Configuration Editor and compare it to the information displayed in the **Win.ini** tab of the System Configuration Utility. Are the contents similar? Yes or No.

10. ___ Which would be easier to make changes in, the System Configuration Editor or the System Configuration Utility? _____

11. ___ You may now close the System Configuration Editor, but leave the System Configuration Utility open.

12. ___ Select the remaining tabs in the System Configuration Utility one at a time. The remaining tabs should be Static VxDs, Startup, Environment, and International. Write a short comment about the contents of each.

Static VxDs _____

_____

Startup_____

_____

Environment_____

_____

International_____

_____

Troubleshooting

13. ___ Select the **General** tab in the System Configuration Utility. Select the **Diagnostic startup** radio button, reboot the PC, and observe the effects. Write a short comment about your observation in the space provided. _____

_____

_____

14. ___ Experiment with changing the settings in the **Selective startup** option. Observe the effects of different combinations when the system is rebooted. Below, write a short comment about the effect on the system._____

_____

_____

15. ___ Select the **Normal startup** option and click **OK**. Do not restart your computer yet. Answer the review questions below, and then shut down the system.

Review Questions

1. List the methods for accessing the System Configuration Utility from the Start menu.

_____

_____

2. What are the three startup options available from the General tab of the System Configuration Utility? _____

3. List at least 10 files that can be bypassed using this utility in a real troubleshooting scenario.

_____

_____

_____

Name _____ Date _____

Class/Instructor _____

Installing Windows 98 Operating System

After completing this lab activity, you will be able to:

✷ Install Windows 98 operating system as an upgrade.

✷ Identify minimum requirements for the installation.

✷ Identify the three common styles of installation: custom, typical, and portable.

✷ Describe the differences between a clean installation and an upgrade.

Introduction

This lab activity explains and walks you through a Windows 98 installation. There are several styles of installations possible, such as a clean installation, an upgrade, an automated setup, and a dual boot system.

There are a list of tasks that should be completed before beginning any software installation or upgrade:

✷ First, read the readme files located on the installation CD. Many times the readme.txt files contain important updated information that did not appear in the printed installation instructions. Some problems are not discovered until after distribution has begun.

✷ Check for viruses. A virus can be resident on a drive and cause many problems that mislead you into thinking the new operating system software has a compatibility problem.

✷ Defrag and scan the target drive. Some operating systems perform a routine disk scan before the installation begins.

✷ Check the software manufacturer's web site for latest updates, known installation problems, hardware compatibility lists, patches, and updates.

✷ Back up important files. This includes backing up system files and data files.

✷ Disable any virus protection software.

✷ Always check for an updated version of the system BIOS.

✷ Open Device Manager and print out a copy of the hardware installed on the computer.

✷ Create a startup disk. This precaution is optional but highly recommended.

There are four types of installation to choose from, Typical, Portable, Compact, and Custom. The type of installation you choose depends on several factors. The Typical installation installs all the software components commonly used by the standard desktop computer. The Portable installation is designed for portable PCs, such as a laptop. It conserves space, at the same time installing the software programs most commonly used in portable computing, such as Briefcase,

Troubleshooting

Direct Cable Connection, and HyperTerminal. Compact installation is chosen when there is not a lot of space available on the hard drive. A Custom installation allows you to individually review and select components to be installed. The Custom method requires a great deal of knowledge about the PC and about Windows 98 options.

When a hard drive has been replaced or formatted, a new installation of Windows 98 is required. To install Windows 98, you must first have system files loaded. If you formatted the hard drive with the **format/s** command, these files will be automatically written to the hard drive. If this is not the case, boot the system with the system floppy disk provided with the Windows 98 installation software. You cannot use the installation CD until the appropriate drivers are loaded. When you boot the PC using the Windows startup disk, you can select the **Start computer with CD-ROM support.** option. This allows the CD to be used in the installation process.

The five major phases or steps to a Windows 98 installation are listed here. Each major step will be discussed as the lab activity progresses.

* Preparing to run Windows 98 Setup.
* Collecting information about your computer.
* Copying Windows 98 files to your computer.
* Restarting your computer.
* Setting up hardware and finalizing settings.

After the hard drive has been prepared, the installation can begin. The CD drive may or may not be self-booting. If the CD drive is self-booting, the installation process will begin when the CD is inserted into the drive. If the CD is not self-booting, the installation will begin from the system disk. After the PC is booted with the system disk, type D:\setup at the command prompt.

■ Note:

In this lab activity, the CD drive is assumed to be drive D:. In reality, it may be designated another letter depending on the hardware installed.

A series of windows is displayed throughout the setup and installation process. The left side of the screen identifies which major step of the installation is presently taking place as well as the estimated time remaining in the installation process. The typical installation takes 30–60 minutes. Let's begin.

Equipment and Materials

* A PC that meets or exceeds the minimum hardware requirements:

    Processor requirements: 486 processor at 66 MHz or greater. The processor must be an Intel X86 family of processors or equal clone. Some clone types are AMD and Cyrix. A Pentium at 120 MHz or faster is recommended

    RAM requirements: 16 MB minimum. 32 MB is recommended

    Hard drive requirements: 200 MB free space. 300 MB free space recommended

    Video requirements: VGA display (640x480) 256 colors. SVGA recommended.

* CD drive (Windows 98 can be installed from floppy disks, but it is not recommended)
* (1) 3.5" floppy disk
* Windows 98 Installation CD and startup disk

■ Note:

Do not use a PC with a SCSI CD-ROM drive. For this exercise, use an IDE CD-ROM drive only.

Procedure

1. ___ Prepare the hard drive for installation. It must be partitioned and formatted before performing a clean installation. If an operating system exists, you simply need to format the drive. If you have installed a new hard drive, you need to first partition the hard drive and then format the partition. You must also install the system files. This can be done during the formatting process by adding the **/s** switch to the **format** command. It may also be done after formatting by using the **sys** command.

■ **Note:**

Do not partition or format the drive without the instructor's permission. Formatting and partitioning the drive destroys any data on the hard drive.

2. ___ Insert the installation floppy (startup disk) and reboot the PC. The installation diskette will prompt you for a choice of CD support or no CD support. Choose the CD support option.

3. ___ Insert the Windows 98 Installation CD into the CD drive. The installation will begin when you enter the word **setup** at the command prompt. The installation program then performs a check of the PC system, including a scan of the hard disk (ScanDisk). ScanDisk checks for errors on the disk drive platter surfaces but does not correct the errors. ScanDisk can only correct the errors when the PC is running in protected-mode. You cannot be in protected-mode until Windows has been completely installed. During the start of the installation process, the PC is in real-mode.

4. ___ During the setup, you will see the license agreement dialog box. You must accept the agreement to continue the installation. If you do not accept, the installation will abort. You will also be prompted to enter the Product Key. The Product Key is printed on Certificate of Authenticity, located on the back of the CD case or on the cover of the installation book. A series of boxes appears in the Product Key dialog box, usually five. You enter the product key in these boxes. As the boxes are filled, the cursor automatically advances to the next box. Do not use the [Tab] key to move from box to box. Be careful when entering the product key numbers and letters. Look carefully at the following symbols: 0, O, l, 1. They are easily mistaken for each other. Any single wrong entry will abort the installation.

5. ___ You will be prompted to select the directory in which you wish to install Windows. The default directory is C:\Windows. Windows can be installed in a different partition and with a different name. For this exercise, use the default directory.

6. ___ Next, what type of installation will be performed? The choices are as follows: Typical, Portable, Compact, and Custom. You will choose **Typical** for this exercise.

■ **Note:**

*You may choose **Compact** if the lab period is short. Check with your instructor.*

7. ___ The next dialog box asks for user information. Enter your name and **PC Repair** for the company.

8. ___ The next dialog box that appears prompts you for specific PC information. This information identifies the PC for a network system. In a network system, each PC must be uniquely identified so that the network can communicate properly. The three pieces of information requested here are computer name, workgroup, and computer description. The computer name can be a maximum of 15 alphanumeric characters and some special symbols. The allowed special symbols are as follows: ! @ # $ % ^ & ( ) - _ ' { } . ~.

Troubleshooting

The computer workgroup is a special collection or group of PCs in a network environment. An example of a workgroup name would be accounting, engineering, or design. The workgroup name has the same restrictions as the computer name. Fifteen characters maximum and the same list of special characters. The computer name and workgroup offer only a limited description of a single PC, especially in an organization with hundreds or even thousands of PCs on a network.

The computer description is used for a more detailed description of the computer. The computer description may include a detailed description of the location of the PC, such as Bld4 room 314, Finance office, or Chicago Melrose branch room 418. The idea is to identify the exact PC in a sea of thousands. The computer description box is limited to forty-eight characters and may contain any letter, number, or special character except a comma (,). The comma is used to indicate the end of a line of data. If you enter a comma in the computer description, the description would end where the comma is placed. For example, if you intended to enter "Chicago Melrose branch room 418" and used a comma to separate "Chicago" and "Melrose," the description would simply be recorded as "Chicago."

All information about the PCs position in a network structure is saved in a database on the central computer known as the file server. The computer must have a name, but entering the workgroup and description is optional. The workgroup field has a default name, but the description field does not.

9. ___ Next, you are prompted to identify the location of the PC. Simply select the country from the long lists of choices. In this exercise, choose United States. Software uses the location information when accessing the Internet. It helps identify the closest web server for faster access.

10. ___ Next, a prompt for making a startup disk will appear on the display. A startup disk is optional but highly recommended. The startup disk would allow you to restart the PC after a system failure in the future. For this exercise, you will make a startup disk. You will need 3.5" floppy disk. Simply follow the instructions on the screen. The system startup disk contains all the files necessary to start your PC. It also contains a generic CD–ROM driver (Oakcdrom.sys) for CD-ROM support while the PC is in real mode. Remember, when a PC is in real mode, most of the system drivers are not available. The CD-ROM driver is a generic design and is only compatible with an IDE CD-ROM. The driver will not support a SCSI CD-ROM drive, nor a CD-ROM connected to a sound card. There are several other drivers available on the installation startup disks that may work for the drive you are using, such as a generic ATAPI/SCSI CD-ROM driver. However, if you are using a non-IDE drive, you will most likely need the manufacturer's driver.

11. ___ Now you can sit back and observe. The system files are now copied and loaded. The system will go through the next major steps without your intervention. You need not interact with the PC until the final phase of installation, when you will be prompted to enter the time zone.

12. ___ After the next reboot of the system, you will be prompted to enter a password and confirm it. Use **Password** for the password.

13. ___ After the installation is complete, the Windows 98 Welcome window appears with options to register the software, connect to the Internet, discover Windows 98, and learn how to maintain you computer. This screen gives the first-time user the option to tour the Windows 98 system. At the bottom-left corner is a small check box that is labeled "Show this screen each time Windows 98 starts." Uncheck the box. Otherwise, the window will appear each time the PC boots. Call your instructor to check your successful installation.

Review Questions

1. What type of installation is designed for a laptop computer? _____

2. What type of installation allows you to choose which components you wish to install?

   _____

3. What is the minimum processor speed required for installing Windows 98? _____

4. Which installation type requires the most knowledge?_____

5. Which installation is used most on desktop PCs? _____

6. Which command is used to start the Windows 98 installation process, **install**, **run**, or **setup**?

   _____

7. Why will the CD not work after formatting the hard drive and rebooting the system?

   _____

8. What is the maximum number of characters that can be used to identify a computer name in the Windows 98 installation? _____

9. What is the maximum number of characters that can be used for the workgroup name in the Windows 98 installation? _____

10. What is the maximum number of characters that can be used when entering the computer description?_____

11. What character cannot be used as part of the computer description? _____

12. What is the name of the generic CD-ROM driver on the system startup disk?

    _____

13. What are the five major steps to a Windows 98 installation? _____

    _____

    _____

Troubleshooting

Name _____ Date_____

Class/Instructor _____

Msinfo32.exe and Dr. Watson

After completing this lab activity, you will be able to:

✴ Describe the options associated with Dr. Watson.

✴ Create a Dr. Watson log file.

✴ Explain how to activate Dr. Watson diagnostics.

✴ Compare two Dr. Watson log files, before and after an error event.

Introduction

In this lab activity, you will run Dr. Watson and look at it under normal conditions and then load and run the program Endless Loop, included on the Instructor's CD. The program is designed to simulate a system lockup by running an endless loop until interrupted. You will activate the Dr. Watson utility and take a snapshot of the programs running before and after Endless Loop is activated. You will also create a Dr. Watson log for viewing.

Dr. Watson (drwatson.exe) is activated from the Microsoft System Information program (msinfo32.exe). Dr. Watson is designed to collect very detailed information about the PC system. That information can be used by the onsite PC technician or transferred via the Internet to a support technician. Many of the options available are only useful to a PC or software manufacturer support technician. Such options address issues such as program threads, and program hooks. While this information may be meaningless to a typical PC technician, it can be valuable to a system programmer who is trying to solve software problems.

When a problem is suspected in a software package, Dr. Watson is activated and produces a log (*.wlg extension) in the Windows\Drwatson\ folder. Viewing the log in a text editor reveals information such as the memory address of the failure and the application that was loading or running when the failure or problem occurred. While Dr. Watson cannot solve all problems related to software programs and memory, it is very helpful, especially in identifying what software programs are automatically loading as the PC is finalizing its booting operation.

Troubleshooting

When activated, Dr. Watson is reduced to an icon resting in the task bar. To access the Dr. Watson dialog box, simply double click the icon in the task bar. Two views of the Dr. Watson dialog box are shown here.

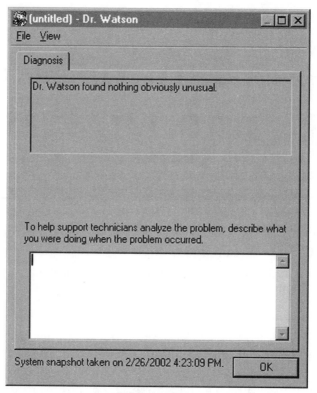

Default view

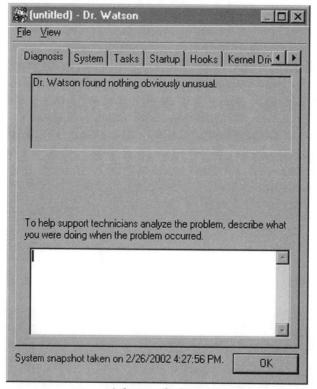

Advanced view

The top view on the previous page is typical when Dr. Watson is first opened. The second view is Dr. Watson after the **Advanced View** option has been selected from the **View** menu. The advanced view gives a very detailed description of many features, such as DOS drivers, kernel drivers, and startup programs.

Many of the tab options allow the user to view items that are not typically used for troubleshooting by the PC repair technician. The most useful information is the list of startup programs and the list of tasks currently running. Dr. Watson does an automatic check of the system and lists any apparent faults under the **Diagnosis** tab. An example of a diagnosis by Dr. Watson is shown here. The suspected cause of the problem is indicated in the following window.

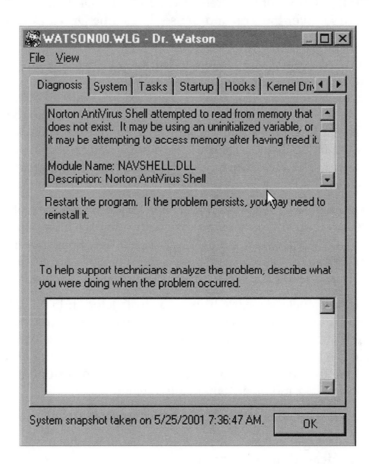

A possible solution for the problem is also indicated in the window, but cannot be seen in the screen capture. Adjusting the scroll bars on the right side of the window would reveal the suggested remedy. Take special notice of the window at the bottom of the Dr. Watson dialog box. The user can type information into the box and then transmit the entire contents of the Dr. Watson screen to technical support.

When a software application creates a system error, a log file named watsonxx.wlg is automatically created. The xx in the filename here represent numbers, which are assigned sequentially to uniquely identify each log file.

Equipment and Materials
* Typical PC with Windows 98 (or later) operating system
* Endless loop program (included on the Instructor's CD)

Procedure

1. ___ Report to your assigned PC station. You will need a copy of the Endless Loop program.

2. ___ Boot the PC and make sure everything is in working order.

3. ___ Start the Microsoft System Information program, **Start | Programs | Accessories | System Tools | System Information**. You may do this by entering **msinfo32** in the **Run** dialog box in the **Start** menu.

4. ___ Select **Dr. Watson** from the **Tools** menu. Watch for the Dr. Watson icon in the Windows task bar, located at the bottom of the screen area. To verify Dr. Watson is in the taskbar, simply move the cursor over the icon and pause. The name Dr. Watson will appear on the screen next to the cursor.

5. ___ To demonstrate how a log of system conditions can be made and stored, activate the Dr. Watson program by double clicking on the Dr. Watson icon. Take special note of the title bar of the Dr. Watson dialog box. It is named "untitled Dr. Watson." This feature is provided so you can easily differentiate between the most recent snapshot, like the one being displayed now, and a snapshot saved as a log. The traditional log file usually saves information in simple text format. Dr. Watson saves the information and then displays it as a Dr. Watson dialog box, not as a text file. Since the information currently being displayed has not been saved, the Dr. Watson dialog box is untitled.

6. ___ From the **File** menu, select **Save As...** and save this system snapshot as Error log1 in the C:\Windows\DrWatson folder. You may manually create a log file at any time while running the Dr. Watson utility. To create a new log file, simply select **New Snapshot** from the **File** menu. To save the newly created snapshot, you must select **Save** or **Save As...** from the **File** menu in the Dr. Watson dialog box. The log file is not automatically saved when it is created manually.

7. ___ Next, get a copy of endlessloop.exe from your instructor and run it. Use the [Alt] [Tab] key combination to return to the Dr. Watson dialog box. Select **New Snapshot** from the **File** menu. Save the new log as Error log2, in the same directory that you saved the previous log. Select the Task tab in each of the logs and compare the tasks that were running at the time of the snapshots. You should see the Endless Loop program listed at the bottom of the second log's list. During a fault, a log file would be automatically created.

8. ___ If you have trouble creating the log files, try using **Help** from the **Start** menu.

9. ___ After saving both log files and comparing the contents, check with the instructor to see if the files should be deleted from the drive.

10. ___ After responding to the questions below, properly shut down the PC.

Review Questions

1. Where is the drwatson.exe file located? Give the path. _____

2. What type of information does the Dr. Watson utility capture? (Hint, look at the tabs.)

_____

_____

3. Where are the Dr. Watson log files saved by default? _____

4. What is the default name of a Dr. Watson log file? _____

5. What is the default maximum number of Dr. Watson log files? _____

Name _____ Date_____

Class/Instructor _____

Virus Test Software

After completing this lab activity, you will be able to:

★ Test a typical antivirus program to ensure it is installed correctly.

★ Build the EICAR virus test program.

Introduction

In this lab activity, you will access the web site at Command Systems Software (www.commandcom.com) and download a copy of the EICAR utility. The utility is designed to test an installed version of any antivirus software.

EICAR (European Institute for Computer Antivirus Research) has jointly developed a virus test program that allows you to see if an antivirus program has been installed correctly and is working. The EICAR antivirus-test file is a simple text file that contains the following symbols. X5O!P%@AP[4\PZX54(P^)7CC)7}$EICAR-STANDARD-ANTIVIRUS-TEST-FILE!$H+H*

You can copy the line of text above using Notepad or WordPad and save it as a plain ASCII text file named EICAR with the file extension of .com, .dll, or .exe. When typing the line of text, be sure to enter the third letter symbol as the capital letter O and not as a zero. All the letters should be entered as upper-case letters.

The antivirus program installed on your computer should prevent you from saving the EICAR file. When the EICAR file is activated, you should see a window similar to McAfee dialog box that follows. The look of the dialog box will vary according to the brand of antivirus software you are using.

Access to file was denied

Infected file name:

C:\MY DOCUMENTS\EICAR.COM

Virus name:

EICAR test file

VirusScan suggests

This infected file cannot be cleaned. You should delete the file and replace it with a clean copy. Your data will not be affected.

☐ Apply to all items

Stop

Clean

Delete

Move File to...

Exclude

Troubleshooting

Seeing a window similar to this window means that the software is working. However, it does not ensure that all options for the antivirus utility are correctly configured. It just lets you know that the general antivirus program is installed and working. For example, it does not mean the antivirus program you are using is up-to-date and contains the latest virus definitions or that the program is scanning e-mail automatically.

If your computer is not equipped with an antivirus utility package, you can download an evaluation package from www.fsecure.com. After downloading the evaluation package, install the antivirus utility following the screen prompts. You can either create the EICAR file or download the test file from most antivirus web sites. The file is free to download and use to test antivirus utilities.

Equipment and Materials

*   Typical PC with Windows 98 (or later) operating system
*   Internet access
*   An antivirus program installed (if you do not have an antivirus program installed, you can download a 30-day antivirus trial version from many different sites, including www.symetec.com, www.mcaffee.com, and www.fsecure.com)
*   Floppy disk for saving EICAR file

Procedure

1. ___ Boot the PC and open Notepad (not Microsoft Word or any other high-end word processor).

2. ___ Type the following list of symbols exactly as they appear and save as a file called eicar.txt to the floppy disk. The string of characters must appear exactly like the list that follows. You may also download this file from http://www.eicar.org/anti_virus_test_file.htm.

    X5O!P%@AP[4\PZX54(P^)7CC)7}$EICAR-STANDARD-ANTIVIRUS-TEST-FILE!$H+H*

    If you have trouble activating the EICAR file by typing the string of symbols, try a downloaded copy. Take special note that the file should be saved as a .txt file not as a .com, .dll, or .exe. If you attempt to save this file as any of these three file extensions, it may trigger any antivirus program installed on your PC. When you wish to use the file for testing antivirus software, you change the file extension to .com, .dll, or .exe. You can name the file anything you wish. It does not have to be named EICAR. You can name it VirusTestProg.exe for example.

3. ___ Test the antivirus program by attempting to save the eicar.com file to the hard disk drive from the floppy drive. (Note that any attempt to save the EICAR file to the floppy drive may activate any antivirus software already loaded on the machine.) The exact reactions to the EICAR program will vary from one antivirus utility to another.

4. ___ Experiment with the EICAR file by changing the type of file extension and by changing your antivirus software settings. You should also try changing one or two characters in the character string inside the EICAR file.

5. ___ Visit the EICAR organization, located at www.eicar.org.

6. ___ After you are done with your laboratory experiments, remove the EICAR test program from the PC and return the PC to its original condition.

Review Questions

1. What type of file extensions are used with the EICAR virus test program? _____

    _____

2. What does the acronym EICAR represent? _____

Name _____ Date_____

Class/Instructor _____

Lab Activity

57

Windows Report Tool

After completing this lab activity, you will be able to:

✳ Explain the purpose of the Windows Report Tool.
✳ Activate the Windows Report Tool.
✳ Modify the Windows Report Tool.

Introduction

The Windows report tool is used to transmit system information to a system provider. The PC technician can gather information about the PC system and transmit the information to a support provider. For example, suppose a user has loaded a software program on the PC, and now the computer locks up at random intervals. The report tool can capture a snapshot of the system, which can then be sent electronically to the tech support provider. The tech support personnel can view the file and determine what may be causing the lockup. Look at the following screen capture.

Windows Report Tool

File   Options   Help

To report a problem, provide the following information and then click Next.

Problem description:

[Describe your problem here]

Expected results:

[Describe what you expected to happen here]

Steps to reproduce the problem:

[Describe the steps necessary to reproduce this problem]

Change System File Selections link

System files will be collected by the Windows Report Tool to help technicians to diagnose the problem.

Change System File Selections

Next   Cancel

Troubleshooting

The typical Windows Report Tool dialog box allows the user to enter text describing the nature of the problem. Also, under the Options menu selection, the user can select from a wide variety of information to include in the data being transferred. The following screen capture shows the variety of information that can be included in the transmission.

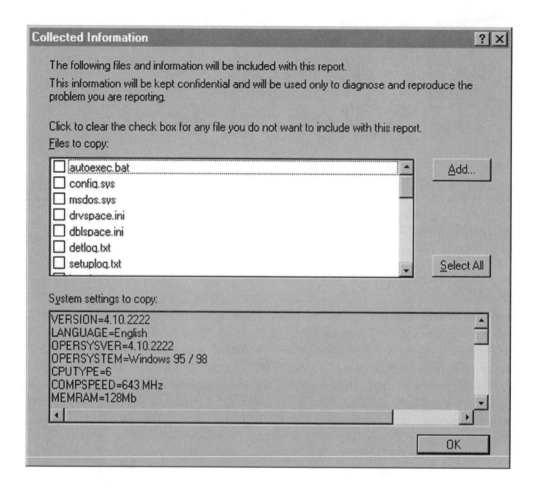

In this lab activity, you will open the Windows Report Tool dialog box and familiarize yourself with the many options. However, you will not transmit the data across the Internet to a support provider. This exercise is simply to make you familiar with the option.

Equipment and Materials

✳ A typical PC with Windows 98 operating system

Procedure

1. ___ Report to your assigned PC. Boot the PC and make sure it is in proper working order.

2. ___ Access the report tool through **Start | Programs | Accessories | System Tools | System Information**. Select **Windows Report Tool** from the **Tools** drop-down menu. You may also reach the Windows System Information screen by typing and running **Wininfo32.exe** in the **Run** dialog box accessed through the **Start** menu.

3. ___ You should see three text boxes in the Windows Report Tool dialog box: **Problem description:**, **Expected results:**, and **Steps to reproduce the problem:**. These boxes are used to record information to send to tech support.

4. ___ Click on the **Next** button located at the bottom right side of the window. A Save As dialog box appears. This window is used to save the data describing the settings of the PC as a file with a *.cab extension. The *.cab extension indicates that the data will be saved as a compressed file.

5. ___ **Cancel** or **Save** the file. The original screen reappears. Locate the **Change System File Selections** link near the bottom of the screen and activate it by clicking on it. A screen will appear allowing you to select specific file to record. You can select or deselect files simply by clicking on the box in front of the selected file. Explore the settings and the information in both windows.

6. ___ Close the Windows Report Tool and answer the review questions.

Review Questions

1. What is the purpose of the Windows Report Tool? _____

_____

_____

2. How is the Windows Report Tool accessed? _____

_____

Troubleshooting

Name _____ Date_____

Class/Instructor _____

Lab Activity

58

Network Adapter Card Installation

After completing this lab activity, you will be able to:

✴ Install a typical network adapter card.

✴ Configure a network adapter card using information supplied by the network administrator.

✴ List the requirements for communicating on a peer-to-peer network.

Introduction

In this lab activity, you will install a typical network adapter card, often referred to as a NIC card. The acronym NIC stands for *network interface card*. After the NIC and the proper drivers have been installed, you will select and install the proper protocols for communication across a peer-to-peer network.

The installation of a NIC became much simpler with the introduction of Plug and Play technology. However, there are still times when you will need to configure the NIC properties manually. At other times, you will need to modify or verify NIC properties. In this lab activity, you will verify NIC properties, even if you are using a Plug and Play card.

The following illustration shows the Network dialog box. You can access the Network dialog box by right clicking on **Network Neighborhood** and then selecting **Properties** from the right-click menu. It can also be accessed by opening **Control Panel** and clicking the **Network** icon (**Start I Settings I Control Panel I Network**).

Networking

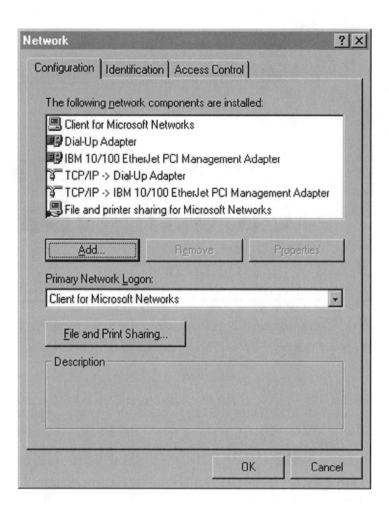

The Network dialog box is used to configure the PC on a network. Below is a partial list of some of the things that can be accomplished through the Network dialog box:

* Select the type of network protocol to be used.
* Install the drivers for the network card.
* Set up print and file sharing.
* Identify the PC and the work group by name.
* Verify and modify Internet properties.

You will use the Network dialog box extensively in the next few lab activities. Be sure you know how to access it easily.

Each network adapter has a unique MAC address used to identify the network card to the network system. The MAC address consists of six pairs of hexadecimal numbers, such as 00 1C DF B7 2C DB. The first three pairs of hexadecimal numbers identify the manufacturer and the last three pairs of numbers uniquely identify the NIC. If two network adapter cards have the same MAC address, the network will be unable to communicate with at least one of the two stations.

The MAC address in the network environment is similar to the unique phone numbers used in the telephone industry. To correctly contact the person you wish to speak to, each telephone must have a unique phone number. The purpose of the MAC address in the network system will become more apparent as you progress through your studies.

After you install the network card, you may not be able to see other computers in the peer-to-peer network. In order to interact with other computers on the network, you will need to set up a share and be part of the same workgroup. Your instructor will assign you a workgroup name.

Equipment and Materials

* Typical PC with Windows 98 operating system
* Network adapter card with a RJ-45 connection
* Cat5 UTP cable with standard RJ-45 connectors
* You will need to access a hub to connect your PC to the other PCs

Procedure

1. ___ Gather all required materials.

2. ___ Before you begin installing the network adapter card, boot the PC to make sure it is functioning properly. If the PC is working properly, shut it down and go on to step three. If the PC is not working properly, notify the instructor.

3. ___ Make sure the electrical power is turned off to the PC before you remove the case cover. Follow all anti-static procedures as prescribed by your instructor.

4. ___ Before you install the network adapter card, look for the MAC address on the card. Write the MAC address in the space provided here. _____

5. ___ Select the appropriate expansion slot (usually a PCI type) in which to install the NIC.

6. ___ Remove the screw that retains the slot cover in place. Save the screw for securing the NIC in place.

7. ___ Insert the NIC into the slot by applying even pressure. Do not rock the card side-to-side while inserting it into the slot. Rocking the card can damage the conductors that run along the edge of the card. Be sure the card is seated all the way into the slot. See the following illustration.

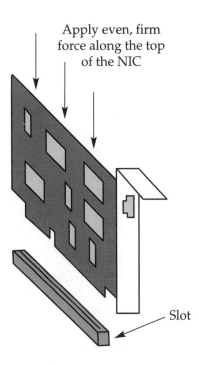

Apply even, firm
force along the top
of the NIC

Slot

Networking

8. ___ Secure the NIC in the slot using the screw removed from the slot cover. Do not skip this step. A loose NIC is one of the most common causes of network problems.

9. ___ Connect the Cat5 UTP cable between the NIC and the network hub.

10. ___ Boot the PC and see if the card is automatically detected and set up. Normally the card will be automatically configured through the Plug and Play Add New Hardware wizard. If the card is automatically detected, simply follow the prompts displayed on the screen. If the card is not automatically detected, you may have to install the driver files from the floppy disk that accompanied the card. If this happens, ask your instructor for detailed instructions for loading the drivers manually.

11. ___ After the card is successfully installed, double click on the **Network Neighborhood** icon on the desktop to view other PCs that are connected to the network. Other PCs may or may not be seen. In order to view other PCs, you must be part of the same network, and those computers must be configured to share files. Below is a screen capture of a Network Neighborhood window, which shows the PCs that are connected to the network.

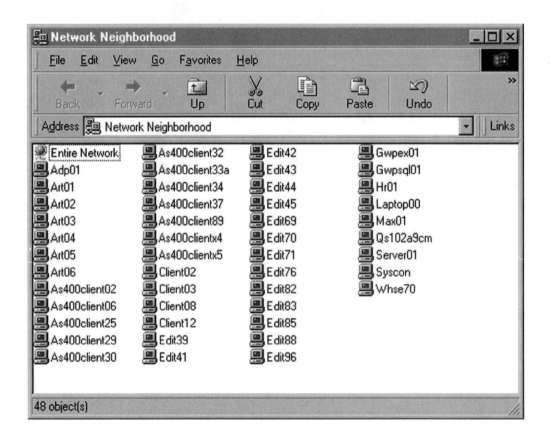

12. ___ Open the Network dialog box by right clicking on the **Network Neighborhood** icon and selecting **Properties** from the right-click menu. This should open the Network dialog box. Take special note of the installed network components listed in the large window near the top of the dialog box. This list contains the network adapter card, the protocols being used, and file and print sharing (if it has been enabled). To add a protocol, highlight Client for Microsoft Networks and then click the **Add** button. This opens a new dialog box that enables you to install additional components, such as other protocols and services.

13. ___ Select the **Identification** tab in the Network dialog box. This screen allows you to verify or modify the computer and workgroup names. A short description for the computer, such as "John's computer in pay roll" or "Building A, Room 212, PC#4,"may be entered into the **Computer Description:** text box. The description is a great help when dealing with hundreds or thousands of computers. The following illustration shows the layout of the Identification tab.

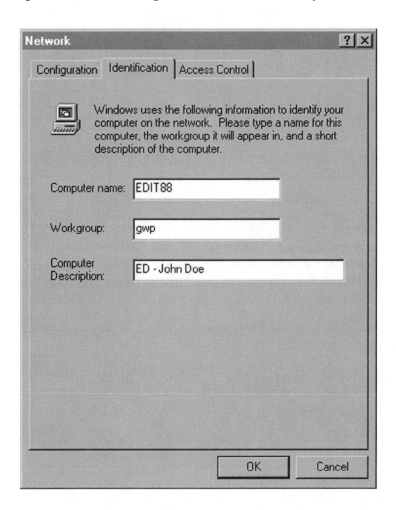

14. ___ Enter the names of the computer and workgroup. This information will be supplied by your instructor. The computer description is optional.

Computer name _____

Workgroup _____

15. ___ After entering the computer name and workgroup, see if the other PCs are visible in the Network Neighborhood window. Remember, the Network Neighborhood window is opened by double clicking the **Network Neighborhood** icon on the desktop.

16. ___ If the other PCs on the peer-to-peer network do not appear, or if your own computer station does not appear in the list, check several items before calling your instructor:

★ First, is the same workgroup name used on all the PCs? Is it spelled correctly on each PC?

★ Second, do you have a good connection at the NIC and the hub?

★ Third, have you enabled file sharing? Check the Network dialog box by right clicking on the **Network Neighborhood** icon and selecting **Properties** from the right-click menu.

Networking

17. ___ Now you will conduct some simple but very important experiments with your network. They will provide you with information to use in future lab activities and troubleshooting.

18. ___ Properly shut down your PC and observe the condition of the LEDs (lights) on the network hub. Pay close attention to what is displayed when the PC is off and when the PC is on. Also, observe the LED on the NIC. Write a short summary of your observation in the space provided. _____

_____

_____

_____

_____

19. ___ Now with the PC booted, remove the network cable from the NIC and observe the LED on the hub and NIC. Record your observation. Replace the cable before proceeding to the next step. _____

_____

_____

20. ___ Open the Network dialog box and select the **Identification** tab. Change the name in the **Workgroup:** text box. Open the Network Neighborhood window and examine the list of network connections. What effect does changing the workgroup's name have on the list? You may need to select the **Refresh** option from the **View** menu before any change can be observed.

_____

_____

21. ___ Change the name of your PC workgroup back to the original one given to you by your instructor. Again, look in the Network Neighborhood window. You may need to select the **Refresh** option from the **View** menu before any change can be observed.

_____

_____

22. ___ You may leave the PC on to assist you in answering the review questions. Check with your instructor before returning the PC to its original condition. The instructor will tell you whether to leave the network adapter card in, or remove it.

Review Questions

1. What happens when a new name is entered in the Workgroup: text box on one of the computers? _____

_____

2. What happens to the LED on the hub when the PC is turned off? _____

_____

3. How is the MAC address identified? _____

_____

4. What is the Computer Description: text box (found in the Network dialog box) used for?

_____

Name _____ Date_____

Class/Instructor _____

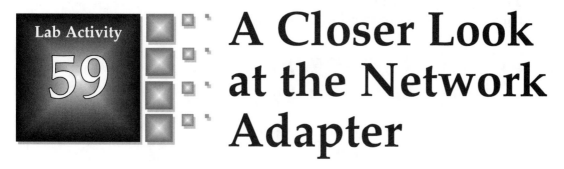

A Closer Look at the Network Adapter

After completing this lab activity, you will be able to:

* Identify the typical protocols associated with the network adapter card.
* Install and remove the TCP/IP protocol.

Introduction

In this lab activity, you will become familiar with the Network dialog box. You will look at how protocols, services, and adapter cards are selected. You will also see how to set the adapter card properties to allow you to communicate with a Novell network from the Microsoft Windows 98 (or later) operating system.

You will be looking at four main areas of network card configuration: the network client, the adapter card, type of service, and the protocol.

* The network client is the network operating system you wish to use for communicating across the network.
* The adapter card is the actual board installed into the PC and used to convert the data into streams of electronic (digital) pulses.
* Network services (in this exercise) are limited to two items, sharing a printer and sharing files.
* The protocol is the software program that allows two PCs to communicate.

The protocol sets the rules for communication between network devices. The protocol sets the standards for dividing the data into packets (also known as frames). Each protocol is designed to package the data into packets in a particular size and order. The packet includes information such as its origin and its destination.

During this lab activity, you will explore how to configure the various components of the network adapter in Windows 98. You will not permanently change any of the adapter's current settings. You will copy down all of the default settings for the adapter card during this lab activity. Later, when troubleshooting PCs and networks, you may use the settings from this lab activity to assist you in diagnosing the problem.

Networking

You should familiarize yourself with common network components before beginning this lab. The following paragraphs describe some of the common network components. Installed network components are displayed by right clicking the **Network Neighborhood** icon on the desktop, and selecting **Properties** from the drop-down menu. This opens the Network dialog box, which lists installed network components. The Network dialog box should appear similar to the one shown here.

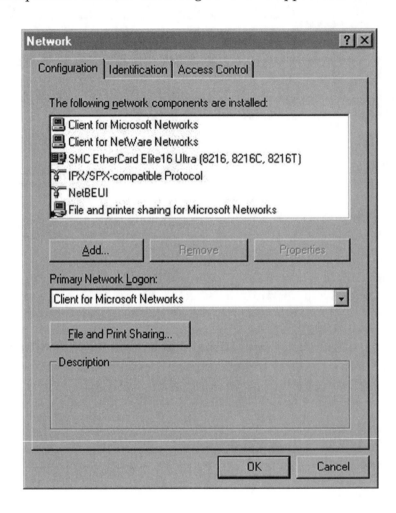

You can use this dialog box to add or remove network components. Network components are items that are configured to work with the PC and the network card. The PC you are using may not have the same components as those shown in the illustration.

The first item in the list is Client for Microsoft Networks. This component gives the PC the ability to communicate with a Microsoft networking system. In a peer-to-peer network using a Windows networking OS, all PCs must have the Client for Microsoft Networks installed.

The next item in the list is Client for NetWare Networks. This component must be installed if you plan to communicate with a Novell network, also called NetWare network. If not, it does not need to be installed and can be removed from the listing. To remove any item from the listing, you simply highlight the item with the mouse, and then click the **Remove** button. Many of the items are included by default when the PC is first set up. Others are added when there is a need for them.

The third item in the list is an SMC Ethercard Elite16. It is the network card installed on this particular PC. When an adapter card is installed in a PC, the software drivers for that card must be installed on the PC system. Often, the necessary driver will be packaged with the network card. If a disk is not available, you can usually download the necessary driver files from the Internet. Without the driver designed specifically for your network adapter card, proper communications will be impossible. For example, you may be able to transmit data across the network but not receive any, or you may be able to see the other PCs on the network but not able to communicate with them.

The next two items, IPX/SPX-compatible Protocol and NetBEUI are two of the many different types of protocols available for use in network communications. The protocol can be thought of as a set of rules that govern the mechanics of communication over a network system. Data is transmitted across networks in what is called packets or frames. A packet is just as the name implies, a packet of information. The specific parameters of the packet are determined by the protocol rules.

The protocol dictates the maximum and minimum lengths for the packets. It also determines the sequence of the packets when multiple packets are sent as part of a total data package. The protocol also dictates how the address of the transmitting PC is encoded, where it is located in the packet, and how many bytes can be used to encode the address. The same is true for the packet's destination address. The protocol also determines where error codes are located inside the packet and how they are used to ensure the complete data packet is delivered as intended. This prevents the message from being damaged or altered. These are just a few of the many functions of the protocol.

The last item in the list is File and Print Sharing and is referred to as a service. For two or more PCs to share data or equipment such as a printer, the file- and print-sharing service must be installed. To install the file- and print-sharing service, click the **File and Print Sharing** button. This opens the File and Print Sharing dialog box shown in the following illustration.

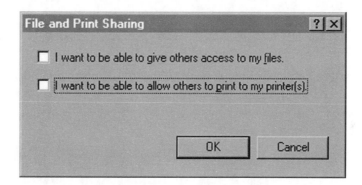

To share a file or printer, put checks in the appropriate boxes. For example, to share a file you must select the check box labeled **I want to be able to give others access to my files** and then click on the **OK** button. This installs the software required to allow you to share files on your PC.

Equipment and Materials

✱ Typical PC with Windows 98 operating system
✱ The PC must have a network adapter card already configured but not necessarily connected to a network
✱ You may also need a Windows 98 Installation CD

Procedure

1. ___ Boot the PC and wait for the Windows desktop to appear.

2. ___ You may access the Network dialog box by right clicking on the **Network Neighborhood** icon on the desktop, and selecting **Properties** from the drop-down menu. You may also open the Network dialog box by double clicking the **Network** icon in the Control Panel. In Windows Me, 2000, and XP, the Network Neighborhood icon is renamed My Network Places.

Networking

3. ___ Open up the Network dialog box on your PC and then list the installed components in the space provided. _____

_____

_____

_____

_____

4. ___ Let's see how to install a protocol. Select **Client for Microsoft Networks** by clicking once with the mouse and then clicking the **Add** button. This should open a dialog box similar to the one shown.

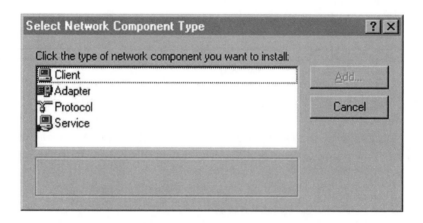

Select **Protocol** from the list, and then click on the **Add...** button. As shown in the following figure, a list of Microsoft-compatible network protocols will appear in the Select Network Protocol dialog box.

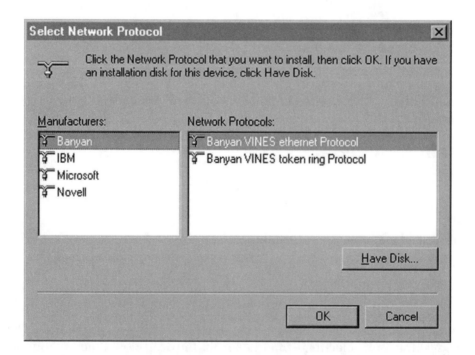

To install one of the protocols, click on the choice once and then click on the **OK** button. You may be prompted for the Windows Installation CD. Also, notice the button labeled Have Disk…. If you need to install an upgrade or patch for an existing network protocol from a disk, click the **Have Disk...** button.

5. ___ Next, add the TCP/IP protocol, listed under Microsoft. If it is already installed, return to the Network dialog box, highlight the protocol, and remove it by clicking the **Remove** button. Then, reinstall the protocol. You may need to review the previous steps and information presented. Practice adding and removing the TCP/IP protocol until you feel confident. If you have difficulty removing or adding the TCP/IP protocol, please call your instructor for assistance.

6. ___ After you are confident with adding and removing the TCP/IP protocol, go on to add file- and print-sharing service. Remove and add file- and print-sharing service several times until you are confident with the process.

7. ___ Now add the NetBEUI protocol component to the network card component list. If it already exists, remove it first, and then add it to the list. Again, practice adding and removing the NetBEUI protocol until you are comfortable with the process.

8. ___ Look at the list of components associated with the network adapter card you made earlier in the lab activity. Be sure the list of components is the same as when you found the computer. If it is not, add or remove components until it does match the list, unless otherwise directed by your instructor.

9. ___ Answer the review questions below and then shut down the PC.

Review Questions

1. What are the four major areas involved in network card configuration? _____

_____

_____

2. How can the Network dialog box be accessed? _____

_____

_____

3. What is a protocol? _____

_____

_____

_____

_____

Networking

Name _____ Date_____

Class/Instructor _____

Lab Activity

60

Creating a Network Share

After completing this lab activity, you will be able to:

✶   Create a share on a peer-to-peer network.

✶   Identify the types of security associated with a peer-to-peer network share.

Introduction

    Sharing files and hardware is the main purpose of a network. In this lab activity, you will set up a network share. You will share a program on your computer with another person in your lab. You will set up a share for a variety of items such as a hard drive, a CD-drive, a directory, and a file. You will also set up the file with rights such as read only, full rights, and access dependent on a password.

    There are two types of shares commonly used in networks, Share-level access control and User-level access control. Share-level access is commonly associated with a peer-to-peer network and User-level access is associated with a centrally administered network, such as one that utilizes a file server.

Equipment and Materials

✶   (2) PCs with Windows 95 or Windows 98 operating system installed and set up as a peer-to-peer network

◾ **Note:**
This is a two-station lab activity.

Procedure

1. ___   Report to your assigned station and power up the PC.

2. ___   After the computer boots, right click on **Network Neighborhood** and select **Properties** from the drop-down menu. When the Network dialog box appears, click the **File and Print Sharing...** button. The File and Print Sharing dialog box will appear. Put a check mark in the **I want to give others access to my files** check box. Click **OK** to accept the changes and close the File and Print Sharing dialog box. In the Network dialog box, click **OK** to accept the changes and close the dialog box.

3. ___   Next, select the **Access Control** tab at the top of the Network dialog box. Activate the **Share-level access control** radio button. Click **OK** to close the dialog box. You will have to restart the computer for the changes that you made to take effect.

Networking

4. ___ When the computer has rebooted, double click the My Computer icon. Right click on the icon for the local hard drive, and select **Properties** from the drop-down menu. Select the **General** tab. In the **Label:** text box, enter the name Station1. The dialog should appear similar to the one in the following illustration.

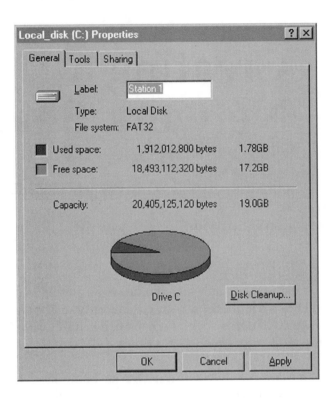

5. ___ Now, select the **Sharing** tab from the top of the dialog box. The dialog box should appear similar to the one shown here.

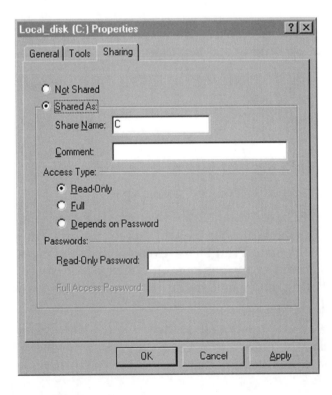

6. ___ With the **Sharing** tab of the hard drive's Properties dialog box open, select the **Share As:** radio button. Next, select an access type by selecting the appropriate radio button in the **Access Type:** area of the dialog box. The access options listed are **Read-Only**, **Full**, and **Depends on Password**. Ask your instructor for the proper settings. Next, enable the share by clicking the **OK** button.

5. ___ After your share for the drive has been set up, go to Windows Explorer and look at the directory structure. If the share has been set up correctly, your C: drive should be represented by an icon similar to the one shown. The icon has a hand under the hard drive to indicate it is set up as a shared device. If this icon is different or not present, call your instructor.

Station1 (C:)

6. ___ After your hard drive has been set up as a share, experiment with the different access types.

7. ___ Try setting up a share for a document. See if you can change the contents of a file that has been set up as read-only by another student.

8. ___ Experiment with the rights of access to directories and entire hard drives. See if the rights still apply to hard drives. If a hard drive is set up as a share, are all files on the drive accessible?

9. ___ Leave the PC on while you answer the review questions. After answering the questions, return the PC to its original condition before shutting it down.

Review Questions

1. What are the three access types associated with a shared device or file?_____

_____

2. How can you identify a file or hardware device that is shared? _____

_____

3. What are the two main types of shares?_____

_____

Networking

Name _____ Date_____

Class/Instructor _____

Lab Activity 61

Internet Connection Sharing

After completing this lab activity, you will be able to:

✶ Install an Internet connection share (ICS).

✶ Explain the purpose of a default gateway or ICS host.

✶ Explain the assignment of IP addresses in an ICS peer-to-peer network.

Introduction

This lab activity will show you how a single Internet connection can be shared by multiple PCs. Internet connection sharing (ICS) is especially useful for a home office and is available in Windows 98SE (Second Edition), Windows Me, Windows 2000, and Windows XP. The ICS program is installed on the host computer only. The host computer connects to the Internet through typical means, such as a modem, ISDN adapter, or cable modem adapter. The connection is then shared with other computers through a peer-to-peer network.

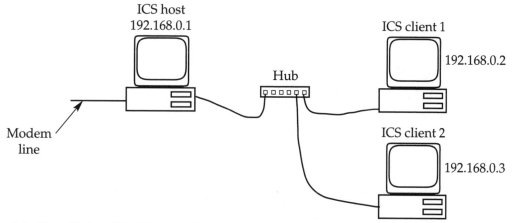

The network is identified as 192.168.0.0 and the subnet mask is 255.255.255.0. The host PC is assigned the IP address 192.168.0.1 and the ICS clients are identified by unique IP addresses between 192.168.0.2 and 192.168.0.254.

In the illustration, you can see how the IP addresses are assigned to computers in the peer-to-peer network. An IP address is composed of four octets. Each octet represents a range of decimal numbers from 0–255. The host is assigned 192.168.0.1; the other PCs are assigned IP addresses such as 192.168.0.2 and 192.168.0.3. In this example, the last octet uniquely identifies

Networking

the individual PC stations, and the first three octets identify the network. Therefore, this network has a subnet mask of 255.255.255.0, which identifies it as a Class C network.

Default gateway is another name for the ICS host. In a large network system, the default gateway is usually the file server. In a smaller ICS network system, the default gateway is an individual computer that connects directly with the Internet and shares the connection with the ICS clients. The default gateway is the only PC seen from the Internet. The gateway or ICS host resolves the names of the individual computers to the assigned IP addresses. In short, the ICS host connects to the Internet, and all messages and downloaded files are transmitted to the host. The host then redirects the downloads to the requested PCs, based on individually assigned IP addresses and names.

There are two ways to assign IP addresses to ICS client PCs, manually and automatically. The TCP/IP Properties dialog box, accessed through the Network Properties dialog box, is where the manual or automatic method is selected. Look at the following screen capture of a typical TCP/IP Properties dialog box. To manually assign the IP address, select **Specify an IP address:**. To automatically assign the IP address, select **Obtain an IP address automatically:**.

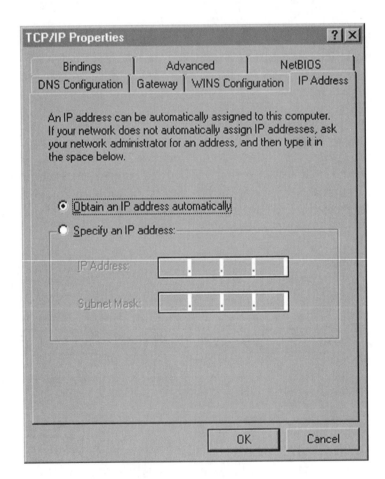

When manually assigning IP addresses, you must access the Network Properties dialog box of each client PC and enter a unique IP address for that computer. The IP address must be within the proper range. For the example Class C network used here, each computer must have a unique IP address between 192.168.0.2–192.168.0.254. You cannot use 192.168.0.0 or 192.168.0.255 for any ICS client. They are reserved addresses used for special network broadcast communications. The subnet mask for each computer must be set to 255.255.255.0. The subnet mask identifies which part of the IP address describes the individual PCs, and which part describes the network.

When assigning IP addresses automatically, you must access the Network Properties dialog box on each PC and select Obtain an IP address automatically from the TCP/IP Properties dialog box. To access the TCP/IP Properties dialog box, access the Network Properties dialog box. Next, select TCP/IP from the configuration listing. If there is more than one TCP/IP configuration listed, select the one that refers to the network adapter, not the dial-up network. Next, click on the Properties button to reveal the TCP/IP properties.

■ **Note:**
If you have difficulty accessing the TCP/IP Properties dialog box, you may use the Start menu's Help program.

Equipment and Materials

✴ Minimum of 2 PCs connected as a peer-to-peer network (one PC designated as the ICS host)

✴ Internet connection for the ICS host

✴ Windows 98 Second Edition, Windows Me, or Windows 2000 Installation CD is required to install the ICS program

✴ 3 1/2″ floppy disk is required to create an ICS client disk

Procedure

1. ___ Report to your assigned PC with the Installation CD for your operating system. (The instructor will identify a computer to use as a host. The host must have an Internet connection.)

2. ___ After booting the PC, open the Start menu's Help program.

3. ___ Open the Internet Tools dialog box located at **Start | Settings | Control Panel | Add/Remove Programs | Windows Setup | Internet Tools | Details**. Select **Internet Connection Sharing** from the components list, which should be similar to the one shown here.

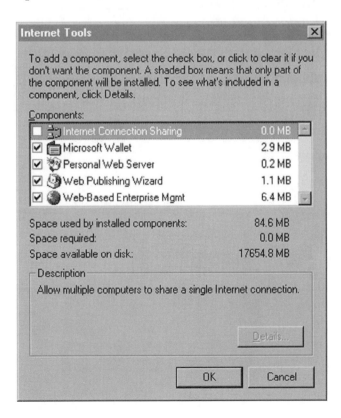

Networking

The Internet Connection Sharing component is only required on the PC acting as the ICS host or default gateway. You may need the installation CD to install the program.

4. ___ After installation of the ICS component is complete, the Internet Connection wizard should start. Simply follow the directions in the onscreen prompts. Through this program, you will create a Client Configuration Disk. That disk can be used to set up the ICS clients.

5. ___ Using the ICS client disk, proceed to set up the ICS clients on the peer-to-peer network.

6. ___ Test the installation by booting all PCs in the peer-to-peer network and then accessing the Internet. The ICS host must be connected to the Internet before the clients can access the Internet.

If the ICS system fails, check the following items:

* Make sure all computers have TCP/IP installed.
* Make sure all PCs are set to obtain an IP address automatically, or that each has a manually assigned address. These two systems cannot be mixed.
* Make sure each PC is using a unique IP address. No two PCs can have the same IP address.
* Make sure file sharing is enabled for each network adapter card.

You may use the troubleshooting feature of the Start menu's Help program to assist you in further diagnostics.

7. ___ When the lab activity has been completed, check with your instructor to see if the PC station needs to be returned to its original state, or if it should be left as a member of an Internet-sharing peer-to-peer network.

Review Questions

1. What does the acronym ICS represent? _____

_____

2. What is the IP address assigned to the peer-to-peer network in this activity? _____

3. What is the default subnet mask of the IP address 192.168.0.0? _____

_____

4. What IP address identifies the ICS host in this activity? _____

5. Does the ICS program need to be installed on all PCs? _____

Name _____ Date_____

Class/Instructor _____

Lab Activity

62

Winipcfg.exe

After completing this lab activity, you will be able to:

✱   Identify the assigned TCP/IP address.
✱   Identify the default gateway.
✱   Identify the subnet mask.

Introduction

When working with a PC connected to the Internet, a technician will often need to verify assigned TCP/IP settings. In Windows 95, 98, and Me, a TCP/IP utility program called winipcfg.exe can be used to reveal information about the PC Windows IP configuration settings of the Internet connection. A similar utility is activated in Windows NT and Windows 2000 environments by running ipconfig.exe at the DOS prompt. You need not know what all the different settings mean, but rather verify the settings when requested by a network administrator.

Equipment and Materials

✱   Typical PC with Windows 95 (or later) operating system (the PC must be part of a peer-to-peer or client-server network)
✱   Internet access through a modem or network

Procedure

1. ___ Boot the PC and wait for the Windows desktop to be displayed.

Networking

2. ___ From the **Start** menu select the **Run...** option. When the Run dialog box appears, type in **winipcfg** and press [Enter]. The IP Configuration dialog box should appear. It will contain information about the PC network adapter being used. A screen capture of the dialog box is shown here.

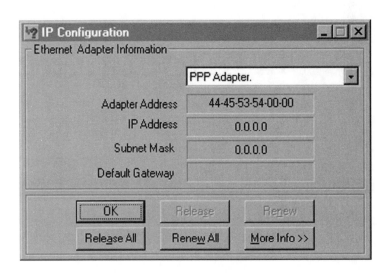

3. ___ Now close the IP Configuration dialog box.

4. ___ Connect to the Internet. There is no need to connect to any particular web site. Simply establishing a connection to the Internet service provider (ISP) will be sufficient.

5. ___ Once again open the **Run** dialog box from the **Start** menu and run the **winipcfg.exe** utility. The IP Configuration dialog box will appear with information about the connection. Record the information in the space provided.

Adapter Address _____

IP Address _____

Subnet Mask _____

Default Gateway _____

6. ___ Now click the **More Info >>** button at the bottom right side of the IP Configuration dialog box. This will reveal additional information about the connection. Record the requested information below in the space provided.

Host Name _____

DNS Server _____

Node Type _____

Subnet Mask _____

Default Gateway _____

Name_____

7. ___ The following are some important points about the information retrieved using this utility:

★ The *host name* is the name assigned to the PC you are using.

★ The *adapter address* is the media access code (MAC) address assigned to the network card. The MAC address is listed as the Adapter Address in the IP Configuration dialog box.

★ The *IP address* is the address assigned to the PC. The PC is usually assigned an IP address from a pool of addresses owned by the Internet service provider. This means the PC may not have the same IP address the next time it logs on to the Internet.

★ The *subnet mask* identifies the size and type of network you are connecting to or passing through. In this case, you are connecting to the ISP network.

★ The *DNS server* contains the software used to translate the domain name into an IP address.

★ When there are many computer stations, such as in a network, they usually connect to the Internet through one designated computer (server). This computer is referred to as the *default gateway*. The default gateway provides the connection between the users' PCs and the Internet.

★ The other information is used in a much more complex network environment. When a connection to the Internet needs to be established from a PC in a large, complex network, the other settings are used. These settings are usually assigned or verified by the network administrator.

8. ___ Now, close the IP Configuration dialog box.

9. ___ Open the IP Configuration dialog box again, but this time through the DOS prompt. At the DOS prompt, type **winipcfg** and press [Enter]. This should display the same dialog box that was opened previously.

10. ___ Return to the DOS window. At the command prompt type **winipcfg/all,** press [Enter], and observe the results.

11. ___ Close the Internet connection and the IP Configuration dialog box. Once again open the IP Configuration dialog box. It does not matter which method you use. Does the PC still have an assigned IP address? _____ Have the other settings changed, or remained the same? _____

12. ___ You may leave the computer on while you answer the questions on the next page. After completing the questions, please return the computer to its original settings and then properly shut it down.

Networking

Review Questions

1. How might you use winipcfg.exe as a troubleshooting tool? _____

   _____

   _____

2. Where would you get additional information about the Internet settings in a corporate network situation? _____

3. In a Windows NT or 2000 setting, what utility provides the same information as winipcfg.exe
   does in a Windows 95, 98, or Me environment? _____

   _____

4. What does the **/all** switch do when added to the **winipcfg** command issued at the DOS
   prompt? _____

   _____

5. What is another name for the Adapter Address displayed in the IP Configuration dialog box?

   _____

6. What is a default gateway? _____

   _____

Name _____ Date_____

Class/Instructor _____

Lab Activity

63

Verify Internet Properties

After completing this lab activity, you will be able to:

✲ Inspect and modify Internet properties.

✲ Assign Internet TCP/IP addresses under the supervision of a network administrator.

Introduction

In this lab activity, you will use either the winipcfg or ipconfig utility, depending on the operating system you are using. Windows 95, 98, and Me use the winipcfg utility. The ipconfig utility is used with Windows NT, 2000, and XP. The utilities are used to verify and modify TCP/IP assignments. When issuing the command, you may use a switch to reveal more information. You may also use the **More Info>>** button on the default window to reveal additional information. Look at the screen captures that follow. They show the typical results of issuing the **winipcfg** and the **winipcfg/all** commands from the DOS prompt of a Windows Me operating system.

The IP configuration dialog box shown in **Figure 1** reveals that this is an Ethernet adapter (network card), and it is tied to a PPP-type protocol. Also displayed is the Adapter Address (MAC address) of the network card. The IP address is assigned to the network card as well as the subnet mask and default gateway. When the **More Info>>** button is activated, additional information is revealed. See **Figure 2.**

Figure 1

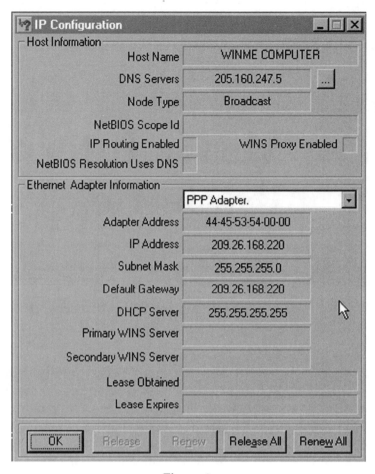

Figure 2

The TCP/IP assignments are the IP addresses used to identify the workstation and other important entities such as the dynamic host configuration protocol (DHCP) server, the default gateway, and the Windows Internet Naming Service (WINS). The DHCP server automatically assigns IP addresses to the network stations. The WINS servers resolve the network's NetBIOS names (computer-assigned names) to IP addresses. Both WINS and DHCP servers are critical for communication on some networks. The network administrator usually tells the tech what to check for. The PC technician is responsible for verifying or assigning the proper IP addresses when performing a network card installation or during routine troubleshooting involving a network connection. You can find out more about these features in your textbook or by conducting an Internet search using keywords such as IP, config, DHCP, WINS, gateway, etc.

Equipment and Materials

✳ Typical PC connected to the Internet either through a network or directly by modem

✳ Windows 98, 2000, NT, Me, or XP installed

Procedure

1. ___ Boot the PC and make sure that it is operating properly.

2. ___ Access the network card and IP assignment information by entering **winipcfg** or **ipconfig** at the DOS prompt. Try using the **/all** switch with the command. A window similar to the one shown in Figure 2 should appear.

3. ___ Write the appropriate information in the spaces provided. Answers will vary from workstation to workstation.

      Host Name _____

      DNS Server_____

      Node Type_____

      Adapter Address _____

      IP Address_____

      Subnet Mask_____

      Default Gateway _____

      DHCP Server _____

4. ___ After filling in the information requested in step 3, answer the review questions that follow. After completing the review questions, shut down the PC.

Review Questions

1. What command is issued from the DOS prompt on a Windows 98 machine to access the network card's IP address information? _____

2. What command is issued from the DOS prompt of a Windows NT machine to access the network card's IP information? _____

3. What does the DHCP server do? _____

_____

4. What does WINS do? _____

_____

Networking

Name _____ Date_____

Class/Instructor _____

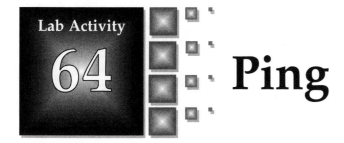

Ping

After completing this lab activity, you will be able to:

* Use the ping utility to verify a network connection.
* Use the ping command to verify that the NIC is operating properly.
* Be familiar with the various ping command switches.

Introduction

The ping utility is a basic network-troubleshooting tool that verifies a connection between the PC and a remote location. The ping utility is run from the DOS prompt. It sends out a data packet to a remote location, which will send a return reply if a connection can be established. Several switches associated with ping are important. Switches added to the ping command determine the size of the packet sent, how many times the packet is sent, how long the packet is allowed to circulate on the Internet or network, and whether addresses are resolved to host names. The time-to-live, or TTL, switch (**-i**) indicates how long the packet will be allowed to travel on the Internet before it is discarded. Without a TTL, the packet would theoretically circulate endlessly. As more and more ping commands are issued, the Internet would eventually be slowed to a crawl because of all the endless ping command data packets circulating. Two of the commands you will most frequently issue are **ping 127.0.0.1** and **ping localhost**. These commands are quick and easy tests for the network card. They ensure that the basic setup is correct, but do not guarantee that the NIC will work correctly as part of the network.

Equipment and Materials

* PC with Internet access or, at the very least, a small peer-to-peer network set up in a lab

Note:
Some network firewalls will prevent the **PING** *command from working correctly.*

Procedure

1. ___ Boot the PC and wait for the Windows desktop to appear. Do not connect to the Internet at this time.

2. ___ Go to the DOS prompt and use Help to identify the switches used with the ping command. Help can be accessed from the DOS prompt by typing **ping /?** or **ping /help**.

3. ___ Go to the DOS prompt, type **ping 127.0.0.1**, and note the response. The command **ping 127.0.0.1** is used to verify that the NIC is working properly.

Networking

4. ___ Now, enter the command **ping localhost** and note the response. Practice the two forms of ping commands and compare the results. In the space provided, write the information that is included when the **ping localhost** command is issued, but not included when the **ping 127.0.0.1** command is issued. _____

5. ___ Now attempt to ping a name of a web site. The instructor can supply you with the name of a web site to use. *Do not connect to the Internet yet.* You will need to go to the DOS prompt to issue the ping command.

7. ___ What is the message received after the ping was sent? _____

_____

◼ **Note:**

Some models of PC with updated versions of software will automatically connect to the Internet when the ping *command is issued.*

8. ___ Now, connect to the Internet and once again ping the chosen site. What response did you get? Write it below. A typical response would be similar to the following.

```
Reply from 127.103.010.12: bytes = 32 time<10ms TTL=128
Reply from 127.103.010.12: bytes = 32 time<10ms TTL=128
Reply from 127.103.010.12: bytes = 32 time<10ms TTL=128
Reply from 127.103.010.12: bytes = 32 time<10ms TTL=128
```

```
Ping statistics for 127.103.010.12:
Packets: Sent = 4, Received = 4, Lost = 0 (0% loss).
Approximate round trip times in milliseconds:
Minimum = 10ms, Maximum = 10ms, Average = 10ms
```

_____

_____

_____

_____

_____

_____

_____

_____

9. ___ Try to ping several other sites and compare the statistics. You do not need to write them all down.

10. ___ Why do you think that there are differences in the reply from the sites? Hint: think about the way the network is designed and what happens when other users attempt to access the same site. The time will vary because of the traffic on the Internet and because the ping route does not necessarily have to follow the same path each time. The main cause is all the traffic moving across the same access lines used for the ping path.

11. ___ Go on to answer the review questions. Leave the PC on while you answer the questions. When you have finished, properly shut down the PC.

Name_____

Review Questions

Now use the **ping/?**, *or* **ping/help** *commands to answer the following questions.*

1. How can the size of the data packet sent be increased? _____

2. What do the letters TTL mean? _____

3. What does the packet's TTL determine? _____

4. How can the TTL be increased?_____

5. How can the ping command be used when troubleshooting a network? _____

   _____

6. What message is generated if the ping command does not receive a reply?_____

   _____

Name _____ Date_____

Class/Instructor _____

Tracert Utility

Lab Activity 65

After completing this lab activity, you will be able to:

* Determine the route taken by a packet.
* Explain how the tracert utility can be used to verify network connections.

Introduction

A very handy TCP/IP utility is tracert, a contraction of the two words *trace* and *route*. The tracert utility reveals more than the simple ping. The tracert command can be issued with the target's IP address or URL name. In the screen capture shown, a tracert command is issued from the DOS prompt. Goodheartwillcox.com is the target of the trace. The IP address, if it is known, can also be used to trace the route.

```
C:\WINDOWS>tracert goodheartwillcox.com
Tracing route to goodheartwillcox.com [64.41.70.90]
over a maximum of 30 hops:
  1    261 ms    247 ms    275 ms  tc101.strato.net [209.26.168.249]
  2    234 ms    247 ms    275 ms  tc102-254.strato.net [64.45.197.254]
  3    247 ms    261 ms    261 ms  host193.strato.net [207.30.98.193]
  4    261 ms    261 ms    261 ms  icrwnpk2-fast-seg2.utelfla.com [209.26.123.228]
  5    261 ms    261 ms    261 ms  208.30.210.21
  6    261 ms    275 ms    247 ms  sl-bb20-ori-0-0.sprintlink.net [144.232.2.232]
  7    247 ms    261 ms    274 ms  144.232.18.246
  8    248 ms    274 ms    275 ms  205.171.27.45
  9    261 ms    261 ms    274 ms  205.171.27.190
 10    274 ms    275 ms    274 ms  205.171.5.67
 11    261 ms    275 ms    275 ms  205.171.21.149
 12    329 ms    357 ms    316 ms  205.171.8.198
 13    316 ms    343 ms    316 ms  205.171.20.114
 14    467 ms    316 ms    302 ms  pos-6-0.ons.siteprotect.com [65.112.64.146]
 15    316 ms    343 ms    330 ms  64.41.70.90
Trace complete.
C:\WINDOWS>
```

The path taken by the data and IP address of the destination are displayed. The amount of time to complete each hop is indicated in milliseconds. The IP address of each network or router along the way is also displayed. The default setting for the tracert utility is 30 hops. A hop is an intermediate connection along the path taken by the tracert packet. Routers are an example of a hop as are the Internet service provider and the final destination. Each hop along the route sends a packet back to the source identifying itself to the source.

This is a handy tool when troubleshooting a large enterprise network. It will verify the route from a PC through the network routers and on through the gateway or firewall. You can quickly determine if the network problem exists on the local network system or in the public system.

Networking

Materials Required

✳ A typical PC with TCP/IP protocol installed (the PC should be part of a network or connected to an Internet service provider)

✳ List of Internet addresses for the tracert exercise (write the addresses provided by your instructor in the following spaces)

_____

_____

_____

_____

_____

◼ **Note:**

Some network firewalls will prevent the tracert utility from working correctly.

Procedure

1. ___ Report to your assigned PC, boot the computer, and make sure it is in proper working order.

2. ___ Test the Internet connection by connecting to any host on the Internet.

3. ___ Access the DOS prompt and trace the routes to the addresses provided by the Instructor. To run the tracert utility from the DOS prompt, type **tracert** followed by the target address and hit [Enter].

4. ___ Take the assigned IP address of another PC station in the lab and attempt to trace the route to the other PC station. Record the final destination IP addresses for each destination.

5. ___ Try using the IP address instead of the URL of the target to trace a route with the tracert utility. Observe the results.

6. ___ Shut down the computer after completing the review questions.

Review Questions

1. How can the tracert utility help in a troubleshooting situation? _____

_____

2. What is the default number of maximum hops? _____

3. What two forms of destination addresses can be used with the tracert utility?

_____

Name _____ Date_____

Class/Instructor _____

Lab Activity

66

Create a Set of Startup Disks

After completing this lab activity, you will be able to:

✽   Create a set of Windows 2000 startup diskettes.

✽   Locate the executable files for making a set of setup disks.

✽   Explain the difference between makeboot.exe and makebt32.exe.

Introduction

Windows 2000 boot disks are also referred to as startup disks. The minimum number of floppy disks required is four. You can make a set of startup disks by inserting the Windows 2000 Installation CD into the drive and then running one of two programs, makeboot.exe or makebt32.exe.

Makeboot.exe is a 16-bit program. It must be executed from a DOS prompt. To run the program, bring up a DOS prompt, access the MAKEBOOT directory on the CD-ROM, type **makeboot.exe,** hit [Enter], and then follow the onscreen prompts. Makebt32.exe is a 32-bit program. It can be run from **Start | Run...**, or by double clicking on the file in Windows Explorer.

You will need four formatted floppy disks to create the set of start up disks. After you create the set of four startup disks, you will test the first disk by shutting down the computer, placing disk 1 in the floppy drive, and then rebooting the system. Your instructor may or may not want you to complete a full installation of Windows 2000. If you do not want to perform a full installation, you can abort the installation right after you are prompted for the second disk. Rather than place the second boot disk into the floppy drive, simply remove disk 1 and shut down the system. The PC should boot normally during the next startup.

The Windows startup disks are a very handy part of a technician's toolbox. They can be used to recover a failed Windows 2000 system. Please note that Windows 2000 Professional and Windows 2000 Server startup disks are not interchangeable. When you label the disks, you should indicate whether they are Windows 2000 Professional or Windows 2000 Server setup disks.

Equipment and Materials

✽   Typical PC with a Windows 95 (or later) operating system

✽   Windows 2000 Installation CD-ROM

✽   (4) 3 1/2" floppy disks, labeled 1 through 4

Windows 2000 and XP

Procedure

Does your instructor want you to do a complete install using the four startup disks you will create? *Yes* or *No?*

1. ___ Report to your assigned computer station and boot up the system. Make sure it is in good working order. If the system is not in good working order, please notify your instructor.

2. ___ Place the Windows 2000 Installation CD-ROM into the CD drive.

3. ___ Open Windows Explorer and access the CD-ROM. Find the two executable files located in the MAKEBOOT folder.

4. ___ Double-click on the **makebt32.exe** file and follow the prompts on the screen.

5. ___ After creating the four startup disks, test the disks by shutting down the computer and booting the system with disk 1 inserted in the floppy drive. Did a startup window labeled "Windows 2000 Setup" appear in the upper left-hand corner of the display? If so, remove the disks and shut the system down once more. If not, call your instructor.

6. ___ Answer the review questions below. You may use the Windows 2000 Help program to assist you in answering the questions. Look in the index under "setup." After completing the questions, shut down the station.

Review Questions

1. What are the names of the two executable files used to make a set of setup disks?

   _____

2. Which directory on the installation CD contains the makeboot.exe file?

   _____

3. Which of the two executable files, makeboot.exe and makebt32.exe, must be run from a DOS prompt? _____

4. What is the complete path name of the makeboot.exe file, assuming that the CD drive letter is D? _____

5. What is the Recovery Console? _____

   _____

6. What is the Recovery Console used for? _____

   _____

Name _____ Date_____

Class/Instructor _____

Installing Windows 2000

After completing this lab activity, you will be able to:

✳ Explain the steps for performing a clean installation of Windows 2000.

✳ Explain the steps for performing an upgrade from Windows 98 to Windows 2000.

✳ Define the terms *server, client, domain,* and *workgroup* as they apply to Windows 2000 configurations.

Introduction

The Windows 2000 operating system uses Windows NT technology. Windows 2000 Professional is a desktop operating system and should not be confused with the network operating systems called Windows 2000 Server, Windows 2000 Advanced Server, or Windows 2000 Data Center. Windows 2000 Professional is designed to be a client on a Windows 2000 Server-type network, but can also be used on a stand-alone desktop system or a small peer-to-peer configuration. In this lab activity, you will install Windows 2000 Professional on a PC. The installation is usually very simple, but can be complicated by hardware compatibility problems and the terminology used by the Setup Wizard. Before you begin the installation, you should familiarize yourself with the following terms:

✳ Server—A server is a centralized computer used to control security aspects of a network and provide services to network clients.

✳ Client—Clients are the PCs connected to the network that depend on the server for certain services, such as Internet access, security log on, access to shared files, and e-mail.

✳ Domain—A domain is a collection of one or more workgroups under one centralized administration. For example, a domain is often an entire company. Some extremely large companies may consist of several domains.

✳ Workgroup—A workgroup is a group of computers that share a common activity or function. Examples of possible workgroups could include an Accounting or Sales Department, a group of students in a particular classroom, or a group of teachers.

Several tasks should be accomplished before you begin a Windows 2000 installation.

1. First, check the hardware compatibility list from the Microsoft web site's technical support. Be sure the hardware devices you are using are on the compatibility list before you attempt to install the operating system. This could keep you from wasting a lot of valuable time attempting to do an impossible install of the operating system. Check the compatibility of your hardware, including the CD-drive, hard drive, and BIOS.

Windows 2000 and XP

2. Decide on the number of partitions (one, two, or more) and the file system to be used (FAT or NTFS).

3. Decide the type of licensing you are going to declare (site license based on a per seat or per server basis).

4. Will this computer be part of a domain or workgroup? If the PC is going to join an existing domain, you will need a user name and password with authority to add a domain computer account. If the computer will be joining a workgroup, you will need the workgroup name.

Your instructor can provide the answers for most of these questions, or you can defer to the default settings. You can also find out more about each of these issues at the Microsoft web site, www.Microsoft.com/Windows2000. There are step-by-step guides available as well as a wealth of technical knowledge for all aspects of Windows 2000 installation, configuration, troubleshooting, etc.

Equipment and Materials

* Windows 2000 Professional CD and product identification key
* Typical PC with at least 133 MHz (or higher) CPU, 2 GB hard disk drive, 64 MB RAM, and a network card installed
* Set of four Windows 2000 startup disks (if the PC supports CD booting, you will not need the four startup disks)
* You will need to know the following information:

    Domain name _____

    Workgroup name _____

    User name _____

    User password _____

    Product ID on the Certificate of Authenticity (COA) _____-_____-_____-_____-_____

Procedure

The sequence of events should follow the list below closely but not necessarily in exact order.

1. ___ After gathering all necessary materials and information, report to your assigned station.

2. ___ Boot the PC with the Windows 2000 startup disk 1. Follow the onscreen prompts until you have installed each of the four startup disks. If you have a PC with CD boot support, you may boot from the Windows 2000 CD. If you are performing a clean installation, run the Winnt.exe program from the DOS prompt to start the installation. The Winnt32.exe program is used to start a system upgrade installation. On the CD, the program is listed as D:\i386\Winnt32.exe or D:\i386\Winnt.exe. For this example, the drive letter for the CD is listed as D:, however, the actual drive letter of your CD drive will vary, depending on your computer's configuration.

3. ___ You will be prompted to accept the licensing agreement. Acceptance is usually given by pressing [F8] at the appropriate time or by clicking the **I Accept** button in the dialog box.

4. ___ Next, you will create/select a partition and format the partition using NTFS5 (Dynamic Disk). (You may do more than one partition, or use a different format if instructed to do so by your instructor.) The setup process automatically checks the hard disk for bad sectors, determines the current file system, and then prepares the disk for installation.

5. ___ The setup process now copies all necessary files from the CD to the hard disk for the completion of the setup process. The next screen to appear after all necessary files are copied is the GUI (Graphical User Interface).

6. ___ The setup program now automatically detects the hardware features of the PC, such as the keyboard and mouse.

7. ___ Next, you will need to enter your regional settings, such as location and time zone.

8. ___ Your name and the name of your organization are requested next.

9. ___ Next, the Product ID is requested. The twenty-five character Product ID is printed on the Certificate of Authenticity (COA). This information is usually located on the CD case, not the CD itself. Be careful not to lose the Certificate of Authenticity sticker.

10. ___ The computer name and password are requested next. You may accept the defaults or enter the ones provided by your instructor.

11. ___ The date and time are requested next. Enter them appropriately.

12. ___ Next, you can enter custom network settings or accept the default settings. Choose the default settings unless otherwise instructed by your teacher.

13. ___ You are requested to supply the workgroup name and/or computer domain name next.

14. ___ The setup program now finishes the installation. That is all there is to the complete installation.

Note:

Performing a system upgrade is very similar to the clean installation. However, you should run a virus check and back up all data before beginning the installation. Also, disable the virus program and screen saver so that they do not interfere with the system upgrade procedure.

Review Questions

1. What are the names of the three Windows 2000 operating systems designed for network server operation? _____

   _____

   _____

2. What should you do before installing Windows 2000 as an upgrade? _____

   _____

   _____

3. What is a peer-to-peer network? _____

   _____

   _____

4. What is a client/server network? _____

   _____

   _____

Windows 2000 and XP

5. What is a workgroup? _____

_____

_____

6. What is a domain? _____

_____

_____

7. What is a clean install? _____

_____

_____

8. What is an upgrade? _____

_____

_____

9. What does the acronym COA represent? _____

_____

_____

10. What is the difference between the winnt.exe program and the winnt32.exe program?

_____

_____

Name _____ Date_____

Class/Instructor _____

Lab Activity

68

Make a Windows 2000 Boot Disk

After completing this lab activity, you will be able to:

✻ Make a Windows 2000 Professional boot disk for a desktop operating system.
✻ Identify the files that must be contained on a Windows 2000 boot disk.
✻ Explain the purpose of ARCpath names.
✻ Identify the parts of an ARCpath name.

Introduction

The following files are necessary to make a self-booting system disk for Windows 2000 professional desktop operating system.

Ntldr

Ntdetect.com

Boot.ini

Bootsect.dos

Ntbootdd.sys

The three core files needed to boot the system are Ntldr, Ntdetect.com, and Boot.ini. If bootsect.dos and ntbootdd.sys are not present, they will not be needed. They are used only for SCSI installations.

ARC Paths

The Boot.ini file contains the Advanced RISC Computing (ARC) paths commonly referred to as the ARC path. These paths point to the operating systems installed on the computer. You can see the ARC path names in the file called boot.ini, located in the root directory. An example of the contents of a boot.ini file is shown below.

```
[boot loader]
timeout=30
default=multi(0)disk(0)rdisk(1)partition(2)\WINNT
[operating systems]
multi(0)disk(0)rdisk(0)partition(4)\WINNT="Microsoft Windows 2000 Professional" /fastdetect
multi(0)disk(0)rdisk(0)partition(3)\WINNT="Microsoft Windows XP Professional" /fastdetect
```

The display above shows multiple operating systems loaded on the same PC. The two ARC paths (last two lines) identify the locations of the different operating systems. If there is only one

Windows 2000 and XP

operating system installed on the computer, there will be only one entry. In the example there are multiple operating systems installed on the same computer.

The ARC path naming convention uses four information fields: Multi( ), Disk( ), Rdisk( ), and Partition( ):

* The first information field in the example above is Multi( ), which indicates that the operating system is installed on an IDE, EIDE, or ATA storage device. If the operating system is installed on a SCSI storage device, the word SCSI( ) appears in place of the Multi ( ).

* The Disk( ) field indicates the SCSI ID number of the drive containing the OS.

* The Rdisk field indicates the ordinal number of the hard disk on which the OS is installed. It is not used for SCSI.

* The Partition( ) field indicates which partition the system is installed on.

To learn more about ARC path naming conventions, see the frequently asked questions (FAQ) Q102873, BOOT.INI and ARC Path Naming Conventions and Usage, located at Microsoft Windows 2000 Product Support web page. Use the FAQ number to locate the material.

Material and Equipment

* Typical PC with a Windows 2000 operating system installed
* 3 1/2" floppy disk, labeled Windows 2000 Boot Disk

Procedure

1. ___ Report to your assigned PC and boot the system. Make sure it is in proper working order.

2. ___ Insert the floppy disk into the drive and use Windows Explorer to copy the following files to it. Be sure to remove the hidden and system attributes before attempting to copy the files.

    Ntldr

    Ntdetect.com

    Boot.ini

    Bootsect.dos

    Ntbootdd.sys

Note:

Remember bootsec.dos *and* ntbootdd.sys *may not be present.*

3. ___ After successfully copying the files, open boot.ini in a text editor and look at the existing ARC path name information.

4. ___ Close the boot.ini file and shut down the system.

5. ___ Reboot the system using the boot disk you just created.

6. ___ Remove the boot disk and then shut down and reboot the system once more.

7. ___ Shut down the system and answer the review questions on the next page.

Review Questions

1. What three files are the core files of a Windows 2000 boot disk? _____
   _____

2. When more than one hard disk drive is installed in a machine, what ARC path field indicates the hard disk drive that the system is installed on? _____

3. Which ARC path field indicates which SCSI drive contains the system in question? _____

4. How are adapter cards or disk controllers indicated in the ARC path? _____
   _____

5. How are individual partitions indicated in the ARC path name? _____
   _____

6. When a SCSI drive is installed, what word replaces *Multi*? _____

Name _____ Date_____

Class/Instructor _____

Make an Emergency Repair Disk

After completing this lab activity, you will be able to:

✳ Make a Windows 2000 Emergency Repair Disk

✳ Identify the contents of the Emergency Repair Disk.

✳ Explain the difference between an Emergency Repair Disk, a Windows 2000 boot disk, and a set of setup disks.

Introduction

In this lab activity, you will make a Windows 2000 Emergency Repair Disk. The disk will contain the necessary files and setup information needed to repair the computer system in the event of an emergency. One such emergency may arise when some of the files required for booting the PC are damaged or missing. This repair disk is not the same as a set of system startup disks or a boot disk. A boot disk simply contains the files necessary to start or boot the system. Sets of startup disks are used to start a clean installation or recover a damaged system. An Emergency Repair Disk contains information about the individual computer system that made it, and should be used only on that system. The boot disks and setup disks can be used on any system.

An Emergency Repair Disk (ERD) stores your Windows 2000 system settings and is used to repair your PC system if the computer will not start because of damaged or missing files. An emergency repair disk contains startup files that are unique to the machine it is made on. If a machine were a close match of another machine, the ERD could be used on the other machine. However, if the machines were dissimilar, it would only further corrupt the startup files.

Windows 2000 and XP

A Windows 2000 boot disk contains only the necessary files to boot a Windows 2000 machine. The Windows 2000 boot disk is not the same as a complete set of system startup disks or the ERD disk. Look at the summary that follows.

Disks	Purpose
Windows 2000 Boot Disks (one disk)	Start or boot any Windows 2000 machine, especially when the CD-drive cannot be accessed. The ARC path name for the disk drive is included in the disk.
Windows 2000 Setup Disks (four disks)	Start the Windows 2000 installation process. Can also be used to access the Recovery Console to repair a damaged system. Especially important if the CD-drive cannot be accessed.
Windows 2000 ERD (one disk)	Used in conjunction with the Recovery Console when making repairs to damaged system. The Recovery Console can be accessed through the set of four Setup Disks or through the Installation CD. The ERD matches the machine it was made on.

You can create the ERD by accessing the wizard located at **Start I Programs I Accessories I System Tools I Backup.** Choosing the **Backup** from the menu activates the Windows 2000 Backup and Recovery Tools utility. A screen capture of the utility is shown here.

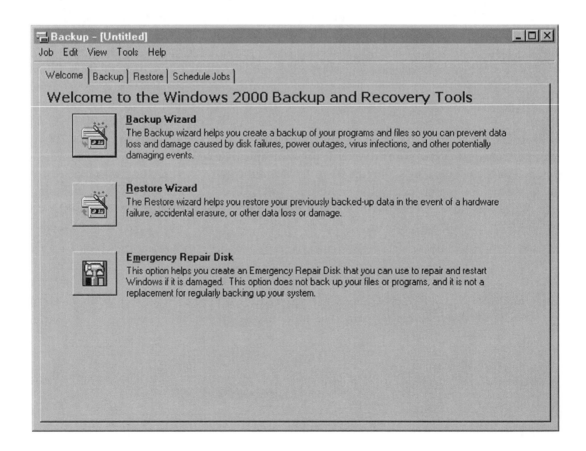

Name______________________________

As you can see, there are several options available from this screen. They are Backup Wizard, Restore Wizard, and Emergency Repair Disk.

In this lab activity, you will select the **Emergency Repair Disk** option. As you can see indicated beside the button, this option is used solely for repair of a damaged system, not as a backup of files or programs. To back up the system files or the entire contents of the hard disk drive, you must select a different option.

The emergency repair disk contains information about the system and guides the recovery console to the appropriate location of files in the registry that are unique since the installation of the Windows 2000 system. The ERD should be updated after any changes in the system, such as new drivers, programs, or system file installations.

Equipment and Materials

- A PC with a Windows 2000 Professional loaded
- 3 1/2″ floppy disk

Procedure

1. ___ Report to your assigned PC.
2. ___ Boot the PC and make sure the system is operating correctly. If it is not, call your instructor.
3. ___ Click on the **Start** button. When the Windows 2000 Start menu appears, select the following sequence to activate the **Start | Programs | Accessories | System Tools | Backup.** The Backup and Recovery window should appear.
4. ___ Answer the following questions based on the Windows 2000 Backup Wizard screen that is displayed. Reply to the statements below with a "T" for True and an "F" for False.

   The Emergency Repair Disk option backs up all files on the PC? _____

   The Emergency Repair Disk is used to repair and restart Windows if damaged? _____

   The Emergency Repair Disk is used to replace regular system backups? _____
5. ___ Place the blank but formatted 3 1/2″ disk in the floppy drive.
6. ___ Click the **Emergency Repair Disk** button and watch as the disk is prepared as an ERD.
7. ___ What label are you prompted to place on the diskette and what information should the label contain? ______________________________
8. ___ View the contents of the diskette and list the names of the files contained on the disk.

   ____
9. ___ Look at the contents of each of the files. When you are prompted to choose a program to open the file with, select either Notepad or WordPad.
10. ___ Shut down the computer and answer the review questions on the next page.

Review Questions

1. What three files are contained on the Windows 2000 Emergency Repair Disk?

   _____

2. Can an Emergency Boot Disk be used to repair any computer running Windows 2000?

   _____

3. How is the Backup Wizard accessed from the Start menu? _____

   _____

Name _____ Date_____

Class/Instructor _____

Lab Activity
70

Windows XP Upgrade Installation

After completing this lab activity, you will be able to:

✶ Upgrade a PC with an existing Windows 98 (or later) operating systems to a Windows XP operating system.

✶ Determine the minimum requirements for a Windows XP installation.

✶ Identify information required for a typical installation.

✶ Explain the Windows XP installation process in general terms.

Introduction

In this lab activity, you will install Windows XP as an upgrade for an existing Windows operating system previously installed on a computer system. Windows XP (eXPerience) operating system was released in October of 2001. Windows XP comes in two flavors, Windows XP Professional, and Windows XP Home Edition. The Windows XP professional is designed to replace the Windows NT and Windows 2000 family of desktop operating systems while the Windows Home Edition is designed to replace the Windows 9x and Windows Me editions. The Windows XP operating system is built on the Windows NT technology, which is more stable than the Windows 9x series.

The minimum requirements for installing the Windows XP operating system are as follows:

✶ 233 MHz Pentium (or higher) microprocessor.

✶ 64MB of RAM (128MB recommended, 4GB maximum).

✶ 1.5GB of unused hard drive space.

✶ VGA monitor.

✶ Keyboard and mouse.

✶ CD-ROM or DVD drive.

✶ A network adapter card (when networking the PC).

Before you begin installing Windows XP, you should check the hardware compatibility list located at Microsoft Tech support (www.microsoft.com/hcl/). Don't assume that because a previous version of Windows is already installed on the PC that the hardware used in the PC is compatible with the Windows XP operating system. Check the listing of hardware for potential problems. Note that Windows XP does perform a hardware check as part of the installation procedure. However, the automatic hardware detection program is not completely reliable. Always check the Microsoft web site for the very latest information.

Near the beginning of the installation process, the Windows XP installation wizard will present a screen giving you an option to connect to the Microsoft web site to check the hardware compatibility list and also look for updates to the operating system.

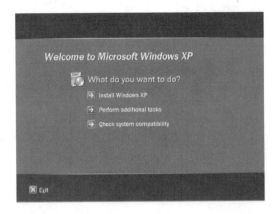

If you select the option to **Visit the compatibility Web site**, a screen image similar to the one that follows will appear.

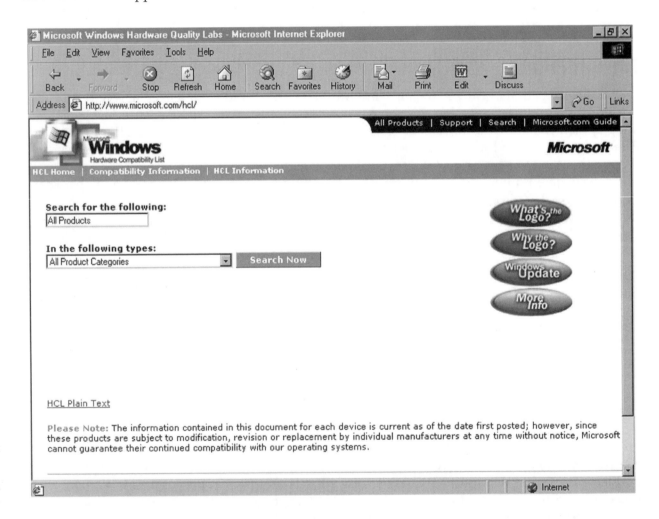

The hardware compatibility web site allows you to search for compatible equipment by operating system and by type of product such as chip set, RAM, displays, and more. The following image is a screen capture of the hardware compatibility list taken from the Microsoft web site. This is a partial list of displays that are compatible with various Windows operating systems. The circle with "Compatible" inside is used to identify the compatible displays by operating system.

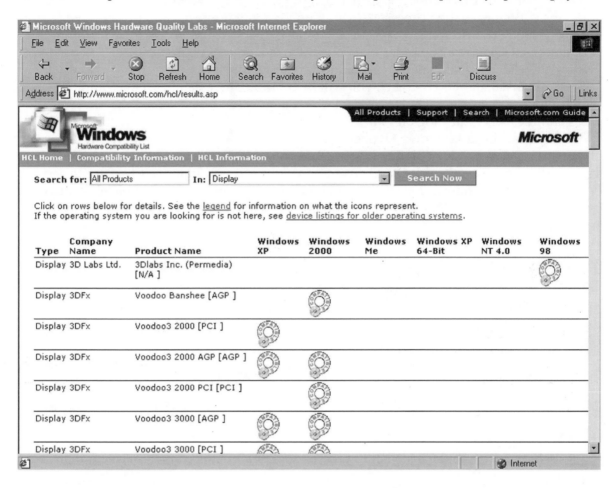

If your specific equipment is not on the compatibility list, you will need to go to the manufacture's web site and download an updated version of the hardware driver that is compatible with Windows XP.

Certain information may be required for your installation of Windows XP. The exact order and specific information can vary depending on whether the PC is part of a network, and if so, what type of network system. Below is a list of typical information you will need before you begin the installation wizard. The following information will be supplied by your instructor.

- ✱ Computer name _____
- ✱ Domain name _____
- ✱ Work group _____
- ✱ User name _____
- ✱ Organization _____
- ✱ Password _____
- ✱ IP address _____
- ✱ Name of DHCP server _____

Windows 2000 and XP

Write the information down on a separate sheet of paper so that you can refer to it during the installation process. During a typical system upgrade, much of the information will be transferred to the new operating system from the old, but not necessarily all of the information listed.

When you start the actual system upgrade installation process, you will insert the CD into the CD-ROM or DVD drive after the PC has been booted. The installation wizard will direct you through the entire installation process. When in doubt about a screen prompt, check with your instructor. Usually choosing the default option will be fine. Because you may be installing the new operating system on a computer in a network arrangement, your instructor will brief you on any particular changes that may be required for the installation.

When the installation is complete, you will be prompted to create a user account. The user account uniquely identifies each user of the PC and allows each user to load their specific settings and files when they log on to the PC.

When performing a Windows XP operating system upgrade, you must perform the upgrade over an existing compatible operating system. The only compatible operating systems for upgrades are Windows 98 (any edition), Windows Millennium, Windows NT 4.0 (with service pack 6 installed), or Windows 2000. Other operating systems are not compatible for a successful upgrade. Some such systems, which are not compatible, are Windows 95, DOS, and various Linux versions.

Equipment and Materials

✱   A typical PC that meets these minimum requirements:

> 233 MHz (or better) processor
>
> 64MB RAM (128MB preferred)
>
> Hard disk drive with at least 1.5GB of unused disk space
>
> Windows 98, 2000, Me, NT 4.0 service pack 6, or XP operating system (either Home Edition or Professional)

Procedure

1. ___ Before you begin the installation process, gather all required materials and then report to your assigned PC station.

2. ___ Boot the PC and check that the machine has the minimum installation requirements. If the PC has the minimum requirements, you may proceed to step 3. If it does not have the minimum hardware requirements, notify your instructor.

3. ___ Access the Read1st.txt file on the CD-ROM. Read the information carefully.

4. ___ With the PC booted to its operating system, insert the CD-ROM containing the Windows XP operating system. The CD-ROM may automatically start the installation process. The automatic startup of the installation will depend on the PC system equipment and BIOS. Wait approximately 2 minutes. If the installation has not automatically begun, start the installation process manually. You can manually start the program by typing and running **D:Setup.exe** from the run option of the start button menu selections. See the screen captures that follow. *(Note: It is assumed here the* D: *is the CD-ROM or DVD device. If this is not the case, substitute the correct drive letter in the command. If you are having difficulty, you can also* **Browse...** *until you locate the program.)*

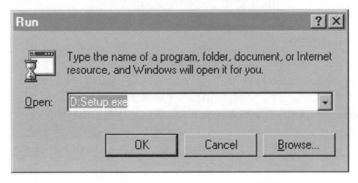

5. ___ Select the **Install Windows XP** from the menu selections by clicking on the item.

6. ___ Next a screen similar to the one that follows should appear. Select the default **Upgrade (Recommended)** from the dialog box.

Select "Upgrade (Recommended)" from the menu

7. ___ Take note of the list on the left side of the screen display. This is a list of the installation activities as they occur during the system upgrade process. The amount of time for the total installation process is also listed. Observe the listing on the left as the installation wizard takes you through the installation upgrade process. You will be prompted for information throughout the installation process. This information will include asking you to accept the licensing agreement and to choose a file system, as well as inquiring about other details such as your regional settings, location, choice of language, name, organization, computer name, administrator password, etc.

8. ___ After the Windows XP operating system is installed, the computer should reboot and you will be prompted to log on for the first time. It is during this time you will have the option to activate your installed copy of Windows XP. You will also be prompted to setup user accounts for the PC. Check with your instructor about the specific requirements of these two prompts. The instructor may not want you to activate the Windows XP operating system. Activation requires using a modem to contact the Microsoft web site and activate the software operating system. This is Microsoft's solution to prevent the pirating of their operating systems. When the system is activated, Microsoft creates a database describing the hardware of the PC system on which the original copy of the Windows XP operating system has been installed. If the specific hardware does not match when activating a second installation on another PC, the installation is disabled.

9. ___ Before ending this lab activity, check with the instructor to see if you will be leaving the upgraded operating system on the PC or uninstalling it.

10. ___ Complete the review questions at the end of this laboratory activity.

Review Questions

You may need to use the Read1st.txt *file located on the Windows XP installation CD to answer some of the following questions.*

1. What is the minimum CPU speed for Windows XP? _____

2. What is the recommended amount of RAM and the minimum amount of RAM required for a typical Windows XP installation? _____

3. What is the maximum amount of RAM that Windows XP can support? _____

4. What is the amount of free hard drive space required for a Windows XP installation? _____

5. What is the minimum monitor resolution required for Windows XP? _____

6. What does the acronym HCL represent? _____

7. From the list that follows, select the items that are recommended you complete before performing a Windows XP upgrade.

   (A) Be sure that an anti-virus program is installed and running during the installation process.

   (B) Perform a virus scan.

   (C) Back up all important files.

   (D) Contact your ISP and notify them that you are installing a new operating system.

   (E) Format the hard drive.

   (F) Access and read the Read1st.txt file located on the CD-ROM.

8. Which of the following operating systems can Windows XP perform a satisfactory upgrade on? Choose all that apply.

   (A) Windows 95

   (B) Windows 98

   (C) Windows 2000

   (D) Windows NT 4.0 with Service pack 6

   (E) DOS 6.0

   (F) Linux

Windows 2000 and XP